Praise for *First Among Equals*

GENERAL MEDIA:

"A big part of this book's appeal is the authors' inherent understanding of how professionals resist being managed."

—Publishers Weekly

"Dozens of self-assessment questionnaires and diagnostic tests help make this an exceptionally practical guidebook on a critical but oft-neglected topic."

—Amazon.com

"For anyone who has been tapped to lead a team of colleagues, this book will be just the basic training needed.

—Southwest Airlines Spirit

BUSINESS MEDIA:

"It's about managing people who don't want to be managed."

—Fortune

"This is a timely, easy-to-read work leavened with action plans and examples"

—Harvard Business School Working Knowledge

"This book would be an excellent handbook for a newly appointed manager in a professional context and a useful refresher for many veterans."

—The Globe & Mail Report on Business

"Promises to be one of the best selling business books of the 2002 spring season!"

—C

D1378238

"Nothing like a leadership book that actually teaches you how to lead. This is one book that you will keep on your shelf for years and the pages will be dog-eared.

—CEORead.com

"When you finish reading this book and the depth of knowledge presented by its authors, you will agree that it is first among equals."

—weLEAD Online Magazine

"The authors offer penetrating insights into the basics of coaching."

—TheBusinessSource.com

The authors of this insightful book provide practical strategies to build, manage, and inspire a team to peak performance!"

—Suite101.com

"If you seriously read and really practice what they preach, you will be in the top 95% of managers world-wide."

—ManagementLearning.com

"Covers the most daunting management challenges imaginable."

—LeadersGuild.com

"Profit from the wide-ranging and thought-provoking points made."

—*Sacramento Business Journal*

"I highly recommend this book for anyone about to be in a leadership role."

—Trendscope.net

"Dozens of self-assessment questionnaires and diagnostic tests help make this an exceptionally practical guidebook."

—RecognizeServiceExcellence.com

"Unlike many business books which discuss theory and not application, McKenna & Maister show you exactly how to be a great group leader."

—StatelineBusiness.com

"The authors draw on years of experience in management to help others become better managers."

—TrustedProfessional.com

First Among Equals is a practical guide that you will refer to often."

—*Business Woman Canada*

HUMAN RESOURCES:

"Practical, applicable, timely and interesting."

—*Training Magazine*

"It is not often that we promote specific books but once in a while, we do read a book which we believe deserves the immediate attention of our readers."

—HR-info.com

"Managing professionals is not easy and this book tackles the subject admirably."

—TeamBuildingInc.com

LEGAL PROFESSION:

"At the risk of sounding trite, this book should be required reading for every group leader who aspires to effective management."

—Law Practice Management

"Too many management texts have a tendency to the vague, the abstract and the pretentious. First among Equals is anything but."

—In Brief Magazine (UK)

"Leaders of professionals will flock to acquire this book."

—Lexpert Magazine

"Contains a wealth of practical advice and checklists."

—Practice Management Advisor—
New York State Bar Association

"May be the first book on management for professionals, and certainly the best."

—Law Firm Partnership & Benefits Report

"LOMAR highly recommends McKenna and Maister's book."

—Law Office Management & Administration Report

The authors deal with issues in a comprehensive 270-page instruction manual that you will not (but should) find in a business school curriculum."

—Houston Lawyer

"It seems unlikely that in 288 pages, the authors could present a thorough guide to group management, but McKenna and Maister easily accomplish the task."

—*New Jersey Lawyer*

"Offers a wealth of useful suggestions on how to be an effective group leader."

—*Wisconsin Lawyer*

"This book will certainly get you thinking about the steps you need to take to turn a group of individual professionals into a well-oiled machine."

—*Massachusetts Lawyers Weekly*

ACADEMIC:

"An important contribution. Topics in this book are unique and have been overlooked elsewhere."

—**Department of Communication—Miami University**

ACCOUNTING:

"Combines compelling cases along with some of the clearest and most effective specific guidelines available in management material to make the concepts come to life."

—*National Public Accountant*

"Offers practical advice, from gaining the confidence of your charges to running and energizing meetings, to dealing with malcontents."

—CAmagazine.com

"A practical guide that professionals and leaders will refer to often for ideas and action lists."

—AccountingWeb.com

"Leaves no nook or cranny of knowledge of the subject unfilled. "

—MarcusLetter.com

"My first thought, where was this 20 years ago when I really needed it? My second was: 20 years ago - what about managing in today's fast paced environment?"

—*Ohio CPA Society Newsletter*

"Offers excellent guidelines on a range of group-related dysfunction's."

—*Accounting Office Management & Administration Report*

"Neither a motivational text nor a pep talk in print, it delivers a strong, positive tone about how to manage groups and the value of doing it well."

—*The CPA Journal*

"Because the book's emphasis is on leadership as a building block process, the text should be read from cover to cover, not piecemeal."

—*Pennsylvania CPA Journal*

MARKETING & COMMUNICATIONS:

"You'll wish every manager and team leader you know would study First Among Equals."

—Ad Genius

"If you don't want to take your role as a leader seriously, don't bother picking this book up. But if you do, there's a lot to work with here."

—Quirk's Marketing Research Report

"This practical guide presents proven strategies along with numerous excellent checklists."

—CorporateLogo.com

INFORMATION TECHNOLOGY:

"CIO's would do well to give this book to IT workers whom they designate team leaders."

—CIO Magazine

"Co-authors McKenna and Maister deliver a guide to help managers improve their own performance and, by extension, the performance of their staff."

—PurpleSquirrel.com

"I highly recommend this book. Keep it close by, because there will be opportunities to use it almost every day."

—Gantthead.com

"Use this book to figure out exactly how to organize your professionals into groups."

—*CIO Insight*

DESIGN:

"A practical guide for professionals on day-to-day leadership concerns."

—*Design Firm Management & Administration Report*

How to
Manage a
Group of
Professionals

F 1 R S T
AMONG EQUALS

Patrick J. McKenna

David Maister

SIMON &
SCHUSTER

London · New York · Sydney · Toronto

A VIACOM COMPANY

First published in Great Britain by Simon & Schuster UK Ltd, 2005
A Viacom Company

1 3 5 7 9 10 8 6 4 2

Simon & Schuster UK Ltd
Africa House
64–78 Kingsway
London WC2B 6AH

www.simonsays.co.uk

Simon & Schuster Australia
Sydney

A CIP catalogue record for this book is available
from the British Library

ISBN 0-7432-6832-6
EAN 9780743268325

Printed and bound in Great Britain by
The Bath Press, Bath

Patrick:

*To my loving wife Monique, who made the
biggest sacrifices in enduring my absences and
supporting my passion for this work; and
To our son David; may you yet find your own
special passion.*

David:

*To Kathy, the eternal source of all that
is good in my life.*

CONTENTS

Introduction .... *xix*

PART ONE
GETTING READY

1. CLARIFY YOUR ROLE 3
   How, exactly, do you add value as a group leader?

2. CONFIRM YOUR MANDATE 11
   Is there an explicit agreement about your rights
   and responsibilities?

3. BUILD RELATIONSHIPS—ONE AT A TIME 27
   What are the key skills you must have?

4. DARE TO BE INSPIRING 45
   Do you know how to inspire people?

PART TWO
COACHING THE INDIVIDUAL

5. WIN PERMISSION TO COACH 59
   How do you get people to accept your guidance?

6. LISTEN TO BUILD RAPPORT 75
   Do people think you are a good listener?

7. DEAL DIFFERENTLY WITH DIFFERENT PEOPLE 83
   How can you understand and respond to people's differences?

8. HELP UNDERPERFORMERS 105
   How can you be useful to those who need assistance?

9. TACKLE THE PRIMA DONNAS 113
How do you deal with difficult people?

10. BUILD SUPPORT FOR CHANGE 121
How do you get people to buy into the need for change?

PART THREE
COACHING THE TEAM

11. CLARIFY GROUP GOALS 131
Does your group have specific, clearly articulated, shared objectives?

12. DEVELOP YOUR GROUP'S RULES OF MEMBERSHIP 137
What do members of your group owe to each other?

13. BUILD TEAM TRUST 151
What gets group members to trust each other?

14. THROW DOWN A CHALLENGE 165
Has your group selected an exciting challenge?

15. ENERGIZE YOUR MEETINGS 175
What are good meeting disciplines?

16. GIVE RECOGNITION 193
How do you acknowledge accomplishments?

17. RESOLVE INTERPERSONAL CONFLICTS 201
What do you do when team members fall out?

18. DEAL WITH YOUR CRISES 207
How do you respond to dramatic events?

PART FOUR
BUILDING FOR THE FUTURE

19. NURTURE YOUR JUNIORS 221
How do you deal with your junior staff?

20. INTEGRATE NEW PEOPLE 231
How do you ensure the success of new hires?

21. CONTROL YOUR GROUP'S SIZE 237
How do you respond to the problems of size?

22. MEASURE GROUP RESULTS 241
How do you measure your group's success?

23. WHY BOTHER? 259
Why would you want to do all this?

Notes on Sources 267

Further Reading 273

Bibliography 275

Acknowledgments 277

Index 281

INTRODUCTION

IF YOU LEAD A GROUP OF PROFESSIONALS, this book is for you. We mean the term "group" to be generic, and not refer to any particular type of organization or structure. Your group might be a geographic unit, or one based around a specific project, client, industry, or discipline. You don't manage the whole firm, but head up, coordinate, manage, lead, or facilitate a part of the firm. You're not people's boss, and even if you are, you don't want to act that way. You have limited, if any, powers to issue instructions, commands or orders, and if you have such authority, you rarely use it. To be effective, you must act as *primus inter pares*, the first among equals.

Since you are managing a group, and not your whole firm, you probably still have client work to do. You must be (simultaneously) a player and a coach. This might be your first experience in managing (or whatever you call it). Prior to becoming a group leader, you were probably expected to focus on your own performance alone. Now it is also your responsibility to worry about (and influence) the performance of others, many of whom were, until recently, your peers (and certainly still consider themselves so). You must also forge a cohesive team out of a group of autonomous individuals.

Group types span a wide spectrum, from the tightly focused mission-oriented team who recognizes a joint purpose and mutual responsibility for that purpose to a group of people who each work on their own projects, owing little to each other, and exist as a group merely for administrative or organizational convenience.

We do not wish to debate when a group becomes a team, since many types of group probably fall between these two categories. **What is important is that *you* come to an explicit agreement on how your group will be defined. We believe that what defines a group (or team) is the set of rules that it is prepared to operate by. In tightly integrated teams, everyone knows the rules and adheres to them with rigor. In loose groups, there**

are few rules, and even those are often negotiable. Throughout the book, we return to the theme of agreeing on how your group will operate. As Jon Katzenbach, the world expert on teaming, put it: "Team performance is more a matter of discipline than togetherness."

This view affirms the finding in David's book *Practice What You Preach*, that success in professional businesses can be shown (statistically) to come from stricter adherence ("discipline") to a set of standards that other groups may also advocate but do not enforce. It was also found that the key to enforcement was the skilled manager, coach, or team leader. If you ask, as you read on, whether "this stuff" can be shown to be profitable, we refer you to that book for the evidence. Here we are concerned with the "how."

Simply labeling a collection of people a group does not make it one. As consultants, we have spent many years trying to convince others that initiatives in business rarely get implemented well unless each group has a leader, a head, a coordinator, or coach whose job it is to manage the team and coach the individual players.

This is not as trivial a point as it may seem. Professional people, inside service firms or within corporations, are notoriously averse to being managed. They are cynical, savvy, and selective. According to Philip Greenspun, an MIT professor and the founder and chairman of ArsDigita Corporation, programmers have huge and fragile egos. He writes:

> Software engineering is different because people at all levels of the organization perceive themselves to be equally intelligent. . . . One of the paradoxes of software engineering is that people with bad ideas and low productivity often think of themselves as supremely capable. They are the last people whom one can expect to fall in line with a good strategy developed by someone else. As for the good programmers who are in fact supremely capable, there is no reason to expect consensus to form among them. Each programmer thinks his or her idea about what to build and how to build it is the best.
>
> A truly great programmer may generate 10 times as much business value as a merely good programmer. Can the organization afford to take someone who can do the work

of 10 average programmers and push him or her into a pure management role? . . . Can the organization afford to put people with weak technical skills into management roles? . . . Since they are still expected to produce designs, software, documentation, and journal articles, the danger is that the new manager will become glued to his or her screen and never look up to see how the project team is doing.

We think Greenspun could have been referring to any of a large number of professional environments. Consider what James Emerson, the distinguished publisher of the *Professional Services Review*, noted:

Based on nearly 30 years of involvement with the professional services industry, I am convinced that effectively leading a group of professionals is a much tougher challenge than most people realize. **Certain characteristics of professionals that allow them to do their jobs effectively create barriers to them being successful in the group setting.**

Most professionals are trained to be skeptical and will almost always critically challenge any new idea, bringing to bear their analytical gifts. Getting agreement on even the smallest issues can be tough.

Because of this, it can be very hard to get technically oriented professionals to think beyond their core competency in order to focus on the big picture. Professionals often want to over-study any problem; first, it satisfies their need to eliminate every last ounce of risk before they make a decision, and second, it gives some professionals an excuse to have endless conversations so they will never be required to act.

Professionals often resist accountability, fearing that it will limit their creativity and ability to find the best solution.

Most professionals like working alone. Keeping a group of professionals in a room is very difficult. They can always leave by saying they have a client commitment when in fact they are not comfortable in the group.

David Swanson of Assante Asset Management observed:

> Working within groups is a good philosophy but I wonder how such an approach can manage the insecurity of the individual's contribution. Individual members contribute to the team but risk losing their own differentiation and possibly their own maximum economic value to themselves and their family. The financial services industry, which I am part of, has never been managed from the top down. It has been entrepreneurial, competitive and transaction oriented. As it moves away from transactions toward fee-for-service planning, it continues to be very competitive but is becoming more collaborative. There is a willingness to nurture a group and its members, yet there is still a fear of not being compensated for the effort.

Unfortunately, the challenge of managing professionals has led many firms and companies to believe that professionals are unmanageable, and as a result, they often give up trying. Group leadership is frequently nonexistent, with group leaders (where they exist) focusing almost exclusively on administrative matters and doing no *managing*.

We recommend precisely the opposite conclusion. **The potential power of having well-coordinated groups is too great to abandon the task. Because managing professionals is complex, it requires *more* attention to management, not less.** Given professionals' quirks, more managerial skill is needed than in some other environments, not less. *What* managers of professionals must do might be similar in other environments (hold meetings, inspire people, listen well, provide counseling). *How* it is done can be quite different, requiring different approaches or an extra degree or two of finesse and style. And the right attitude!

We will try to show that, to succeed in your role, you will need a willingness to get most of your fulfillment from the success of others. You will also need a special set of skills: the ability to influence other people's emotions, feelings, attitudes, and their determination. Unfortunately, in many firms, these are not the criteria usually applied in selecting group leaders. All too often the most senior, the best business-getter, intellectual luminary, or financially savvy person is chosen. As a result of this historical (and sometimes political) reality, some firms have found it necessary to appoint two people to lead a practice. One (called something like the practice chair) is the "titular head," the luminary, often well known in the marketplace, whose primary focus is representing the group to the marketplace. This person bears no coaching responsibilities, but is backed up by the real group leader, who does the co-ordinating, counseling, and effectively runs the practice. This is a perfectly acceptable solution. In this book we are assuming that you are the person really doing the day-to-day managing and coaching.

If you recognize any of the issues highlighted in the sidebar, and want to address them, this book is for you. We will try to help you eliminate the barriers and provide you with the knowledge you will need to perform your leadership role effectively.

In our respective previous writings, we have both tried to make the case for management, and for group leaders. Apart from some comments in chapters 1 and 2, this book does not repeat those arguments. Instead, it addresses a question we often receive when the case for management is accepted: "OK, we have agreed to have managed teams with group heads focusing on coaching their teams. How do we help them learn how to do it?"

We describe here what group leaders must do and, in as much detail as we can provide, precisely how to do it.

While there are many excellent books available on how to be a manager or a coach, the overwhelming majority of them are written with a corporate setting in mind, where the group head has a significant amount of "position power" or recognized authority. This is not the case in many firms, particularly professional firms, where managing (as opposed to administering) is a relatively new concept. Such leaders often don't have subordinates or employees, or don't think of them that way. They have peers, collaborators, colleagues, co-workers, and perhaps, partners.

In addition, many managers inside corporations, such as engineers, human resource advisors, marketing departments, finance professionals, information technology officers, and many others face a similar challenge. They are asked to lead highly educated, autonomous, energetic people who may respond to being influenced or coached, but resist being "managed."

Our goal in this book has been to provide an introduction to the basics of being a group leader in a professional setting (not just inside professional firms). **This is a book about "doing."** It is not concerned primarily with

Test your group's effectiveness with this quick quiz:

1. Do members of the group share in knowing why your group exists, where it is going, what it's trying to accomplish, what its core priorities are?

   Or are they non-committed, grudging participants, perhaps because they feel that membership in the group is irrelevant to their individual performance and individual compensation?

2. Do people believe that they can really depend upon and count on each other, and do they feel confident about each other's capabilities and efforts?

   Or do they feel that relying on each other's goodwill and expertise is either naive or dangerous?

3. Do people share their collective wins and losses with each other?

   Or do they only claim personal victories while rationalizing negative outcomes with excuses and finger-pointing?

4. Do members of the group genuinely listen to each other's ideas and opinions?

   Or do they simply defend and promote their own positions?

5. Do people publicly honor and recognize each other's efforts and contributions?

   Or are accomplishments taken for granted?

6. Do members of the group value each other's time?

   Or do they behave in a way that suggests that other's time doesn't have much importance to them?

7. Do group members hold agreements and promises made as sacred?

   Or are agreements and promises only made expediently, such as "maybe, if it's convenient"?

8. Do people help each other succeed and grow, and then share in the excitement of each other's accomplishments?

   Or are such concerns deemed irrelevant?

9. Do people hold each other to high standards of performance and provide each other with straight feedback, coaching, and compassion?

   Or do they fail to insist on high standards or to coach poor performance, and confuse caring for people with indulging them.

10. Do group members behave as if their own success will be enhanced by the success of the group?

    Or do these people act as if their own needs and those of the team are contradictory concepts?

11. Do people in the group share client contacts, information, tools and other resources with each other?

    Or do they tend to hoard and protect turf?

12. Are members of the group recognized for contributing to the team purpose?

    Or do group members feel that they are better off pursuing their own personal agendas, even though outwardly participating?

13. Does the group get the authority, the resources and the support to do what it was organized to do?

    Or is a lot of time wasted playing political games to overcome internal bureaucracy?

14. Do the members define themselves as members of the team?

    Or do they feel an affiliation only with the firm or their occupation?

theories, concepts, or insights. It's the book we wish we had read when we were first given the challenge of leading a group!

WHAT WE DON'T DISCUSS

There are many fascinating and complex issues about how groups function within the context of the firm as a whole. Among the topics we have encountered are these:

1. Should groups be organized by discipline, by industry, or by geography?

2. What are the special challenges of multisite, international or global groups?

3. How do you handle the complexities of matrix management when groups intersect or overlap?

4. Should groups be treated as profit centers?

5. How do you prevent balkanization of a firm if the groups are too strong?

6. What role should group heads play in the executive committee of the whole firm?

These questions, while indeed important, are beyond the scope of this book. We have tried to write for *individual* group leaders about the execution of their role, and not write for firm leaders who are dealing with firm-level structural and process issues. That's another book!

A NOTE ON TERMINOLOGY

In attempting to write for group leaders in a wide variety of professional settings, we found ourselves constantly struggling with terminology, both because some contexts are different, and because different professionals use different terms for the same thing.

For example, lawyers, consultants and accountants use the term "billable hours," while marketing communications firms refer to "utilization rates" or "chargeability." Some in-house professionals use none of these terms, but the concept of time spent directly serving (in-house) clients should be readily understandable and apply easily.

A related problem arises with the concept of "non-billable time"—hours spent at work that is not directly related to a client project. We have sometimes used the term "non-production time" or "non-reimbursed time." We can't promise that we have always used the right language, but we hope the concept is clear.

We have also been fairly free with our use of the words "manager," "leader," and "coach." Vast oceans of ink have been spilled trying to arrive at precise definitions of these terms, and we have no intention of joining in. We have been concerned with exploring appropriate behaviors, attitudes, skills, and actions, not with nomenclature.

Other words get in the way. Some professions rely heavily on making distinctions between "partners" and "associates." Law firms use the word "staff" to mean non-lawyer employees, while accounting firms use that term for entry-level professionals. We have tried to avoid all such language and write about managing people. We occasionally differentiate between junior and senior people, but that's the only distinction we make.

We hope that even if our terminology is ambiguous (or not that which your business usually uses) it does not interfere with the clarity of our analysis and our advice.

Finally, we stress that this is a joint work. Where it is necessary to refer to things we have done separately, we refer to ourselves as Patrick or David. Otherwise, it's "we."

HOW TO USE THIS BOOK

We recommend reading this book straight through, since it is intended as an integrated work, not a "manual" of disconnected chapters. The book is divided into four sections, presented in the order in which you need to think about the issues.

Part One is all about clarifying and understanding your role. As we note, success in helping your group succeed is mostly about *you*. Not *them*.

Part Two deals with the activities you must engage in to coach, lead, inspire and guide individual members of your team. As we note in the text, you will only be able to deal with your group once you have developed strong working relationships with each of its members.

Part Three turns to team management; dealing with your colleagues collectively as a group.

Part Four addresses the issues of building for the future: managing juniors, dealing with the problems of size, and monitoring your group's success.

Another way of viewing the book's contents is to examine how frequently you will need to do the things we recommend. Some chapters (particularly those in Part One) you might need to sort out only once. They are your "setup" (getting your mandate, establishing the round rules on which your team will operate, etc.). Other chapters (on setting a compelling challenge, building support for change, or tackling prima donnas) cover things you might need to do periodically. Finally, there are those chapters (on such topics as coaching, running meetings, giving appreciation and recognition) that you will need to do continuously. We hope it is clear which category each activity falls into. (We will review these categories in the final chapter.)

Finally, the contents of the book cover a wide range of skills and activities, from the "mechanical" (how to run a meeting) to the deeply emotional (issues of trust, relationships, meaning, and inspiration). We think it important that a group leader develop abilities in all these areas.

Laura Holmes of Smythe Dorward Lambert, an international change management consultancy, commented to us:

> An ongoing debate exists between what is the role of a manager versus the role of a leader. The real distinction lies not in the title, but in how you do your job and approach the people around you every day. The range of activities that group leaders face goes from basic requirements (setting goals and measures, running effective meetings, evaluating performance) to the challenging choices one must make (inspiring through times of change and uncertainty, advising people on career development, negotiating out of a group conflict). It is not an either/or situation. **Group leaders need to be skilled at management basics *and* inspirational, motivational leadership to deliver successful business outcomes.**

That's our view too!

PART ONE

GETTING READY

THIS FIRST SECTION is about you and your role. It might be the most important part of the book, because if you don't get this right, nothing else will work.

1. Clarify Your Role
   How, exactly, do you add value as a group leader?

2. Confirm Your Mandate
   Is there an explicit agreement about your rights and responsibilities?

3. Build Relationships—One at a Time
   What are the key skills you must have?

4. Dare to Be Inspiring
   Do you know how to inspire people?

chapter I

Clarify Your Role

How, exactly, do you add value as
a group leader?

BENJAMIN HAAS is the managing partner in the Chicago office of the human resource consulting firm Towers Perrin, which has about 8,500 employees in seventy offices worldwide. He articulated the core truth about being a group leader:

> The reality is that a leadership role is fundamentally different from the individual contributor role. A leader has fundamentally got to be somebody who is effective at making things happen for other people.
>
> It's a real different mind-set in terms of what you do and how you impact the business. A leader has to bring a certain energy and optimism to the business. Part of our job is to build energy and enthusiasm. A leader must create a sense of shared ownership. The kinds of people we're managing want to feel like they are owners and not employees.
>
> Another key ability is to assess people and determine what's going to be the right role for each individual that

> meets their needs and also allows them to contribute effectively to the organization.

We could not agree more with these comments. Your job as a group leader is to help your people, and your team, win.

Prior to becoming a group head, many people will have been asked to spend their whole working lives focusing on their own individual performance. The transition to being responsible for the performance of others is a difficult one for many to make, particularly since, in all likelihood, they still carry *some* client-service or production responsibilities. **There is an issue here both of attitude (willingness to focus on other people and their success) and of skill (the ability to win influence over other people without being domineering). Skills can be taught; attitudes are harder to change.**

John Schoenewald, CEO of AFSM International, noted:

> To be effective, a leader must show he truly cares about others—not only caring what the employee does but, as important, how he does it. I have seen leaders who are consumed with themselves and their personal goals. This is especially common in high-tech services. They don't have time nor do they take the time for coaching, as they are goal-oriented and desire results through technical solutions. In the high-tech services industry, technicians as well as managers, for the most part, fall into the category of loners. They are individuals who would rather work independently. That's why they choose a technical field and not the sales profession. This situation creates a challenge for effective teaming. Most technical teams I've managed have all the correct ingredients for success, but they try to achieve team results through individual efforts.

The best group leaders see themselves as catalysts. They expect to achieve a great deal, but know that they can do little without the efforts of others. It is challenging to manage a group of people with different skills, diverse experiences, a variety of work styles, and sometimes, conflicting priorities. Casey Stengel, the renowned former manager of the New York Yankees, once said, "Getting good players is one thing. The harder part is getting them to play together." As we shall see, it requires commitment, curiosity, and courage.

In order to help other people succeed, you will need a willingness to get most of your fulfillment from the success of others and a special set of skills: the ability to influence other people's emotions, feelings, attitudes, and their determination.

Jack Newman, now retired from managing a substantial and well-integrated group at global law megafirm, Morgan, Lewis & Bockius, clearly understood his role:

> It's significant that I have two business cards. One is mine. The other is the group's. There are twenty lawyers on that group card, and it fits into the client's pocket just as easily as mine does. On that card, the client can find the right lawyer for the right question. Subliminally, the very existence of the card sends a message about the importance of the group as a group.

So, how do you help other people succeed (and play as a team)? Part of the answer may be about substance or content (they don't know what to do or how to do it), but this is rarely the biggest issue. **Most often, you will be working with highly talented people who do know what to do and how to do it, but just aren't doing it.** The causes may be numerous (fear, suspicion, lack of drive, attitudes, problems at home, or structural firm impediments) and you will find that most of the barriers have to do with feelings, attitudes, and emotions.

Your role, therefore, and your essential skill, will be to help people fulfill their potential by influencing these feelings, attitudes, and emotions. If you accomplish this, the raised performance level will result (among other things) in greater financial success for your people, you and your firm.

Note, however, that while money (or profitability) may be your goal, it is not what you must manage. What you must manage in order to get money is the energy, drive, enthusiasm, excitement, passion, and ambition of your people. Your primary skill (and the test of all your activities) must be whether or not you are able to raise the level of commitment and drive of those you influence.

Among the contributions you can make are the following:

a. Create energy and excitement

b. Be a source of creative ideas, and stimulate creativity in others

c. Forge teamwork

d. Help develop a common purpose that everyone can buy into

e. Help to solve problems and break down barriers for team members—make it easier for them to succeed

f. Act as a sounding board—help people think through their issues

g. Enforce standards (deal gently, promptly, but firmly with noncompliance)

h. Be a conscience ("gentle pressure") when self-discipline fails

i. Be a constant source of encouragement to improve effectiveness, quality, and efficiency

How would you rate yourself at each of these? How would those you lead rate you?

WHAT A LEADER SPENDS TIME ON

So, you are the leader of your group! Your goal is to help, but what do you actually do to accomplish this? Which of the following possible activities are you expected to do? Do your team members expect you to do these things? Do those you report to agree that you should be doing them?

1. Spend unscheduled, informal time with individual people (senior and/or junior), serving as coach, to help them develop themselves and their practice.

2. Be knowledgeable about the development of junior people and be ready to suggest reassignments between projects in order to build skills and advance their careers.

3. Be in touch with other group members' clients to help them grow relationships, and to monitor client satisfaction and act as a conscience for everyone to excel at client satisfaction.

4. Help members of the team differentiate themselves from other competitors in a meaningful way that clients recognize and value.

5. Help people to stay current with the trends affecting the client industries they serve, the changes that will affect these clients, and their demand for the group's services.

6. Monitor the profitability of assignments conducted by group members and discuss results with them.

7. Devise methodologies to capture and share knowledge acquired while serving clients both within the group and across the firm.

8. Help the group explore new and innovative ways of using technology to better deliver services and reduce costs to clients.

9. Spend time recruiting, interviewing, and attracting potential recruits (junior and senior).

10. Spend time following up and actively helping members of the group execute their planned activities.

11. Initiate and run regular meetings to collectively plan the group's activities and initiatives for the coming quarter.

12. Conduct formal performance appraisals of other (senior) people in the team for purposes of compensation.

13. Conduct counseling sessions with people on the basis of these performance appraisals.

14. Celebrate individual and group achievements—the minor wins, not just the home runs; the good tries, not just the successes.

You will immediately see that most of these are time-intensive activities. In fact, we suggest that, as an exercise, you estimate how many hours in a year each activity would take, given the size of your group and the nature of its activities. You may find that there's not enough time to do them all, and you will have to choose: Will you try to do them all to a middling level, or will you try to do a selected few superbly? (We recommend the latter!)

As you review this list of activities, we invite you to ask yourself a few questions:

a. Which of these activities are most likely to raise enthusiasm, excitement and, hence, performance?

b. Which of these activities do those you counsel (or coach or lead) accept as valid (i.e., agree that you should perform them)?

c. Which of these activities do your superiors expect you to perform?

d. Have we left activities off our list that you think should be part of your leadership role? What else could you be doing that would raise the performance of your group and the individuals within it?

A group leader does not have to do all of the items we have discussed here. **There are many versions of group leadership. However, if the group and the leader are to succeed, it is necessary to agree upon (and write down) the leader's role, responsibilities, accountabilities, and performance measures.** You need to come to agreement both with those you supervise and those you report to. It is remarkable how infrequently this is done. (We discuss in the next chapter additional things that you need to negotiate with your firm leadership to fulfill your role properly.) The single biggest (and most certain) source of failure for a group leader is not having agreement in advance about what he or she should do!

Since many professional firms (and professional groups within corporations) do not have a history of activist group leaders, it is essential that to arrive at precise answers to these questions. You may think that everyone understands your role, but we have learned that it is safe to assume that while each person may be absolutely clear on what you should be doing, there as many different views as there are people you must deal with.

Group leaders cannot and must not attempt to impose their own view of their role on others: this will be doomed to fail. In a professional environment, people must cede permission to be coached, and this can only be done if the role, and its limits, are agreed upon and well communicated in advance.

THE "VISION THING"

Many management texts, and many of our clients, suggest that one key contribution of a leader is to provide or create a "vision." We are skeptics here, not on any theoretical grounds, but simply because as longtime consultants we have seen many professional environments, and have rarely met managers or leaders who have pulled this approach off. To us, a leader talking about his or her vision sounds too much like "Follow Me!"—an appeal that is unlikely to work in professional environments.

We concede that there may be those individuals who, through personal charisma or the painting of an irresistible future, can get large numbers of professionals to follow them. We just don't think many people can pull it off. We call it "The Moses Strategy"—going up into the mountain, receiving the word of God, and bringing it back to the children of Israel, saying "Here is the word of God. Get excited!" If you remember your Bible, you may recall that even Moses had to do it twice before he could get the attention of his audience!

Our point of view, based upon the most effective managers we have seen, is that they don't say "Follow me!" Instead, they say "Let me help you!" The management writers call this "servant leadership."

The key point is that the central goal of either approach is to get your people enthused, excited, and energized. Unless you have a very special skill, then we suggest you focus on what excites each of your people, not (just) on what excites you.

Here's how David described the group leader's role in _Managing the_
Professional Service Firm:

A business group is like a sports team, filled with talented athletes who will only win if they truly fulfill their potential. People in business, like athletes, when left to their own devices, don't accomplish as much as they do when they are supported by a good coach.

The best managers really do add a very special value. First, through their actions, individual people accomplish more, and focus on more important things, than they would if left to their own devices. Second, the talents of powerful individuals are shaped into even more powerful teams, learning from and supporting each other.

How do good coaches achieve results? Effective practice leaders recognize that you rarely "turn on" people (or get them to change) through speeches, vision statements, or inspirational group meetings. They know that the only truly effective way to influence people is one-on-one, i.e., highly individualized, closed-door counseling. Above all else, they pay attention to the individual. They are close enough to what the individual is doing to be able to offer substantive suggestions. They are always "dropping by" to discuss "how's it going?"

Effective coaches go out of their way to celebrate successes and triumphs. They make constant use of approval, visibility, recognition, and appreciation. However, to be effective, good coaches must also be demanding. When a good athlete successfully jumps over the high bar, a good coach celebrates the accomplishment, and then— raises the bar! ("Come on, you can do it.") Coaches must be simultaneously chief cheerleader and chief critic—one without the other is insufficient. Part of the skill of coaching is knowing how high to raise the bar, judging for each individual, separately, what next challenge will be stretching but achievable.

Good coaches build teams. Since most players will probably be more focused on their own personal performance, it is up to the coach to look out for the overall best interests of the group. The coach must identify opportunities for joint activities. This inevitably involves the coach in trading favors. ("Help us out on this one, and I'll do my best to look after you next time.") Good coaches pay significant attention to how the group's resources are being deployed, and whether or not all the bases are being covered.

Leaders are needed to be the _guardians of the long-term_. They are valuable when they act as the _conscience_ of their colleagues: not necessarily giving them new goals, but helping them achieve the goals they have set for themselves. The manager's role is to be the _reminder_, the _coach_, and the _supporter_ as individuals and teams struggle to balance today's pressures with longer-term accomplishments.

chapter 2

Confirm Your Mandate

Is there an explicit agreement about your rights and responsibilities?

IF YOU ARE VERY LUCKY, the concepts of managed groups are well established in your firm or company. It is clearly understood exactly why the group exists, what your role is, the terms and conditions under which you will operate, and precisely what your rights and obligations as group leader are. Unfortunately, this is not always the case.

Professional groups are often difficult to run because no one knows the ground rules under which they will operate. The conditions necessary for you to do what is asked of you might be missing. In fact, the way some firms are run ensures that effective group management is close to impossible. Before you can effectively manage your group, you must ensure that you have reached agreement on what we call your "terms of engagement" or your mandate.

We stress that there is a choice here, and that you cannot adopt a simple checklist approach to this task. There are too many kinds of groups and teams inside professional businesses to generalize. Some group leaders might be in charge of a distinct profit center, or specific geographic location. Others might be in a matrix organization and be responsible for a collection of people who also belong to other operating units. Still others might belong to "task teams" that only exist for a few months or years. However, in each of these situations, our advice is to follow the processes we recommend to establish the ground rules under which you and your group will operate. **You may think everyone around you already shares the same view of your mandate, but it is worth checking!**

Some professional businesses recognize the importance of groups and group management. John Graham is the CEO of Fleishman-Hillard, a prominent public relations firm. In a presentation to The Conference Board, Graham commented:

> Not only do people want to be associated with the best, but we want to be part of something larger than ourselves. That desire isn't satisfied by being one of 50,000 employees. It's satisfied by being part of a team. What makes a group of people a community or a team? Open communication; an opportunity for input and to influence decisions; and personal knowledge of others in the group.

However, in many professional businesses the form of group management in use today does not really deserve the word management. People are loosely grouped into practices, departments, or operating units, and the role of the group head is primarily administrative, not managerial. As a group head, you are expected to monitor short-term financials such as utilization, billing discipline, and receivables, but have little or no authority to supervise the activities of other people in the group, especially not other senior people.

Senior people jealously guard their autonomy to use their own time as they see fit, and cede no authority to anyone on such things as how they will staff their own projects or what practice development activities they will conduct.

There is no expectation (and certainly no requirement) that group members will act collectively and make joint decisions (with mutual responsibility to each other) on such things as practice development, development of junior staff, or building tools and templates of benefit to everyone in the group.

Since in this situation your freedom to act as a group leader is severely circumscribed, it is often the case that you are allowed no extra time to fulfill the group leadership function. You are expected to be as busy on client work as any other senior person in the group, to have the same responsibilities in revenue generation, and you are appraised based on your personal accomplishments as an individual contributor rather than your success as a group leader.

The leaders of one firm we worked with said it this way:

> We remain committed to developing effective groups as one of our primary, long-term goals. However, our most critical issue is that this firm is exceedingly busy with client work right now and we grow concerned that, lip service notwithstanding, many of our group leaders will forsake spending time on their management responsibilities in favor of serving clients. While we have told them about the priority we place on their managing their groups, there is still an overriding sense throughout this firm that serving clients is rewarded above all else.

We also hear from various group leaders:

> We're never really sure of what it is that firm management expects of us. Group leaders here have never been given any formal outline or guidance on what the job really is, how much time we are expected to steal away from our individual client work, or even where we are expected to devote that time.
>
> When I first agreed to take on this role I thought that it was an acknowledgment of my having the most expertise in this particular area. Now they seem to want me to spend time on everything but that which will enhance my expertise.

In many firms the concept of groups is floundering. The firm sprays (a little) training on their group managers, then sends them back into an unchanged environment and prays that something good will happen. The real challenge is to provide a supporting structure that transcends prayer.

THE RULES YOU WILL OPERATE UNDER

To avoid these problems, you need to clarify some terms of engagement that you must clarify with your group, and with those you report to, before you are ready to begin. Don't be afraid to raise these issues and resolve them. Unless you do so, immediately upon accepting the role, you will be doomed to failure!

In addition to agreement on your role (discussed in chapter 1) your terms of engagement should include (at least) these things:

1. Time to do the job

2. Your right to coach

3. Your performance criteria and compensation

4. Input on the compensation of team members

5. Valuing everyone's nonreimbursed time

6. What you need from your firm leader

1   TIME TO DO THE JOB

Probably the single biggest source of failure in making professional groups work is not giving the group leader the time to do the job. In many firms, group leaders are expected to be as fully busy on client (or production) work as anyone else in the group.

As a result, they continue to view their own individual performance as job one, and their coaching responsibilities as a secondary, lesser responsibility which they get to if, and only if, time allows. Not surprisingly, since most professional people live busy work lives, something has to give, and that "something" is almost always their group leader responsibilities.

As one group leader said:

> I'm doing this job on faith. The faith that someone is going to remember at the end of the year all of the time I have put into doing this job. And the faith that I'm not going to get

> screwed at compensation time because I don't have the numbers I would have had if I'd practiced full time.

The real problem here is not the group leaders, but firm management. Too many firm executives say (publicly and privately) that while they buy the concept of group management, they are not prepared to take any risks with the firm's economics. Management is not prepared to give assurances to the group leaders that if they spend time on the role and do it well, the group leaders won't be penalized for a drop-off in personal production or revenue generation. Firm management is concerned that they might create a financial "black hole" by moving some of the managing, coaching, and mentoring activities to group leaders.

If a firm's leaders seriously want to develop effective groups and believe that time spent on managing these groups is capable of producing profitable benefits, then (like the most successful firms we have observed) they must allow for and acknowledge the importance of each group leader's "management" time.

Having said this, we are not advocating the time-worn adage that "you get what you pay for." Many people accept the responsibility of leading a group because they believe it would be rewarding. They find intrinsic gratification in teaching and guiding younger people, in helping their colleagues become even more successful, and they genuinely want to do an outstanding job of building a group that may become a symbol of their "legacy." The single most pressing issue for these group leaders is simply one of receiving some fair degree of protection. They don't want to invest time for the benefit of the group, only to be short-changed personally at compensation time for not having contributed more client-service or revenue-producing time.

It is easy to show that allowing group leaders the time to manage can be immensely profitable for the firm, which will make more money from having a well-managed group than from having the incremental production of the group leader. Here's the calculation for a single group:

> Consider a group leader who is responsible for a group containing ten senior and ten junior professionals, with total

revenue of, let's say, $8 million and a profit of $3 million. (Naturally, you should substitute your own numbers in this example). Let's assume that the plan is for the group leader to reduce his or her personal production by 500 hours in a year.

Five hundred hours represents about one day a week of the group leader's time. We'll assume the group leader keeps up all other activities, including business development, but reduces his or her client-service (or fee-earning) time by the 500 hours.

Let's assume that the practice leader's billing rate (explicit or implicit) is $400 per hour. This means a loss of $200,000 in the practice leader's revenue production. (It is not necessary to assume that the firm bills by the hour, but let's assume the notion of an implicit billing rate can be used in this example.)

The group (or firm) has lost $200,000 in fees, but gained an extra day a week to manage an $8 million business. What is the probability that, with one day a week available (week-in, week-out, throughout the year) to focus on managing an $8 million business, generating $3 million in profit, the group leader could recoup a multiple of this $200,000 investment?

If the group leader has *any* managerial skill, the probability should be very high, perhaps over 99 percent. If he or she *couldn't* create that benefit with a day a week available to work with twenty (or so) people, then there is only one option available. He or she should resign as group leader!

Notice that we are not talking about full-time group leaders. As Jon Katzenbach, who for many years worked at McKinsey, observed to us:

A professional service leader who is also actively serving (demanding) clients brings two strong advantages to the coaching of others. The first is simple credibility, since he is successfully doing the kinds of things that he will be coun-

> seling and coaching others to do. The second is that his actions will speak louder than his words, often making the words unnecessary.

In fact, the calculation just given is a worst-case scenario. We have argued for many years that most professionals, even senior ones, spend a significant amount of time doing work that could (with proper supervision) be delegated. Estimates given to us by our clients of the amount that could be done by someone more junior range up to 50 percent or more of each senior person's time.

What this implies is that, **by restaffing the projects that the group leader continues to supervise, he or she could continue to be in charge of every engagement he or she is currently doing, retain all current client contact time, and still free up enough time to be an effective coach and leader.** The economic sacrifice to the firm and to the group leader is negligible. The process of giving up some fee-earning activities simply encourages the group leader to delegate those tasks that most likely could (and should) have been delegated in the first place.

Management (when done properly) clearly adds value and raises profits. Think of it this way: You hold a large block of stock in a publicly traded company. Imagine that this company has just made a public announcement that they are disbanding the management team and devoting all of the management team's time to helping with production. Is that a buy signal for you as an investor, or a sell signal?

There needs to be a clear understanding of (at least approximately) how much time the group leader will spend in managing and coaching activities, just so that there is no "second guessing" later. One approach which we have seen work well is to set a "minimum-maximum requirement" for the amount of non-client-service time that should be devoted to coaching matters. Setting both upper and lower limits is important. The minimum is meant to represent a sincere expression by firm leadership signifying the importance of the responsibilities. The maximum is an indication that any additional time taken to coordinate the group's efforts or to coach individual people will not be viewed as an acceptable excuse for diminished personal performance.

The group leader is told:

> *"We expect that coordinating and coaching your group should require that you devote no less than X hours over the coming year. However, we don't expect that you should need to devote any more than Y hours. We want you to spend the greatest amount of that time working one on one with individual group members. Your coaching role should involve either helping guide them with their personal career aspirations, working with them hands-on to help them complete the various projects they volunteered to undertake, or going out with them to visit their clients and help prospect for new clients."*

2 YOUR RIGHT TO COACH

As we shall show, **a major part of the group leader's real value comes from discussing individual performance and engaging in effective follow-up with individual members of the group.** Many groups spend a fair degree of time and effort in planning their future activities, but without follow-up, little is implemented.

The value that the group leader brings to each member of the group here is to act as a conscience mechanism. The group leader serves to remind them of projects that they undertook to complete, to offer genuine hands-on assistance, and help implement projects that could have substantive and profitable consequences that would benefit everyone in the group. However, you must not take for granted that group members (or management) will automatically assume that you have the right to engage in this informal, one-on-one interaction.

A similar issue is your right to visit your colleagues' clients (preferably with them) as a means of quality assurance and as an opportunity to role model client contact skills. You need to ensure that everyone agrees that it is within your marching orders to engage in such behavior. You need to determine what kinds of coaching interventions are or are not deemed to be acceptable.

In some professional contexts, this "right to intervene" is taken for granted as the natural obligation of a group leader. In others, it must be negotiated. Whichever is true for you, be wary of making assumptions. Make sure your rights to act in designated ways are clear to everyone. Start by clarifying them with your firm management. In subsequent chapters, we will discuss how to clarify them with your team.

3 YOUR PERFORMANCE CRITERIA AND COMPENSATION

We think it wise to align the incentives for the group leader with the best interests of the firm. This is simply done. Group leaders should be measured and appraised predominantly by how well their group has done, with their own personal statistics being deemed a lesser performance target. Group leaders should still be expected to practice—and generate revenues—as much as they like, but personal accomplishments should no longer be the primary element in their appraisal. Only improving the group's success represents a complete fulfillment of the role. If they can help the group succeed while still carrying a full book of business, so much the better. But if they cannot do both, then it is clear that the number one priority is the group!

For a variety of reasons, this simple solution is not yet possible at many firms, where there can be a profound mistrust of any person not carrying a "full load," which is always defined in terms of production, the only valued activity in the firm. The reluctance to allow a group leader to reduce his or her production hours significantly usually results in the introduction of a larger number of coaches, each spending a small amount of time with a small team. This has the merit that you are more likely to get group teamwork and cooperation started in smaller groups (say, five people, for illustration). The concept of the "player-coach" is reinforced in smaller groups.

Each group leader needs to feel confident that his or her performance appraisal as a group leader will be given significant weight in his or her performance appraisal. This is necessary to keep the group leader's eye on the ball; moreover, everyone else in the group must understand that the group leader is not getting a free ride through reduced production hours.

With respect to compensation, the group leader should not receive "position pay." **No one should automatically be compensated more highly for taking on a group leadership role. Group leaders should be paid more if they do, in fact, raise the performance of their team. They should not be paid more merely for the assumption of the role.**

If there were position pay for group leaders, their groups would likely initiate a palace revolt, fearing—or assuming—that their leaders would just top-up their own individual compensation, refocus on their own client priorities, and abandon their coaching responsibilities. The issue for group leaders, in some environments, is not so much about compensation as it is about protection.

4 INPUT ON THE COMPENSATION OF TEAM MEMBERS

Another element is necessary to get a group system off the ground. Group leaders must have a formal role in providing input to the firm's performance appraisal and compensation system.

The irreducible core of a group leader's activities is getting the team to plan its activities and then (what is most important and most time-consuming) to follow up with each team member to ensure that agreed-upon activities are indeed executed. Coaches should be encouraged to rely primarily on such qualities as personal charm, interpersonal influence, and inspirational charisma to ensure that their team members pull their weight.

However, it would be naive to believe that these leaders will not occasionally have to deal with severe degrees of noncompliance, such as refusing to show up for group meetings or failure to deliver on promises to the team.

What, then, should the group leader do? The best solution is to require each leader to provide formal input to the firm's performance appraisal and compensation system. The group leader should not, in our view, determine compensation and cannot be the sole source of performance appraisal. However, he or she does have the opportunity to comment on how well each team member has contributed to the collective effort.

Karl Kristoff, vice president of the law firm of Hodgson Russ, had this to say about providing input on individuals' compensation:

> Practice leaders at our firm have the ability to provide input into determining an individual's compensation. They have not always had as much ability in that regard as they are gaining now. I think that's part of a shift in culture that we're going through in the firm as a whole. However, this year, for example, as we are beginning to think about compensation decisions, each of our group leaders have met with the com-

mittees who set compensation to talk exactly about the contributions, billable and otherwise, of each member of their groups.

5 VALUING EVERYONE'S NON-REIMBURSED TIME

The next essential component of the group leader system is that the firm must credibly convey to its people that activities conducted with non-billable (non-reimbursed, non-production, or non-fee-earning) time by all group members (not just the group leader) are valued, monitored, and considered an essential part of their performance appraisal.

Much of what groups do to create their future success involves investment of non-reimbursed time in activities that build the future of the business. Obvious examples include various kinds of marketing activities, development of tools, conducting training programs, and so on.

Unfortunately, what happens in too many firms is this: The team meets and lays out a wonderful plan for marketing, training, and tool development. Then, the group leader comes around a few weeks later and says, "Hey, Fred. How's that article going that you promised to write?" And Fred replies, "Well, I've got some more client work to do, so I'm too busy to write it. Client work trumps everything else, right? At least that's what the compensation committee believes, and I've got to protect myself. Sorry, coach!"

So the article never gets written, and all the other team members reason the same way. They might just as well not have had their planning meeting. They might just as well not have had a group. They might just as well not have a group leader.

The point here is not about working more hours, since every person is already spending some (and sometimes significant) non-fee-earning time. The point is that the essence of having groups is the willingness of individuals to contribute at least a portion of their non-fee-earning time to the group effort, and agree to be held strictly accountable to the group for what they have promised. They don't have to promise a lot, but what they promise, they must do. Where everyone in the group commits to investing roughly equal amounts of non-reimbursed time, no member is doing more than the others or is left to feel taken advantage of.

Note that the primary obligation and accountability is neither to the group leader nor to firm management. The obligation is for team members to keep their promises to their team. The role of the group leader (and firm management) is to be the conscience: monitoring and helping people keep their promises.

 ## 6 WHAT YOU NEED FROM YOUR FIRM LEADER

Another key to the success of group leaders and their groups is the attention, commitment, and dedication of the firm leadership. This is particularly true if the traditions of groups and group leadership are not yet well established in your firm. So what should you ask your firm leader to do, to help you perform your role?

Firm leaders should:

a) Be front-and-center, continually letting people know that having effectively functioning groups is one of the firm's highest priorities

b) Encourage those who are reluctant to get on board

c) Volunteer to attend group meetings

d) Be an enthusiastic cheerleader.

e) Develop a group leaders' council

f) Schedule periodic progress reviews.

a) Be front-and-center; let people know that this is a high priority

For an initiative to garner the attention it requires, your firm leader must continue to provide hands-on support. He or she, above all others, must let people know that developing effective groups is something the firm takes very seriously. The firm leader must articulate to everyone the desirability of high-performance groups and how they can benefit both the firm and (more importantly) the individual careers of the people involved.

Firm leaders must keep communicating the message until everyone tells them they are overdoing it. First, we hear. Then, we understand. Then we believe. If firm management stops telling everyone about the importance of group effectiveness, everyone will conclude that management was not serious after all. Good communication does not necessarily guarantee success but poor communication (or firm leader abdication) probably guarantees failure.

b)   Encourage get those who are reluctant on board

It is imperative that some effort be directed to the informal opinion leaders in the group. If a firm leader can convince them of the need for high-performance groups, others will quickly determine that this is a good thing to support. How does your firm leader get them on board? Find a way to get them involved in the process, calling upon them to participate in some meaningful way. If this doesn't work, then a personal appeal from the firm leader may at least neutralize their disruptive capabilities. They should be asked to suggest ways in which to keep group functioning on a positive and constructive course. (We will have more to say on dealing with prima donnas in chapter 9.)

c)   Volunteer to attend group meetings

Your firm leader's most powerful management tool is attention. What he or she devotes attention to and invests time in is usually deemed as important! **There is no substitute for the enthusiasm that can result from having your firm leader show interest in a group's activities by volunteering to attend one of their meetings as an "outside observer."**

Firm leaders should review their calendars and determine how many of those group meetings they can drop in on over the next month. Their presence will signify to a team that its progress is something they are seriously interested in. By attending the entire meeting they will gain some firsthand experience at observing how the group reacts and what significant issues are unearthed.

d)   Be enthusiastic cheerleaders

Your firm leader's second most powerful tool is to serve as cheerleader. Firm leaders should talk to each group leader about what they have observed from sitting in on other groups' meetings. That will demonstrate that group effectiveness is important to them, as well as signal to group leaders who are not holding meetings that their commitment to moving forward is genuine.

Firm leaders should send e-mails to a group's leader and its members acknowledging the good action ideas that the group generated and indicating that they are looking forward to hearing a progress report at the next meeting. That will provide the additional catalyst to drive team members to follow through on activities they volunteered to implement.

e) Develop a group leaders' council

Increasingly firms have come to recognize the challenges of finding the means by which to facilitate the exchange of communications, information, and knowledge among and between the departments, groups, and industry teams that make up their firms. Many firms have initiated some form of "group leaders council" that meets for a couple of hours (at least quarterly) to review and discuss what is going on within their various groups. This council can be an excellent venue for group leaders to assist each other by sharing common experiences and common challenges.

f) Schedule periodic progress reviews

Firm leaders should schedule a review meeting every six months with all group leaders to discuss progress, get specific feedback on action plans, and offer suggestions to enhance performance. Setting the meeting date well in advance signals to everyone the importance of being able to report specific results.

Terms of Engagement Questions:

1. What is my minimum-maximum requirement for the amount of non-reimbursed time that I should devote to group leadership activities?

2. Can we agree on what my rights are, as group leader, to interact with group members (and their clients)? What's acceptable, and what's not?

3. To what degree can I be assured that my compensation will be be based entirely or in large part on my effectiveness in helping the group succeed?

4. Can we agree that I will be allowed to provide individual performance appraisal input on each member of the team and that my input will be accorded serious consideration irrespective of that individual's personal production?

5. Can we agree that firm management will communicate internally that activities conducted with non-reimbursed time are valued, monitored, and considered an essential part of each person's performance appraisal—and that group leaders will be called upon to provide their input?

6. Can I have the assurance of firm management that my efforts as group leader will be supported by:

   a) a clear articulation of the importance of strong groups within the firm, and a clear articulation of my mandate and powers as a group leader

   b) active encouragement provided to everyone to get them on board with the initiative

   c) the attendance of firm leaders at periodic meeting of the group

   d) an ongoing and visible demonstration of acknowledgement to those groups making progress

   e) the initiation of a group leaders' council to facilitate communications and information sharing

   f) the scheduling of periodic progress reviews

chapter 3

Build Relationships— One at a Time

What are the key skills you must have?

YOUR TECHNICAL COMPETENCE and knowledge will determine a small portion of your effectiveness as a group leader. The overwhelming determinant of whether or not you will be effective has to do with your people skills—interpersonal, social, and emotional.

We have asked numerous professionals to tell us about their most trusted mentor, teacher, advisor, or leader. What specific characteristics and behaviors made them believe that this was someone that they could really put their faith in, someone that they would feel comfortable going to for advice? Here is a sampling of some of our clients' responses, provided here in their words, not ours.

> One important aspect of a great practice leader for me is how interested that person *really* is in your life. For example, if you tell this individual about something significant that is going on in your personal life, do they follow up and find out what happened?

Anyone can tell you to cheer up. There are lots of people who will tell you that when things aren't going well. It makes them feel good. But see who really goes out of their way to acknowledge when things are going well with the contribution you made on some important project. The real coach is someone proud of your accomplishments, not jealous of your success, or taking credit for it behind your back.

When the chips are down and it's you against them, most will scramble to protect their own interests. But your trusted advisor is that individual who is supportive and has some ideas or a plan to help both of you, not someone who only looks to save their own butt.

A true coach is someone who is honest and will tell you something you may not want to hear. This requires that rare individual who is willing to have you be upset with them if it will help you.

Your effectiveness in being a group leader (or coach) is more about you than it is about the person you are coaching. In particular, **your success as a leader will turn on whether or not you are received by your people as a trusted advisor. If they so view you, then you can make a lot of mistakes and still have a big impact.** But if they view you as somebody trying to play the role of boss or cop or technical expert, telling them what they are doing wrong, then you are going to fail.

In your role as coach, you will need to deal with your colleagues with the same sort of delicacy and forethought in your phraseology that you would do in dealing with your most powerful clients. You must take a deep breath every time you go into a colleague's office and ask yourself, "Why am I here? What am I trying to accomplish?"

Here are some other questions you should ask yourself:

1. How many of those that you have the responsibility to coach would consider you their trusted advisor?

2. Do you actually like the people you are coaching—and do they know you like them?

3. Do the people you are seeking to coach actually view you as being someone who cares about others? Do they think you care specifically about them?

4. Can you help your people to visualize and articulate their dreams?

5. Are you investing time toward building a strong relationship?

6. Do people feel comfortable admitting their flaws to you?

7. Do you always act and offer your advice in the best interests of your people?

1 HOW MANY OF THOSE THAT YOU HAVE THE RESPONSIBILITY TO COACH WOULD CONSIDER YOU THEIR TRUSTED ADVISOR?

What are the characteristics of trusted advisors? What makes a person somebody you would turn to, eagerly and positively, for advice, guidance, and counsel?

In *The Trusted Advisor*, David and his co-authors made a list of common traits of trusted advisors. Here (changing the language from dealing with external clients to that of dealing with team members) is the list:

Trusted advisors:

1. Seem to understand us, effortlessly, and like us

2. Are consistent: we can depend on them

3. Always help us see things from fresh perspectives

4. Don't try to force things on us

5. Help us think things through (it's our decision)

6. Don't substitute their judgment for ours

7. Don't panic or get overemotional: they stay calm

8. Help us *think* and separate our logic from our emotion

9. Criticize and correct us gently, lovingly

10. Don't pull their punches: we can rely on them to tell us the truth

11. Are in it for the long haul: the relationship is more important than the current issue

12. Give us reasoning (to help us think), not just their conclusions

13. Give us options, increase our understanding of those options, give us their recommendation, and let us choose

14. Challenge our assumptions: help us uncover the false assumptions we've been working under

15. Make us feel comfortable and casual personally, but they take the issues seriously

16. Act like a person, not someone in a role

17. Are reliably on our side, and always seem to have our interests at heart

18. Remember everything we ever said (without notes)

19. Are always honorable: they don't gossip about others (we trust their values)

20. Help us put our issues in context, often through the use of metaphors, stories, and anecdotes (few problems are completely unique)

21. Have a sense of humor to diffuse our tension in tough situations

22. Are smart sometimes in ways we're not

As you examine this list, here are a few questions for you to consider:

1. Would you agree that this is what a client would appreciate in a trusted advisor?

2. Would you also agree that this is what your team members would appreciate?

3. Would you agree that, if you acted in this way, they would be more likely to accept your influence?

4. How well does this list describe how you currently act in guiding, counseling, encouraging, and supervising others?

You will notice, of course, that a few of these items are about intellectual skills (e.g., help people see things from a new perspective). You will also notice that many more of them call for emotional, social, interpersonal, and verbal skills. It's a challenging role!

A trusted advisor helps you see things a new way. Notice that this is different from telling you what to do. The added value of the coach becomes: "This person helps me view things in a different way than I've viewed before. He or she doesn't try to force his or her answers on me." A trusted advisor says "Have you thought of this? Have you thought of that? If I were in your shoes maybe I'd think this might be a good idea."

Ron Daniel, McKinsey's managing director from 1976 to 1988, had this to say at a conference of McKinsey directors:

> My message—in talking about how leaders and followers interact—is a simple one:
>
> I believe that a follower in looking to a leader must have (1) professional respect for him and (2) personal trust in him—if the leader is to be effective in his role.
>
> Respect and trust, however, are only the price of admission. Beyond that a leader must demonstrate behavior that suggests (1) a willingness to make a real investment in the professional development of junior people and (2) a genuine concern for the junior person as a human being.
>
> These interactions between leaders and followers are fueled and facilitated by active and regular communications.

While a coach needs many attributes and skills, one attribute dominates the list: whether or not those you are trying to influence must trust your motives. If people think you are truly trying to help them, they will listen to you; if they think you are nagging and exhorting them in order to make yourself look good, they will resist your influence.

2 DO YOU ACTUALLY LIKE THE PEOPLE YOU ARE COACHING—AND DO THEY KNOW YOU LIKE THEM?

One of the characteristics listed earlier is that our trusted advisors tend to like us. A trusted advisor is somebody who you think is basically on your side. **So, do you actually like the people you are counseling and do they think you like them? If they don't, then your effectiveness as a coach will diminish, no matter how valid is the intellectual rigor of your comments.**

What happens when you try to be a coach to somebody you don't actually like? You could try to think positively—to focus on the positive aspects of the person and try not to dwell on the parts that you don't like. It is said that good acting is not lying—it is finding that small part of the character that you can relate to and ignoring everything else. You don't have to like everything about the character; but if you can find that one little bit that you can relate to, you can focus solely on that bit and achieve the necessary empathy.

Can you like everybody? No. But if you can't find *anything* that you like or can relate to in someone then you cannot coach that person. There are group leaders we know who've told us that they dislike some of the people they're coaching. They ask, "How do I deal with this dumb idiot?" Our response is: "If you think he is a dumb idiot, there's probably not much you can do." Unless you can find something you can empathize with, you will not have an influence on him. That's a tough message. You can't influence people you despise, because most of us are too transparent. We're just not that good at faking it.

3 | DO THE PEOPLE YOU ARE SEEKING TO COACH ACTUALLY VIEW YOU AS BEING SOMEONE WHO CARES ABOUT OTHERS?

Can the skills of a coach or a trusted advisor be learned or do you have to be born with them? As with most skills in life, our answer follows the "10-80-10" rule. For most skills, 10 percent of people are naturals—you don't need to teach them a thing, they've always done it that way. Another 10 percent will never learn it because they basically don't want to. You can get them to read all the books but they are still not going to do it well. They are "nonparticipants." The good news is that most of us are part of the 80 percent in the middle. We are neither naturals nor nonparticipants, but we *can* learn new skills if properly guided.

What is *not* teachable is another key requirement of trusted advisors and coaches: that he or she is viewed as honorable, honest, trustworthy, consistent, dependable, and has an interest in others. Those are not behavioral descriptors, but character descriptors. A worldwide study that David conducted showed that the most successful managers were notable less for their beliefs and actions than for their underlying character.

Were you chosen to be a group leader because you are seen by those around you as honorable, trustworthy, a person of integrity, someone who cares about others? If you are viewed that way, you will be forgiven a lot of mistakes. If you are not viewed that way, then no matter how many books on coaching you read, you will fail. Character is probably not easily changed (or teachable) among adults with many years of work experience.

There are a lot of group leaders who fail this test. They fundamentally are not interested in the other person. They are coaching solely because they want to raise the group's financial performance and not because they want to help the individuals within the group. Some of them don't even like their colleagues; they think of them as billable-hour machines.

A coach who talks only about work and never about personal matters will have less influence on us. If someone's going to have influence, we've got to believe that when she offers us a critique (and gives suggestions on what to do) that she really, actually cares about us. Maybe she doesn't like everything about us, but she has to care. Make an analogy with a client. You have more influence over a client if he thinks you care. You don't have to like everything about him, but you have to care about him, and about his success.

Every time you go into a meeting, role-play a little mantra in your head:

> "My goal for this meeting is to help this person, my goal for this meeting is to help this person, and my goal for this meeting is to help this person."

If you have influence only if people think you care about them, you have two options. **Either you actually do care about your people, or you are remarkably good at faking it**—making others think you care when in fact you don't. There are a few "natural seducers" in the world that can pull this off. That option is not available to the rest of us. That's why coaching is so hard.

 ## CAN YOU HELP YOUR PEOPLE TO VISUALIZE AND ARTICULATE THEIR DREAMS?

To influence people, you must make them *want* to do something. How is this achieved? Dale Carnegie gave us the secret when he wrote: "He or she who can get people to dream can conquer the world." A large part of getting people to show energy is to get them to fervently desire something, the new dream. You can't just say, "thou shalt be energized." That doesn't work very well. Much more powerful is to help create the tantalizing dream:

> *"How would you like to have this kind of work? These kinds of clients? This kind of reputation? Let's talk about where you want to be three years from now: in what way could your work life be better? What would you like to have that you don't have now?"*

The response you're looking for is: "Wow, is that possible?" And you say "Well, work with me and we can get you real close." The job is to get them to choose a goal, because of course the minute they choose a goal, you get what we call "nagging rights." Suppose one of your people says, "I really would love to build my skills in these areas, develop my expertise here, and have the following kinds of work within three years." You can then say, "Okay, let's talk about that. What would be your first logical step? What help would you need from me? Let's think it through together."

If you can discuss with each of the people in your group what they want to achieve with their careers and help them determine for themselves the first logical steps, you can then come back a month later and say, for example, "By the way, how's that article going that you said you were going to write?"

You need to understand each of your people in such a way that you help each one develop an individualized, stretch goal, custom-tailored, that they will accept as exciting and as challenging. They must believe that they should do it for themselves, because it is in their very best interests, not just for the firm or group. If you can't pull that off, you will never be effective as a practice leader.

5 ARE YOU INVESTING TIME TOWARD BUILDING A STRONG RELATIONSHIP?

Whether or not someone is willing to accept your coaching depends upon whether or not you have a relationship with that person. If you do, they'll accept their input, or at least listen. If there is no prior relationship, if it is just a transaction, they'll pretend to listen, but they'll resist all the way.

We think relationships between human beings follow similar principles whether we are talking about business life or personal life. **Ask yourself: what are the actions, secrets, and rules of romance in your personal life that build strong, deep, long lasting relationships?** In short, what do you do to build a great relationship? Here are a few of the responses we elicited from a group of professional group leaders when we posed these questions:

1. You need to be available as a sounding board to your romantic partner. You don't need to be critical. Listen before you react.

2. Work really hard at listening and understanding.

3. Do the unexpected occasionally; don't take each other for granted.

4. Discuss your common values.

5. Communicate honestly, openly and frequently.

6. Spend time with each other, with no agenda.

7. Show your appreciation regularly, but not in a formulaic way.

8. Find ways to have fun together.

9. Don't let problems fester. Catch them and discuss them early.

Would you agree that these principles of great relationship building in personal life have their counterparts in work life? What other rules of relationship building with friends, romantic partners, and family members would you identify? Do you apply those same principles at work? Are you as considerate, supportive, sensitive to feelings, understanding, and loyal to those you lead as to those in your personal life? These questions are not about what you "should" do in any moral sense. The point is simply that you will have greater influence on others to the extent that you behave in this way.

How well do you pass these tests in building relationships with each of your people?

1. Show interest

2. Understand your colleague

3. Spend time off the issue

4. Give of yourself

I. Show Interest

In romance, you show interest by asking questions, listening, and getting the other person to do the talking. In other words you can't initiate a relationship if you go in there with your agenda too explicitly showing. The essence of romancing another person is getting him or her to talk about what they want to talk about. It's not that you're not going to get to your agenda, but rather it's an issue of timing.

2. Understand Your Colleague

The essence of building a new relationship is that you need to understand this other human being as fast as you can, so that you can figure out how to customize your language and change your behavior to have influence.

3. Spend time off the issue

Take them out for drinks, take them out for a cup of coffee, talk to them about their lives and their practice and shut up! Just listen. The more you can learn about people, about what they like and don't like, what they respond to and don't respond to, then the more able you are to figure out the right things to say to have influence. Try to find your common ground. We are not saying you never have an agenda, but you keep it to yourself until you have done the things that win you permission to coach.

4. Give of yourself

If you want to earn somebody's trust and confidence in a romantic relationship, you do a little something to test the waters. You make a gesture of good will. But you can't get what you want from the other person if you haven't first given. Which leads us back to the conclusion that before you can get somebody else to change his or her behavior you have to ask yourself how you can actually help this person.

It must not have the appearance of a barter deal: "I'll do this for you if only you'll do that for me." That's too crass and it doesn't work. It can't be "I'll help you now, and I want this right away." You build relationships by being seen to be willing to invest in the relationship.

 ## 6 DO PEOPLE FEEL COMFORTABLE ADMITTING THEIR FLAWS TO YOU?

You cannot be a good coach if people don't feel comfortable talking about their flaws and weaknesses in front of you. A good test of coaching is: are they coming to you, or do you always have to go to them? They will only come to you if you're even tempered, you're even keeled, you're there to help, and they can confess weakness to you.

Cliff Farrah, a strategy consultant with experience at Kaiser Associates, Oracle, A.T. Kearney, and EDS, says:

> One approach to get people to acknowledge their flaws and weaknesses to you is to adapt your response to the timing of when they acknowledge the issue. I've got a "free pass" rule. As long as issues are raised early, I will be nothing but supportive. No one is perfect, and by getting advance warning, we can deal with most things and compensate for individual weaknesses. I've yet to run across a situation that couldn't be fixed. But I make it painful for people who don't admit flaws/weaknesses in advance of it becoming an issue. When I get blindsided, I make people very uncomfortable, to the point that it now rarely happens in my practice. I preach using the carrot, but I carry a big stick just in case.

Most of coaching is about emotions. If you can make somebody want to do something, you've done maybe nine tenths of your job. Showing them how to do it is the easy part. The main job is helping them overcome their fears and concerns. If they say, "I'm worried about this," it doesn't help to simply say, "Don't worry about that!" You've got to help people deal with their worries and their fears.

A good coach needs to have emotional courage. This means that you've got to be willing to be a human being to your colleagues, rather than stay in your leader role. **Many people, when they first become group leaders, are surprised by the amount of emotional investment it takes.** You ride on a lot of roller coasters. But to do the job properly, you've got to come across as being on an even keel. This is very hard when one person is telling you about this dramatic event and another is telling you about that tragic occurrence and you'd love the freedom to react with your emotions.

But the minute you do, you're dead, because as a group leader, you are an emotional amplifier. If somebody has a little problem, that's OK. But as soon as the group leader says we have a problem, everybody else thinks we're going bankrupt. Or the minute you think something is going partic-

In *True Professionalism*, David outlined this related attribute of a successful coach:

If your job as a leader is to influence and motivate my colleagues (and me), then you must infect us with your personal enthusiasm. (And I don't mean an exclusive enthusiasm for money.) If I am to follow you and accept your influence, I expect you to be passionate about our work, be fascinated with clients and their problems and care deeply about accomplishing something meaningful. If "making money" is your exclusive goal, you will be a bad leader. (Perhaps a great financial officer, but a bad leader!)

I don't want the head of my practice (or firm) to be a cold, calculating "businessperson." I want someone who is not afraid to *care*—about clients, about quality, about senior *and* junior people. Someone who will take the job because they want to make a difference in people's lives, not because they want the position, the title, the power. I want someone of whom it will be said "This is a better, more exciting place to work since he or she took over. He or she believes in things that I can believe in—and it is proven every day because we do things differently now." Give me someone like that, and I'll agree to accept you as my coach.

ularly well, everybody else relaxes and thinks: "Fine, I don't have to work so hard."

7 DO YOU ALWAYS ACT AND OFFER YOUR ADVICE IN THE BEST INTERESTS OF YOUR PEOPLE?

Nobody wants to be coached by a know-it-all. One of the very best ways of being an advisor is to let the person know that you don't have all of the answers all of the time. It requires you to be open to confessing your shortcomings and acknowledging your personal vulnerabilities. In making such an admission, you will immediately be perceived as sincere and credible. A great way to give advice (after admitting your own personal infallibility) is to say, "There are things I don't know and there are things I know I know. And this is something I know I know."

In *Practice What You Preach,* David was able to identify what group leaders must (at a minimum) do to create a success culture. Her are some of those actions.

1. Act as if not trying is the only sin.

2. Act as if you want everyone to succeed.

3. Actively help people with their personal development.

4. Allow your people to try different skills and experience different things.

5. Always do what you say you are going to do.

6. Believe in, and keep the faith with, what you say your mission is.

7. Never talk down to anyone, senior or junior.

8. Facilitate, don't dictate.

9. Give credit where credit is due.

10. Lead by example; be what you want others to be.

11. Manage people in the way that works for each individual, not just how you like to manage. You don't have to be a chameleon, just adaptable.

12. Show enthusiasm and drive; they are infectious and addictive.

13. Take work seriously, but don't take yourself seriously.

14. Work the halls and get to know everyone.

15. Speak regularly about your vision and philosophy so people know where you stand.

16. Let people know you as a human being, not just as their leader.

Certain other qualities were expected of group leaders in the most financially successful offices. The original (longer) list contained the following:

1. Be demanding but make sure your demands are driven by the common good, not your personal interests.

2. Be willing to take money from short-term profits to fund people's workplace satisfaction.

3. Build your organization and its roles around the people you have and then fill in the gaps around that.

4. Create a "casual, relaxed, collaborative" environment, but also a professional one.

5. Be an intermediary for your people to get cooperation for them from elsewhere in the organization.

6. Make sure your people know the firm will take care of them in a crisis.

7. Show sensitivity to what people are going through.

YOUR STARTING ACTION PLAN

Your starting action plan should proceed as follows:

1. Schedule time to meet informally (no agenda) with each person.

2. Discuss their career goals, ambitions, and desires

3. Look for your opportunity to obtain "nagging rights."

I. Schedule time to meet informally with each person

Set aside a few hours each week to make informal, unscheduled visits with each and every member of your team, seniors and juniors. Start your efforts quietly with minimal fanfare, taking small steps, and building incrementally.

Make your visits casual events. Drop in to people's offices, ask questions ("What are you working on?"), show concern ("How can I help?"), and take supportive action. **Follow up immediately on any actions that you agree to take, so that people can see that you are reliable and that they can depend on your word.** Doing what you say you will do, when you said you would do it, sets a powerful example.

Here are some further questions that you can ask, as you spend time with your people.

What can I do to help you

1. Make things run more smoothly?

2. Make better use of your skills?

3. Save you time or increase your ability to get things done?

You probably will not want to ask these questions verbatim. It is the spirit of the questions that must come through, but your vocabulary has to be far less formal. Get out there often. Sporadic visits don't produce lasting results. Be sensitive to the fact that people will observe your first few visits with skepticism, especially if you have not been known for visiting with people in their offices in the past. The relationship will not really form until a pattern of productive visits and productive outcomes has been established. You need to convey that you are trying to connect, not impress or confront.

2. Discuss their career goals, ambitions, and desires

In the most successful firms, each individual acts as if he or she has a personal strategic career plan. Each has thought through what their special value on the marketplace will be, what will make them more than just one more practitioner in their specialty and how they plan to achieve this vision of personal career progress.

In such an environment, the organization of groups serves as the icing on this cake of individual, energized, directed efforts. Unfortunately, in too many groups the individuals have no such commitment to a personal development plan. **Your job as a coach is not to develop a career plan for your group members, but to ensure that they each develop one for themselves.** This takes nothing more than engaging in private closed-door meetings with each professional to discuss:

> *"What, precisely, is it that is going to make you special (or even more special) in the marketplace over the next few years? Would you like to develop an expertise in a particular technical or industry area, in certain types of transactions, or in the problems of certain types of clients? You probably can develop cutting-edge expertise in any one of these, but not all of them simultaneously. The choice is yours. All that anyone here can ask of you is that you focus and stretch—that you pick a career-building goal and work towards it."*

By pursuing this approach practice leaders are ceding to individuals, as they should, the autonomy to determine their own professional lives. By requiring answers, they ensure that each individual's efforts are energized and directed. Teams, then, can be configured around members who have a common vision of their personal development goals, career strategies, designated specialties, or standards of excellence.

In theory, such an approach could lead to each individual pursuing a very different personal vision of excellence. In practice, this is rarely the case. The practice leader who poses these questions does not just accept whatever the professional says, but instead plays the friendly skeptic role. For example, he may point out that a person has chosen something that no one else in any (existing or contemplated) group wants to pursue, and ask, "Do you really want to try to develop that specialty alone? Some of your colleagues are committing themselves to developing a practice in a related area: would being a part of that team fulfill your ambitions?"

From this approach, a set of teams can be constructed from the enthusiasms of individuals. **As one of the best managers we have met told us: "I'd rather have a set of messy teams filled with enthusiasts than an analytically correct set of teams filled with dutiful citizens."**

Ask each of your people:

1. What is it that they want to do that would make them distinctive in their competitive marketplace and even more valuable to their clients?

2. What kind of support would they need from the firm and from the group in order to achieve their desired distinctiveness?

3. What specific form of professional and personal training and development do they think that they might benefit from?

4. What do they feel has been their most significant professional (and personal) accomplishment up to this point?

5. What was their biggest dream when they first entered the profession and what is their greatest source of pride now?

6. What are their outside interests, what is their family situation, their spouse's background, and how supportive are their spouses with respect to their career pursuits?

7. What are their personal views on the characteristics that make for an effective coach?

8. Would they actually appreciate some coaching assistance, and if they would, in what specific areas?

9. What is their personal and candid assessment of your personal strengths and weaknesses?

10. What is their personal and candid assessment of their colleagues within the practice team?

11. How well do they think the group currently performs, and what are their recommendations for improvement?.

From this kind of information you should be better able to determine what you could do as the group leader to support each person's individual career aspirations and efforts.

3. Look for your opportunity to obtain "nagging rights"

We all routinely draw up "wish lists" of things we "intend" to do (and which we generally fail to do). What will get us to take action? For most, the answer lies in supplementing self-discipline with some form of external conscience. **We must willingly, knowingly, voluntarily, give someone else "nagging rights" to keep us honest on the goals we set for ourselves.**

Robert E. Gilbert, of Miller Canfield Paddock and Stone, one of Detroit's oldest law firms, noted:

> The problem is, for many professionals, words are action. Professionals make their living uttering or writing words; that's their stock in trade. But in management, action is action, and you have to overcome the tendency, reinforced by years of education and training, of most professionals to substitute words for action. My challenge, therefore, is to get the groups to *do* something.

Nagging rights don't have to be negative or punitive. In fact they work best when they're not. The key is the willingness of the individual to accept accountability, just as an athlete voluntarily agrees to be coached. A coach will exhort, demand, insist on one more practice, one more try. Yet the athlete gives permission to the coach to be demanding, because the goal is one the athlete chose. It's nothing more than saying "I believe in this goal. Keep me honest. Force me, if necessary, to do my best." Only in this way will superior accomplishments result.

chapter 4

Dare to Be Inspiring

Do you know how to inspire people?

YOUR GROUP WILL BEST ACHIEVE peak performance by unleashing the power of your people. This is not done by managing them, nor by leading them, but by inspiring them.

There are countless texts on leadership, covering everything from how everyone can be a leader, to the immutable laws of leadership. While these texts have something to offer a struggling group leader, they rarely seem to articulate fully what Marvin Bower brought to McKinsey, making it the most renowned management-consulting firm in the world. Nor how a succession of revered leaders guided Goldman Sachs to become (eventually) the global powerhouse that it is today. While few of us may achieve that level of accomplishment, it is sad that so few even aspire to it.

Jack Welch, the recently retired chairman and CEO of General Electric, said:

> The job of any leader is to build self-confidence in the people around him. Make those people feel twelve feet tall. Clap for every achievement, no matter how small, with everybody around you. That's a hell of a lot more important than some finite strategy.

There are rare individuals in every profession who strive to create big dreams. Dreams that are steeped in a strong set of personal values, in setting high standards, and in striving to lift the spirits of human potential. This is not about management, and it's not just about leadership either. It goes beyond whatever the words "management" and "leadership" might convey to us.

Let's look at a couple of examples of extraordinary individuals who have something to teach us about the way in which they connect with their people.

A precocious composer, Benjamin Zander has had the distinction of conducting the Boston Philharmonic. Zander sees himself more as a teacher than as a leader or maestro. Much of what he has to say suggests an understanding of what it takes to inspire talented people, both musicians and other high achievers.

> It wasn't until I was about forty-five that I realized something amazing: **The conductor doesn't make a sound. The conductor's power depends on his ability to make other people powerful.** That insight changed everything for me. I started paying attention to how I was enabling my musicians to be the best performers they could be.
>
> My job as a conductor is to teach musicians to be expressive performers of great music. In any performance, there are always two people onstage: the one trying to play, and another one who whispers, "Do you know how many people play this piece better than you do? Here comes that difficult passage that you missed last time—and you're going to miss it again this time!" Sometimes that other voice is so loud that it drowns out the music. I'm always looking for ways to silence that voice.
>
> I've developed a simple technique to quiet that second voice. Every fall, on the first day of class, I make an announcement: 'Everybody gets an A.' There's only one condition: Students have to submit a letter, written on that first day but dated the following May, that begins: 'Dear Mr. Zander, I got my A because. . . .'

In other words, they have to tell me, at the beginning of my course, who they will have become by the end of the course that will justify this extraordinary grade.

That simple A changes everything. It transforms my relationship with everybody in the room. We're giving out grades in every encounter we have with people. We can choose to give out grades as an expectation to live up to, and then we can reassess them according to performance. Or we can offer grades as a possibility to live into. The second approach is much more powerful.

The A is easy to misunderstand. People say, "Oh, you mean it's just pretending that everybody is the same." It's not that at all. Nor is it about pretending that people can do things they can't do. The letters that students write to me about what they will do to deserve their A give me much richer information about how the students stack up against their dreams. They write, "Suddenly I'm not shy anymore, and I enjoy playing," or "I'm no longer depressed by criticism." That's the kind of information that I need to help them perform at their best.

One way I know if I am performing well is to look in my musicians' eyes. The eyes never lie. If the eyes are shining, then I know that my leadership is working. Human beings in the presence of possibility react physically as well as emotionally. If the eyes aren't shining, I ask myself, 'What am I doing that's keeping my musicians' eyes from shining?'

Our second example comes from the comments delivered by Leo Burnett at his firm's annual breakfast meeting in 1967. Through thirty-six years under its spirited founder—during the last four of which he held the title of founding chairman—the Leo Burnett Company created some of history's most enduring advertising, ranging from the Marlboro Man to Kellogg's Tony the Tiger, to the "friendly skies" of United Airlines.

Somewhere along the line, after I'm finally off the premises, you or your successors may want to take my name off the premises too. You may want to call yourselves "Twain, Rogers, Sawyer and Finn" . . . or something. That will certainly be okay with me if it's good for you. But let me tell you when I might demand that you take my name off the door.

That will be the day when you spend more time trying to make money and less time making advertising—our kind of advertising. When you forget that the sheer fun of advertising and the lift you get out of it—the creative climate of the place—should be as important as money to the very special breed of writers and artists and people who compose this firm of ours—and make it tick.

When you lose that restless feeling that nothing you do is ever good enough. When you lose your itch to do the job well for its own sake—regardless of the client, or the money, or the effort it takes. When you lose your passion for thoroughness . . . your hatred of loose ends. When you stop reaching for the manner, the overtones, the marriage of words and pictures that produce the fresh, the memorable, and the believable effect. When you stop rededicating yourselves every day to the idea that better advertising is what the Leo Burnett Company is all about.

When you are no longer what Thoreau called "a firm with a conscience"—which means an organization of conscientious men and women. When you begin to compromise your integrity—which has always been the heart's blood— the very guts of this firm. When you stoop to convenient expediency and rationalize yourselves into acts of opportunism—for the sake of a fast buck.

When you show the slightest signs of crudeness, inappropriateness or smart-aleckness—and you lose that subtle sense of the fitness of things. When your main interest becomes a matter of size just to be big—rather than good, hard, wonderful work. When your outlook narrows down to the number of windows—in the walls of your office. When you lose your humility and become big-shot weisenheimers, a little too big for your boots.

When you disapprove of something, and start tearing the hell out of the individual who did it rather than the work itself. When you stop building on strong and vital ideas, and start a routine production line.

When you start believing that, in the interest of efficiency, a creative spirit and the urge to create can be delegated and administered, and forget that they can only be nurtured, stimulated, and inspired. When you start giving lip service to this being a "creative firm" and stop really being one.

That, ladies and gentlemen, is when I shall insist you take my name off the door.

Although Burnett died in 1971, his spirit continued to motivate thousands of intensely loyal Burnetters in more than sixty offices worldwide. "Leo had that ability, like a good athletic coach has, of making you do better than you thought you could," recalled his wife, Naomi. To this day, Burnett still offers shiny red apples on all reception desks free of charge, a legacy from Leo and as a homage to his spirit.

THE LESSONS

Notice what Zander and Burnett were offering. Zander described the actions of an inspired and inspiring leader:

Enable people to be the best they can be; allow people to aspire to their dreams; ensure that their eyes are shining; and wake them up to not remaining complacent.

From Burnett the message was similar, albeit with different words:

Never lose that itch to do your best; never stoop to acts of opportunism for a fast buck; never lose your humility; never stop building on strong ideas; and never forget that

> the creative human spirit needs to be nurtured and stimu-
> lated.

If you seek to inspire your people, Zander and Burnett suggest a common element: it all starts with spending time to build and nurture a relationship, above and beyond the immediate task at hand.

Pete Friedes, the retired CEO of Hewitt Associates, puts it this way:

> Leaders or managers need to understand that every sin-
> gle interaction they have with one of their people is on two
> levels: the content level (whatever they are talking about)
> and the trust level (either building it or destroying it). For
> example, when managers talk inappropriately about others
> not present, or show they are willing to cut corners, or de-
> ceive "just a little," they are destroying trust with everyone
> who hears it directly and more people later. Likewise, if they
> are always straight with people, in all situations, they are
> building trust, which can only be done over some period of
> time.

Years ago, Friedes pointed out to David that every conversation you have with someone advances, diminishes, or leaves neutral your relationship with that person. Accordingly, you must ask yourself, every time you talk to someone, two questions: "Did I deal successfully with the matter at hand, and what did I just do to my relationship with that person?"

Here are a few more important questions to reflect upon:

1. Do you show a genuine interest in what each of your group members wants to achieve with their careers?

2. Do you show an interest in the things that mean the most to your people in their personal lives?

3. Are you there for your people in their times of personal or professional crisis?

4. Do you informally "check in" with each of your people every so often?

5. Do you offer to help when some member of your group clearly needs it?

1 DO YOU SHOW A GENUINE INTEREST IN WHAT YOUR GROUP MEMBERS WANT TO ACHIEVE?

Think about each member of your group. Have any valued people left recently or announced that they are about to? Are some people, with a lot of talent and potential, performing at a level far below where you think they should? If the answer to either of these questions is affirmative, then the chances are that you have failed to pay attention to something these individuals want or need to jump-start their careers.

Some years ago, Patrick was beginning to work with a group. One of the valued younger partners had just announced that he was leaving. The group leader was shocked: "I had no idea Alan was unhappy or looking at other opportunities." Patrick and the group leader got together to debrief the session. The group leader was still stunned by the loss. One of the other young partners came in. As she was sitting down, the group leader asked her, "Did you have any idea Alan was unhappy or wanted to leave?"

She took a deep breath and said: "Geez, Mike, I thought you knew. He's been wanting to pursue developing a more international presence for our group for at least the past ten months that I know of, and he just wasn't feeling like he was getting the kind of support he needed for what he wanted to do." Alan ended up not only walking away from this firm with a few more clients than he had brought in, but he also took a couple of the more valuable juniors with him. It took this group some time to bounce back from the loss of clients and to replace the talent who had left.

One of the most effective managers of professionals that David ever met was Don Groninger, at one time the general counsel for Bridgestone/Firestone, he ran a legal department of around thirty people. He was always looking for ways to advance the careers of his people, even (or especially) if this meant their being promoted to top corporate positions and hence leaving his group. In the words of one of his people:

> He had a deep insight into people and could discover and nurture strengths that others might not see. He paved the way for you to take on stretching challenges, expected you to produce results and, without ego, trusted you to run with the ball, calling on him only when you felt the need to.

> He did not micro-manage. But when you asked for guidance what you received was the wealth of his "book learning" as well as his "street smarts." I don't know that he was ever wrong in the advice he gave me.

Don once had his entire group evaluate him as a manager (see chapter 22), disclosing the results to everyone in the group, and obtained the highest scores that David had ever seen for any group leader in a firm or corporation. And then he improved the following year!

Paying close attention to what people want and need in developing their careers is a critical part of any group leader's role. ("Allow people to aspire to their dreams"—Zander; and "never stop building on strong ideas"—Burnett) Unfortunately, too few bother.

2 DO YOU SHOW AN INTEREST IN THE THINGS THAT MEAN THE MOST TO YOUR PEOPLE IN THEIR PERSONAL LIVES?

Even though we have been working with groups for many years, we are still struck by how little interest many group leaders display in the personal lives of their own group members.

When your group members start talking about personal issues, do you show anything more than a perfunctory interest in what they have to say? How much do you really know about their families? What about their leisure-time interests? Do you explore with them what they are keenly passionate about? Do you ask questions that get them talking about their personal interests?

You may be saying to yourself, "Well, I'm not sure I agree that people who have a good working relationship really need to talk to each other about this kind of stuff." However, our experience is that you cannot build a successful business enterprise if everyone always stays in role, and deals with everyone else solely on a functional, logical, rational basis. Professionals love to retreat into their discipline and avoid messy emotional stuff, and it can be tempting to think that they do not want you know about their emotions. The reality is that you cannot separate the human being from the performer. ("Are you sure that their eyes are shining?"—Zander)

We once asked a top leader in a professional firm what most surprised him about taking on the managerial role. What had he not anticipated before he took the job?. His answer? **"I learned more about the personal lives of my people than I ever thought I would know! It turned out to be essential in order to get the best out of people."**

3 ARE YOU THERE FOR YOUR PEOPLE IN THEIR TIMES OF PERSONAL OR PROFESSIONAL CRISIS?

All of us confront crises and make important transitions in our lives. A family member goes into the hospital, a child is having a particularly difficult time at school, a marital relationship is faltering, or a spouse has just been offered an important career move that could necessitate the relocation of the family to a new city. Such issues can lead to behavior that suggests a sudden disinterest in the work. At the other extreme, some people may bury their personal issues in workaholic traits, burning the proverbial candle at both ends.

Right now, as you read this, it is very likely that some member of your group is facing some significant crisis or transition. Are you aware of it? What kind of support are you offering? Maybe you're an exception, but if you're like many of the managers we've worked with over the years, you probably haven't always been there for your people when they needed you. Pay attention, and help where you can!

4 DO YOU INFORMALLY "CHECK IN" WITH EACH OF YOUR PEOPLE EVERY SO OFTEN?

We all face those day-to-day situations when client work gets overpowering, when the firm's internal systems seem to make it harder rather than easier to get anything done, or when a technology glitch makes us wish we could retreat to far simpler times. These frustrations don't have a devastating effect, but they do preoccupy us. One thing that helps immeasurably is having someone notice and say: "You look a little distracted. What's going on?"

If a group leader just takes a few minutes to listen, something special can happen. The person has a chance to "vent." To get whatever is bugging her off her chest. It may not solve the problem, but she'll probably feel somewhat better. The burden has been lifted a little. If you're the person listening, it doesn't take a lot of time or effort. But for the individual who is the fortunate recipient, it's special. It's like being given a battery recharge just when you needed it the most.

Do you notice when members of your practice team are preoccupied, frustrated, or distracted and take the time to check in with them? ("The creative human spirit needs to be nurtured and stimulated"—Burnett) Most group leaders don't do this anywhere near as often as they should.

5 DO YOU OFFER TO HELP WHEN SOME MEMBER OF YOUR GROUP CLEARLY NEEDS IT?

If your team is at all typical, you and the other members are very busy people. You all work hard and sometimes you're stretched to the limits of your capabilities. This can cause well-meaning people to make small, but important, mistakes.

Someone on your team has just landed a monster project with a deadline coming at him like a high-speed train. Meanwhile, two serious glitches have just cropped up that could never have been anticipated. At a time like this he is liable to need a helping hand. The question is, are you going to make some time available to help?

By help, we don't just mean a few minutes of being sympathetic, empathetic, compassionate, and a good listener for your teammate. You must offer to pitch in and lighten the load. As busy as you are, do you take on some of your colleague's headaches to help him through the rough period? ("Pay attention to how to enable people to be the best they can be"—Zander)

Once again, in too many work groups, the answer is probably, "No." You don't have the time. You don't offer to help out. At best, you might be counted upon to arm-twist some other member to pitch in. And there goes your credibility and influence as a leader and coach. **You want people to accept your influence in the future? Help them now!**

SUMMARY

Group leaders are responsible for creating an inheritance, a legacy, which passes into the custody of the next generation. Their fundamental purpose should be to inspire others.

Those, like Zander and Burnett, who inspire, do so because they wish to serve others. Inspiration comes from within and the group leader's job is to create the environment which can invite it. Inspiration is not derived from selfish motives, but from caring about people, caring about our relationships with those people, and caring enough to intercede and see if we can coach people to perform better than they thought they ever could. To be an effective coach requires patience, persistence, and permission.

PART TWO

COACHING THE INDIVIDUAL

WE NOW EXPLORE, in more detail, your leadership, management, and coaching activities. We examine first how to deal with individuals, and defer to the next section how you deal with groups.

This is not a random order. You cannot and must not attempt to deal with your group until you have built a relationship with every individual in it.

5. Win Permission to Coach
   How do you get people to accept your guidance?

6. Listen to Build Rapport
   Do people think you are a good listener?

7. Deal Differently with Different People
   How can you understand and respond to people's differences?

8. Help Underperformers
   How can you be useful to those who need assistance?

9. Tackle the Prima Donnas
   How do you deal with difficult people?

10. Build Support for Change
    How do you get people to buy into the need for change?

chapter **5**

Win Permission to Coach

How do you get people to accept your guidance?

WHILE INDIVIDUALS MAY ENJOY the good fortune of accepting a specific public honor or peer award, their acceptance speeches are usually filled with many "thank you's" to those who coaxed, coached, and inspired them into delivering some measure of exceptional performance.

Take the case of actress Helen Hunt, in her Oscar acceptance speech for *As Good As It Gets,* who singled out and thanked Larry Moss, an acting coach with whom every working actor wants to study. Here was Hunt, a multiple Emmy Award winner who had been in front of the cameras since the tender age of nine, unafraid to admit to her peers that she couldn't have gotten to where she was without Moss.

For his part, in a *Los Angeles Magazine* interview, Moss stated:

> One of the things that excites me about coaching is that I'm totally fascinated by each individual. To me, they're all unique. They all have strengths and weaknesses. I get to coach people and get them to see their own value.

Indeed, in Hollywood, Moss is known for his ability to locate an actor's particular skill and then show him or her how to use it.

Award-winning performances don't happen spontaneously. It takes years of hard work to hone one's skills and develop one's techniques. Most of us would benefit greatly from having a coach like Larry Moss, someone who sees the talent that lies hidden within us and who is able to draw those latent skills and abilities to the surface. Individuals believe their performance improves when someone takes a personal interest in helping them perform better.

Note that coaching is an activity, not a title or position. It is the process by which you help another person fulfill his or her potential. It requires that you judge well when to intervene, and when to stay away.

Coaching is what is required when some member of your group:

1. Is unclear about his or her career path

2. Asks for advice, assistance, feedback, or support

3. Is taking on a new task or responsibility

4. Appears frustrated or confused

5. Seems indecisive or stuck

6. Is performing inconsistently

7. Expresses a desire to improve

8. Performs below acceptable standards

9. Has a negative attitude that is impeding their work and the work of others

Strategy consultant Cliff Farrah notes:

> In my experience, the best thing a new group manager can do is to establish a norm with all team members that regular one-on-one coaching is a standard, non-negotiable part of life. I've found that, with a regularly scheduled meeting, the opportunity to provide coaching is expected, and welcomed, in contrast to those coaching moments that are triggered by an event. I have a half-hour scheduled with each member of my team that I am directly responsible for on a

> regular basis. Depending on the team, this can be weekly,
> monthly or quarterly. Any regularly scheduled meeting held
> less frequently than quarterly loses its effectiveness.

Before you can even begin to develop and stretch your people's talent, you must assess whether you have earned "the right" to be able to do so.

Here's what Daniel J. Fensin, the managing partner of accountants and consultants Blackman, Kallick, Bartelstein, had to say:

> I have tried to make it a habit of never taking credit for
> anything. My partners will come to me for support, and I'll
> help them as much as I can in terms of guiding them, in
> terms of doing whatever they need, whether they need a pat
> on the back or a kick in the behind. They come to you for
> what they need, and it's your place to give it to them.
>
> When they have a success, it's their success. Don't get in
> the way of their success. Even if you absolutely handed them
> that success, it's their success. They need that because it
> gives them confidence to go and achieve other successes. If
> you stand in the way of their success, they will not trust you.

Preparation (planning what you are going to say and how you are going to help) is an important part of any effective coaching process. However, many coaching opportunities may be spontaneous, requiring quick action in order to assist a situation or prevent a problem from arising. Whether you have five minutes or five hours to prepare, it is usually constructive to consider the purpose, timing, and place of your coaching initiative.

Rob Duboff, whose long experience includes a senior executive role at Mercer Management Consulting and the top marketing job at Ernst & Young, commented:

> The key, to me, is thinking through your strategy before
> a meeting with one of your people. You should decide the
> one or two points (no more) that you want to get across,
> and invent a technique to make them memorable. Of
> course, you also need to take into account, as you plan your

> strategy for the meeting, the key thing that motivates each team member: money, substantive recognition, a simple pat on the back.

There are many challenging dimensions to coaching. Successful group leaders learn how to straddle the line between "too little" and "too much." Here are some basic steps that may help in your winning permission to coach:

1. Ask how things are going
2. Confirm that the individual is ready for coaching
3. Ask questions to clarify the situation, and offer your support and help
4. Offer information as appropriate
5. Listen actively
6. Help this person identify possible courses of action
7. Agree on the next step
8. Offer your personal support and confidence

1. Ask how things are going.

"Hey Jan, how did your meeting with the client go?"

Your aim is to find out what is on an individual's mind. Your best approach is to be informal and open-ended. Helpful questions begin with phrases like: "What's happening with . . . ?" or "What did you find out about . . . ?"

Identify an opportunity to help someone expand on his or her skills, knowledge, and abilities. Look for signals or cues indicating that coaching could add value. Take time to tune in to the need behind the words.

2. Confirm that the individual is ready for coaching.

"Do you have a few minutes to discuss this? Would you be interested in talking about what happened? Perhaps I can help. Is this a good time or do you want to schedule something later today?"

If a person mentions several issues, focus on the one that the person seems most interested in or concerned about. Ask straightforward questions to gauge the person's readiness and interest.

Let the person know that you are available to provide guidance feedback. This allows the individual to be prepared to listen or gives ᵗ dividual an opportunity to postpone the discussion if the timing is baᵈ. this person does need to postpone the discussion, make sure you schedule a specific time.

3. Ask questions to clarify the situation, and offer your support and help

> *"How much progress have you made so far? What happened as a result? Let's make sure that I understand. You called the other firm, found the documents that were submitted last year, and you've shown them to the people in our group."*

Phrase your questions carefully so they do not pressure the person or imply a negative reaction. Begin each question with words like *when, what, where, who,* or *how much.* Frame questions that will draw out facts. Try to build awareness, not to solve the problem. Determine if the individual has the right information to move forward. Avoid questions that may evoke a negative reaction (questions that often start with *how* or *why*) as they tend to put people on the defensive.

4. Offer information as appropriate.

> *"I don't know if this would be helpful, but two immediate alternatives jump to my mind . . ."*

Offer only necessary information, providing whatever this person needs to choose a course of action. Respond briefly, being careful to take your cue from the other person. How much information you provide will depend on the situation. To help someone resolve a substantive issue might require that you provide a fair bit of detailed instruction. To help with a creative solution, you might want to simply provoke the individual's thinking in different directions.

5. Listen actively

If necessary, make some brief notes. Don't interrupt with your own ideas. Should the individual stray from the topic, ask a question that will help refocus the issue. This keeps both of you on track, but it still allows the individual to lead the discussion. From time to time, summarize what you have heard.

6. Help this person identify possible courses of action

> *"What steps could you take to reduce the confusion? What other actions can you think of? What if our client could proceed without this type of protection, would that affect the way you approach this situation? Let's look at the arguments for and against each of these options."*

Avoid offering any of your own ideas until after the person you are coaching has finished. Encourage her to think aloud. Ask for off-the-wall as well as practical ideas that might be considered.

You may want to make a list of the ideas generated, without commenting on their feasibility. Help her weigh the pros and cons of each option.

7. Agree on the next step

> *"Okay, so which of these alternatives do you favor? What's your next step? When do you think you can have that ready by? What obstacles might you have to deal with in completing the arrangement?"*

Prompt the person to make a firm commitment to action. Clarify what specific steps he is planning to take, and by when.

8. Offer your personal support

> *"Now, I've seen you handle glitches far more difficult than this, but as you get further into it, I'm available if you want to talk, I'll touch base with you next week following your Tuesday meeting with the client."*

Conclude by expressing your continued interest, your confidence in your colleague's ability to solve the issue, and your offer to help, if and where you can do anything that would support her in accomplishing her objective.

It is important to know when not to engage in coaching. If you don't have a relationship of mutual respect and trust with an individual you should probably take some remedial action to build trust before offering any coaching assistance. Trust is the single most important element in a successful coaching relationship. But gaining another person's trust does not come quickly or effortlessly. Trust can not be faked. As a group leader, you need to continually work at building a foundation of trust by being open, honest, and credible in word and deed with all your colleagues.

You should also not try to coach when, for whatever reason, you are angry about a situation, or when your colleague is very busy or under a deadline pressure. Timing is everything.

Remember, your involvement will be valued to the degree that you take a genuine interest in the person and offer guidance (or direct him or her as to where to get help), and do that in a dynamic, uplifting, enthusiastic, positive and optimistic manner.

You need always to demonstrate that you believe in your colleague, especially when communicating corrective feedback. **If you want to win a person's permission to be coached, you must see the potential in that person and be able to express your confidence in what you believe they are capable of achieving.**

People who have been coached to believe that they can succeed become more confident in selecting challenging goals. They work harder, and persist longer when faced with obstacles. A large portion of the coach's role is to see the potential for greatness and to enthusiastically communicate that expectation, both verbally and nonverbally. As one group leader commented to us:

> I think you've got to come to this role every day feeling that you can make a difference and just getting that enthusiasm throughout your group. I think enthusiasm becomes contagious.

You must also create a safe environment so that others feel comfortable expressing feelings and opinions.

CREATING A SAFE ENVIRONMENT

You need to be the catalyst to push individuals to stretch and grow, and then provide safe opportunities for them to refine their skills.

Giving Corrective Feedback

Even for the best coaches, it can be excruciatingly difficult to tell people that their behavior or performance is not up to an acceptable standard, or that they are hindering the group's performance, or that they are not adequately following through on their commitments. This is the stuff that interpersonal conflict, hurt feelings, and dysfunctional groups are made of.

Whether your task is providing positive or corrective feedback to a member of your group, it should be given in a manner that is useful to the recipient, and should always be "constructive." The most effective steps to keep in mind when giving corrective feedback are:

1. State the purpose of your feedback. This helps set the focus for the feedback and also lets the person know what your intentions are.

2. Describe your observations and perceptions. Be specific, brief, and clear about the behaviors, incidents, facts, or perceptions upon which you base your point of view.

3. Jointly agree on the subsequent action to be taken. Think of this as a plan of action. Your willingness to help can make it more effective.

4. Summarize your discussions and show your appreciation. Receiving feedback is just as hard as giving it. Let recipients know you appreciate their openness, their willingness to discuss the issue, and their willingness to move constructively forward.

If you aren't crystal clear about what this behavior change should look like, you won't be able to identify improvements or provide useful feedback.

Always focus on the problem, situation, or the behavior, never on the individual. Describe in precise terms the situation when the behavior occurred. For example, "John, at our meeting earlier today there were three times when . . ." Refrain from using words like "always" and "never." If you say, "John, you are always late for our group meetings," John will view your message as a personal attack, become naturally defensive, and attempt to prove that there have been occasions when he was on time.

There are ways to deliver corrective feedback without it coming across as a personal attack. When presented well, the feedback can actually strengthen relationships, enhance communication, and resolve conflict.

A good group leader should be aware when a person needs to be nudged out of his or her comfort zone. Without an element of renewing challenge, any talented person will become bored and apathetic.

One group leader tells us that she refers to this as a precise balance of skill, confidence, and challenge. When a group leader raises the bar for performance, the individual is likely to feel more intrinsically motivated about the increased challenge. **The group leader also needs to provide a safety net by creating situations for the individual to master these new challenges successfully. You need to provide dress rehearsals and opportunities so that people can safely practice new skills.**

When this leader's group decided that it would call upon each of its significant clients to get some measure of that client's level of satisfaction, it spent some time together rehearsing how it would execute the initiative. The leader observed:

> It's a form of learning by doing. We determined a series of questions that would be most appropriate to ask our clients in one-on-one meetings. We determined which two people would be at which meetings. Then we role-played various scenarios where one of our other people who knew the client very well would play the role of client. We practiced how we would handle difficult responses should they arise. In the end we were all far more comfortable that we were ready to undertake the exercise having done it first as a team in a non-threatening environment where we could make mistakes and learn from them.
>
> My role as the coach is not to lecture my people on how to conduct effective client meetings, but rather to pull the lessons out of them. People don't remember what you tell them; they remember what they experience. They don't remember what I say. They remember what they say.

The most important element in performance is confidence. Rehearsal allows the opportunity to build confidence and perfect technique. Set up frequent opportunities for others in your group to actually "practice" a new skill in a nonthreatening context.

Cliff Farrah reported to us the value of role-playing and rehearsing in his (consulting) business:

> Every professional sells in one way or another. For example, a new recruit will (without a doubt) be asked what he or she does either on a plane, at a holiday party, or at a bar. We all know how hard it is to talk about what we do even to each other, let alone to a stranger when you may only have a few minutes to convey your value. Therefore, at the end of every team meeting I save time for a "who and what are we" session. We spend 30 to 45 minutes role-playing the typical conversation that happens in the business development process—what to say, what not to say, how to deal with the toughest questions (around things like price), and ultimately how to move a conversation to someone else in the firm for further discussion if appropriate. At the end of the role play we talk about what worked and what could be improved upon. This is unbelievably effective and exciting.

Great group leaders work to get people to create vivid mental pictures of their personal success. However, setting goals and envisioning success isn't enough. Research by the psychologist Albert Bandura proves that both goals and feedback are necessary to improve performance. The group leader is responsible for keeping everyone on track by regularly monitoring performance and providing frequent, timely, and specific feedback.

Aside from regular group meetings, many group leaders rarely have as much time as they might like for lengthy formal sit-downs. Therefore it is important to take advantage of those brief informal moments—in the hallways, on the elevator—to find out how some member of the team is coming along. Instead of limiting your role as coach to annual performance reviews, find ways to incorporate coaching moments into every meeting, conversation, and even voice-mail and e-mail messages. Chances are the information you will get will be timely and present opportunities for valuable coaching.

Use metaphors and stories to explain concepts and provide encouragement. Teaching without a metaphor is like driving without any markings on the road. Tell stories about what others have been able to accomplish.

Serve as a role model. If you are seeking to have someone voluntarily take on a project or execute some course of action, make sure that they see you stepping up to bat first. If you are asking someone to make a behavior change, be the first person to exhibit this new behavior.

FORMAL COUNSELING

Of all the ways of improving a group's success, informal, unscheduled, one-on-one counseling is the most powerful. Done well, it can help ensure that all people are making the most of their talents and capitalizing fully on their potential. However, there can sometimes be a role (if not an actual requirement) for formal, structured counseling.

Unfortunately, formal reviews tend to focus overwhelmingly on the "look back" *appraisal* function (frequently because they serve as an input to reward decisions), and contain only a minimal "look ahead" *counseling* component. People frequently complain about ineffective goal-setting, ambiguous performance criteria, and a lack of feedback (of any sort.) As one disgruntled professional expressed it:

> It's as if we were archers being judged on our ability to hit a target with a few arrows every day. But the target is hidden in the mist. And the results of our daily shots are consolidated and given to us at the end of the year. Then we are rewarded or punished for the accuracy of our aim and exhorted to improve.

Any counseling process can (and should) be designed to *help* people, creating the opportunity for people to:

1. Reflect on and learn from the past year's accomplishments

2. Obtain constructive feedback, positive or negative

3. Receive personalized advice on how best to advance their careers

4. Receive guidance in setting realistic but stretching personal goals for "growing their assets" and making a contribution to the firm.

Consider Bevan Ashford, a seven-office UK law firm based in Bristol. Its chief executive partner, Nick Jarrett-Kerr, describes the firm's people-development approaches:

Until 1996, I personally sat in on every appraisal of every fee earner in our Bristol office. These annual appraisals each lasted two to three hours. That meant as much as three hundred hours of my time every year! It's something I just can't do anymore.

So we looked for alternative solutions to maintain quality and commitment in this area. One idea we came up with was competency-based self-appraisals. They're very challenging for the fee-earners to fill out, and they help us focus in on very particular personal professional issues.

We do psychological testing as well. We look for behavioral indicators, which we find very useful in making team assignments. We do a variety of testing and evaluating. For example, we categorize both partners and fee earners in order to assess where they're at in terms of skill levels. It's a dynamic process, the whole point of which is to determine what we need to do to get each lawyer to the next tier.

Here is a five-step process that we think is generally applicable.

Step 1. Specify performance criteria

Step 2. Design the counseling process

Step 3. Hold the counseling meeting

Step 4. Engage in career planning

Step 5. Set goals and plan actions

Step 1. Specify performance criteria

The first essential element of any effective counseling system is a shared understanding of what aspects of performance the group wishes to stress. There is often much ambiguity here.

Examples of formal criteria might be:

1. Profitability of work supervised

2. Client satisfaction on work supervised

3. Coaching on work supervised

4. Contributions to practice development

5. Contributions to the success of others

6. Personal growth (career strategy)

The first three categories, it will be noticed, relate to the person's performance in managing and supervising client work. Not coincidentally, these three performance indicators coincide with the three traditional goals of most professional groups: client service, financial success, and professional satisfaction.

The remaining three performance categories (practice development, helping others, and self-improvement) are somewhat more subjective and therefore need to be judged.

Notice that the fifth performance category is "contributions to the success of others." One of the eternal risks in any performance appraisal and counseling system is that it encourages an excessive focus on individual performance and destroys teamwork. To counteract this, **each person should be asked to point to specific ways in which he or she has contributed to the success of others.** Someone who cannot meet this criterion should be deemed as having failed to meet his or her obligations as a member of the group.

To gauge whether someone is truly contributing to the success of others, you could ask the following questions:

1. Does this person inspire and engender enthusiasm in other members of the team?

2. Does this person keep the other members of the team informed about what they have learned while working with clients that may be of value to the others?

3. Does this person give freely of his or her time to help others handle unexpected client emergencies or tight deadlines?

4. Does this person make it a point to publicize the superb work done by other team members?

5. Does this person work with others to set clear goals, make plans, and establish objectives for those projects that he or she leads?

6. Does this person exhibit technical competence and provide counsel-advice when others ask for assistance with technical questions?

7. Does this person provide direction to team members on new projects and help them set priorities?

8. Does this person actively seek new ways to improve what we do in the group?

9. Does this person treat the other members of the team with respect?

10. Does this person give recognition to team members for their contributions and efforts?

11. Does this person follow through to see that (internal or client) problems get solved?

Step 2. Design the Counseling Process

The process should begin by inviting the person being counseled to conduct a self-evaluation. Most of us (not all) are more critical of our own performance than anyone else would be. However, when someone else criticizes our performance, we are likely to become defensive and offer any excuse for our apparent weaknesses. It is important that "good performance" is taken to mean *improvement* and not just sustaining a given level of result. Counseling discussions should then focus upon year-on-year changes, not just the latest year.

You should also provide the goals and action plans from the person's previous counseling session. The simple gesture of saying "We haven't forgotten the goals you set last year, here's what you said and what we agreed to" conveys a powerful message about the seriousness of the process.

Step 3. Hold The Counseling Meeting

Since providing help (not just providing feedback) is your key objective, ask yourself the following questions: "If I rate this person lower than the top on any performance category, do I have an action idea for her to do to improve, and do I also have an idea about how I can help her improve?" If you can't answer these questions affirmatively, then you're not ready for the meeting!

The person being counseled should be invited in advance to rate herself on each of the performance categories. In the meeting you can discuss and compare your evaluations. Differences in the person's self-perception and your perception should be discussed and documented.

You should listen carefully to the person's views and not prejudge this individual's performance or jump to conclusions. Your goal is not only to observe what the performance has been, but also to determine *why* it has happened, so that you can help with future improvement.

If your group uses a structured form for counseling sessions (in general, a good idea), include a section which rates not only accomplishments but also specific skills.

The form could include the following:

1. Communications skills (ability to express thoughts in a logical, fluent, and concise manner)

2. Counseling skills (tact, the ability to explain, to persuade others in a nonconfrontational style, see the other person's point of view, keeping client informed, listening well, etc.)

3. Creativity and innovativeness

4. Planning and organization (ability to get things done)

5. Leadership (motivation of subordinates, effectiveness in delegation and supervision)

6. Cooperativeness and team play

7. Drive, self-motivation

If a counseling session is to be constructive, the suggested areas for improvement need to be as specific as possible.

Step 4. Engage in career planning

Career planning ("Where's my career going?") cannot and should not be separated from performance evaluation ("How am I doing?"). Together, you and the individual you are counseling should identify which career track offers the greatest opportunity to make the person distinctive and valuable, and to make a contribution to the group. Think through, together, how that person can make himself special in the marketplace.

Forcing a discussion on career plans will make the counseling process more long-term, and will signal to everyone the need to develop special skills or a focus that will make them different, distinctive, and more valuable.

Step 5. Set Goals and Plan Actions

It is important to force discipline by designing (and documenting) concrete action plans where each action item has a specific due date, a tracking measure (i.e., a milestone that shows whether the action has been performed or not), and an estimate of the time required to perform the action. This discipline helps to highlight ambiguous goals ("Become better known") and also to reveal actions that might be infeasible because of time limitations. The objectives and plans thus created form the beginning of the appraisal and counseling system for the following year.

The test of successful counseling is simple: Does the person being reviewed know *specifically* and *precisely* what to do to improve his or her performance in the coming year? If so, then the coach has done the job properly. If not, then the counseling has failed, and so has the coach. Accordingly, it is a good discipline for the counseling process to end with a statement signed both by the individual and the counselor affirming that the individual does know where to go from here.

chapter 6

Listen to Build Rapport

Do people think you are a good listener?

YOU PROBABLY THINK OF YOURSELF as a reasonably good listener. But if you were to ask those you work with for their candid feedback, what would they really say? You might be pleasantly surprised, but all too often the people we work with say that we need to work on our listening skills. And some may even say we *really* need to work on them.

In *The Trusted Advisor*, David and his co-authors provided a list of good listening habits when dealing with clients. We think it applies equally well to listening to those you coach. Here it is:

WHAT GOOD LISTENERS DO

1. Probe for clarification
2. Listen for unvoiced emotions
3. Listen for the story
4. Summarize well
5. Empathize
6. Listen for what's different, not for what's familiar

7. Take it all seriously (they don't say, "you shouldn't worry about that")

8. Spot hidden assumptions

9. Let the other person "get it out of his or her system"

10. Ask, "How do you feel about that?"

11. Keep the other person talking ("What else have you considered?")

12. Keep asking for more detail that helps them understand

13. Get rid of distractions while listening

14. Focus on hearing your version first

15. Let you tell your story your way

16. Stand in your shoes, at least while they're listening

17. Ask you how you think they might be of help

18. Ask what you've thought of before telling you what they've thought of

19. Look at (not stare at) the person as he or she speaks

20. Look for "congruency" (or incongruity) between what the person says and how he or she gestures and postures

21. Make it seem as if the other person is the only thing that matters and that they have all the time in the world

22. Encourage by nodding head or giving a slight smile

23. Show awareness and control of body movement (no moving around, shaking legs, fiddling with a paper clip)

How many of these tests do you pass? How many do your people think you pass? Ask them: you may be surprised!

Active listening is the ability to pick up, define, and respond accurately to feelings expressed by the other person. It is a technique that reduces defensiveness, and acts as a defuser in emotional exchanges. When active listening is employed, people feel that they are being understood. This frees them to explore their own feelings, to express their ideas, and to rely less on defensive behavior. The effects of active listening include a comforting effect for the individual being listened to, and a promotion of a sense of rapport and trust.

We all want to be heard. However, a case can be made that active listening is even more important for professionals than those in other walks of life. Professionals, as we have noted, value their autonomy and resent being told what to do or how to do it. They may accept guidance, but only if their self-respect is not threatened. Professionals are willing to accept the views of others, but often not until after they have had the chance to express their own views.

Professionals, highly trained in their technical discipline, often like to present a façade of detached, logical analysis. However, they can be (and are) as emotional as any other human being, and not only have technocratic opinions on what's going on, but also have deep feelings about them. As a group, however, professionals are often likely to think that showing their feelings is somehow "unprofessional." Don't be fooled.

You might observe (or suspect) that a member of your group has sensitive feelings on some issue. Often, the act of verbalizing these feelings clears the air and allows constructive discussions to resume. The experience of being heard and understood can be a catalyst to developing trust.

When you listen actively, you try to understand what someone is feeling or what his or her message means. Then, you put this understanding of the message into your own words, and feed it back to the individual for verification. You do not send a message of your own; you feed back only what your colleague's message meant. Active listening, like any skill, can be learned and improved with practice.

Keep in mind three critical steps that will help you listen actively:

1. Ask questions and encourage dialogue

2. Listen intently, making a written note of the situation, problem or request

3. Summarize and paraphrase your colleague's situation, problem or request

I. Ask questions and encourage dialogue.

Often, especially during coaching discussions, **people find it difficult to articulate or communicate their feelings about sensitive situations. Yet**

a critical part of your role as a group leader is to get people to share their issues, and how they feel about them, with you.

One way to get a dialogue started is to ask questions, seek clarifications, and show respect for your colleague's views. Not only do you learn more about what someone means by asking questions, but you also succeed in showing your interest in what the other person is saying. Properly selected and phrased questions can dramatically further your relationship. These questions may be either open-ended or closed.

Open-ended questions are phrased to draw a wide range of responses on a broad topic. They attempt to encourage the person to expand or elaborate on needs, wants, and problems—and cannot be answered by a simple yes or no:

"What type of meeting schedule would best meet your needs?"

Use open-ended questions to encourage someone to share thoughts, feelings, and opinions. By doing so you enhance your chances of learning what is really important to them.

Closed questions require narrow answers to a specific inquiry. The answers to these questions are typically yes, no, or some other brief answer:

"Would a quarterly meeting of the group better meet your needs?"

Your questions should be sufficiently open-ended that they elicit detailed answers. Once you get answers, you should encourage your colleague to continue talking. This involves making sure colleagues understand that you're interested.

Seeking clarification not only prevents misunderstandings, it shows people that you are interested in them as individuals. You might say: "Could you go back over that one more time?" or "Can you explain that in a little more detail?"

When someone disagrees with us or doesn't see the world as we do, we want to dig in and defend our position. Sometimes we are so intent on voicing our own point of view that we simply forget to listen to what the other person is saying. By demonstrating a willingness to consider the other's viewpoint, we contribute to the dialogue. You and your colleague may not agree on everything, but the door for further communications remains open.

You can show respect for the person's views in a variety of ways. Maintaining eye contact is one of the most important. A nod of your head when your colleague makes a particular point can confirm that you're listening and understanding. A brief "yes," or "good point," also encourages the individual to continue the dialogue. Attention is not only directed to the words spoken, but also to the thoughts and feelings of the person. To listen in this manner requires a suspension of personal thoughts and feelings in order to give attention solely to listening. It means, figuratively, "putting yourself into someone else's shoes." It requires you to indicate (both verbally and nonverbally) that what the person is saying is really being absorbed.

2. **Listen intently, making a written note of the situation, problem, or request.**

If you think you know what an individual is going to say because you've confronted the same situation with this person a number of times in the past, you probably won't listen actively. ("Here he goes again.") Instead, your thoughts will wander or you will start preparing an answer before the person has finished speaking.

Try to ensure that meetings and coaching discussions with colleagues will not be interrupted. Listen with pen and paper in hand. Taking notes can convey a sincere interest in the individual's situation and provides you with a written record of the meeting from which to seek confirmation of the main points. However, don't overdo it. The act of writing things down can be interpreted as removing your attention from the other person and may convey an impression of excessive formality.

3. **Summarize and paraphrase your colleague's situation, problem, or request.**

Your colleague, at some point in a typical discussion, may look to you and ask, "Okay, now do you understand?" An excellent way of confirming, understanding, and projecting empathy is to summarize and paraphrase the person's situation. You might say: "Let me confirm what I heard you say, to make sure I've got it right," or "If I understand you correctly, you need to have help in completing your project for next Friday's group meeting. Is that correct?"

Confirming understanding by way of paraphrasing is critical to active listening because it serves as a check to make sure you leave the conversation having really understood what the person said. However, your colleague could react with annoyance, suspicion or anger if you were to paraphrase everything he or she said. You would not paraphrase someone who asks, "What time is it?" by repeating, "I hear you asking for the time!"

Be careful how you react, or whether you should react at all. If your colleague feels ignored, talked down to, attacked, or blamed, you will lose your effectiveness. If he is explaining something to you and you feel confused, it is a signal to paraphrase: "If I understand, your concern is that you are . . . ." At that point he will either agree or modify your version.

If you are presenting your summary of what you understand to be the situation and the other person disagrees, or vice versa, treat these as signals to pause and listen carefully before restating your own views.

DEALING WITH BAD LISTENERS

Certain people may be counted upon not to hear a thing you have said or even understand the basic points that you may be raising. They are either unreachable, stubborn, or impossible to convince. Then there are also those who switch to "auto pilot" and become immune to input from anyone; who are unwilling or unable to see the possibility of some other way of looking at things. Because they might not see the merit of your point of view, they cannot accept your counsel as legitimate, or react constructively to your attempt to offer guidance. It can be very difficult for even the most gifted coach to maintain a constructive dialogue with such people. The following are all signals of poor listening:

1. Avoiding eye contact or continually responding with a vacant stare

2. Appearing absorbed in other activities or allowing interruptions to disrupt the conversation;

3. Repeated yawns, looking at one's watch, giving "Yes, but . . ." responses, or not responding to the topic at hand.

Effective coaches may use several techniques to communicate with those who are not good listeners:

1. The direct approach
2. The preventative approach
3. The therapeutic approach
4. The punitive approach
5. The indirect approach

1. The Direct Approach

This approach requires that you confront the issue as soon as it becomes apparent. You might try saying:

> *"I don't feel that you are hearing me and I'm not sure what else to do. Do you have any suggestions?"*

Or, if you are aware that this particular person is usually sensitive to other people's feelings and values constructive relationships, you might express your feelings:

> *"It upsets me when you don't seem to pay attention to what I'm saying."*

2. The Preventative Approach

If in the past you've had difficulty getting someone to listen, you might try asking:

> *"I know I haven't always been successful in communicating to you my point of view in the past, but could we try again? Can I ask that you try to hear my point of view on this issue?"*

3. The Therapeutic Approach

The therapeutic approach is an attempt to have the other person reflect upon his or her behavior in the hopes that the reflection might bring forth an acknowledgment and behavior change. It requires you to say something like:

"You seem to give an impression of not focusing on our discussion. Do you have any idea why this happens?"

4. The Punitive Approach

There will be times (rarely, of course) when, as a practice leader, you have to flex your authority (formal or informal) in order to get your colleague's attention and to convey the seriousness of the matter under discussion. Those situations, hopefully rare, may require that you pose some form of ultimatum:

"If we can't discuss this issue without interruptions, I will just have to make a decision and proceed without your input."

5. The Indirect Approach

Finally, we must accept that each of us has very different styles of working, of interacting, and of communicating. Some people prefer the written word to verbal communication as they may feel that it allows them to reflect before responding. And there are those with whom you will never comfortably relate, often because of a difference of style. In those instances, two alternatives may be appropriate:

1. Write (a note, a memo, an e-mail) to the individual to express your concern or convey your views and ask for their response

2. Use a third party (one of your colleagues) who has the confidence of this individual

We advise you to use the written or indirect approaches sparingly. It is all too tempting to lean on these tactics for our own comfort, to avoid confrontations. The content of your message may be communicated, but it will not convey emotion or serve to build trust and a relationship with the person you are trying to help.

chapter 7

Deal Differently with Different People

How can you understand and respond to people's differences?

NOT EVERY INDIVIDUAL can be managed (or inspired) the same way. A manager must learn to deal with each individual according to the things that energize that individual.

Consider, for example, the concept of "commitment." You have to be committed *to* something. What could people be committed to (beyond their own short-term self-interest)? Figure 7-1 shows some options.

Figure 7-1: *FORMS OF COMMITMENT*

Committed to:	Label:
The Group's Strategy	Vision
The Group	Loyalty
You	Gratitude
Peers	Team Spirit
Subordinates	Responsibility
Client	Service
Work Itself	Pride

Some individuals might be committed to what your group is trying to accomplish—that is, to your strategy. They want to be part of achieving that vision and will give of themselves (beyond the norm) to achieve it. Alas, not everyone can be reached this way. Some people are impervious to "the vision thing."

On the other hand, some other people may feel a strong loyalty to the group (independent of strategy) and will go the extra mile to demonstrate their commitment to the group.

Of course, many people are not susceptible to appeals to vision or loyalty, but among this group might be those who *do* feel a commitment to *you*. Perhaps there was a time when you were particularly helpful to them, and they feel that they are in your debt. They won't knock themselves out for the group or for a vision, but they'll do whatever you ask out of a sense of gratitude to you.

Sad to say, some of your people do not feel this way about you. Are they lost souls? Not at all! Their commitment might be to their colleagues and co-workers. They will stay late to contribute—not for you, but out of a sense of "being in this together."

Then there are the "non–team players" who are immune to this appeal. Can you still get their enthusiasm? Absolutely! There are people who feel a strong sense of responsibility for those who work for them (i.e., their subordinates), and will try mightily to ensure that they are looked after.

But what if someone doesn't respond to vision, loyalty, gratitude, team spirit, or responsibility. Are there yet other alternatives?

We can think of two more. First, a commitment to the client. Some people will do everything they are supposed to, and more, not out of loyalty to the group or firm, but because they believe in truly looking after their clients and their clients' interests.

Finally, there are those who don't seem to care about the group and don't even care about the clients. These people you can sometimes "get on the hook" with the challenge "Bet you can't do this!" Such people's commitment is to their professional pride.

What all this shows is that people are different and must not all be treated the same. Nevertheless, there are ways of thinking about groups of people (categories, if you insist) that can help you get started in understanding each individual you must deal with.

A WAY OF THINKING ABOUT TYPES OF PEOPLE

Think back to the last group meeting that you attended. Everyone gathered in the boardroom for lunch and it was about 12:10 p.m. before all of your people grabbed their sandwiches and got settled. Remember how each of your people started into that meeting?

There is usually a Dorothy, who wants to know precisely how long this month's meeting is going to last, because she has some important client matters that need her immediate attention, and after all, why do we really need all of these sit-down meetings?

Meanwhile, Anthony is quizzing everyone on how their weekend was and what each of them was up to. Amy is studying the agenda and wondering aloud why certain written reports could not have been sent around on Friday so she could have had the weekend to study them. Then there's Elliott, who wants to tell everyone the story about how cleverly he handled an important client matter last week.

And then there's you, the group leader. You're sitting at one end of the table, trying to figure out how you are ever going to magnetize this particular room full of compasses, such that they are not all pointing in different directions.

These people, each probably critically important to the overall success of your group, think, communicate, decide, and behave differently. They also use their time differently, handle emotions differently, and deal with conflict and stress differently. Not necessarily worse—or better—than you might. Just differently.

The group leader who fails to take these differences into account will rub people the wrong way, miscommunicate, and consequently experience great difficulty in establishing rapport and trust.

BLENDING DIFFERENCES AND SIMILARITIES

Fortunately, **people's behavior is not nearly as random as it often may appear. We are much more predictable, even in our apparent differences, than most of us would ever want to admit.**

While your people may behave very differently from one another, they can be surprisingly predictable if, and only if, you take time to understand them and where they are coming from (their particular style), and are then prepared to adapt your style to complement theirs.

We are not suggesting that you will be able to foretell each person's every move. Nor do you need to know for sure how a particular person will react. When you are dealing with people, there are no certainties, but there *are* probabilities.

Have you ever noticed how a professional gifted in dealing with clients behaves when first meeting with a prospective client? She will probably begin to modify her behavior patterns to reflect that which she observes about the other party. That is an important element of what makes her so accomplished. She instinctively recognizes that people like people who are like them!

The very same principles apply, whenever you seek to develop any productive relationship. It follows then that we need to learn a bit more about how and why people (especially those we want to manage and coach) behave the way that they do.

GUIDELINES FOR UNDERSTANDING PEOPLE'S BEHAVIOR

Psychologists have come up with a variety of concepts to help us explain and understand behavior. Many leading accounting and consulting firms have taught techniques developed by Dr. David Merrill in the 1960s for enhancing interpersonal skills in order to improve client relations and develop their people's management capabilities. We have found this approach to be particularly helpful. What follows is not original to us, nor is it necessarily the best for everyone. However, we think it an excellent place to start in trying to understand different people and how they like to be treated.

Merrill discovered that two clusters of behavior, "assertiveness" and "responsiveness" are extremely helpful in predicting how individuals are likely to behave. In its most practical form, an individual's level of *assertiveness* (not aggressiveness, which is very different) is the degree to which he or she is seen by others as being forceful or directive. Quite simply, across a broad continuum, there are those at one end who "tell" and those at the other end who "ask."

More assertive "tell" people will often speak louder, more rapidly, and more often. They will exert pressure for a decision, for taking action, and are pointed in expressing opinions, making requests, and giving directions. They are slightly more risk-oriented and often more confrontational. Assertive people feel no hesitation in interrupting and attempting to take control in the middle of a discussion.

Meanwhile, less assertive people (absolutely no value judgement implied) will tend to ask questions, are more subdued in their expressions and posture, speak more softly, have less intense eye contact, and want to study a situation before making any decision. They "ask," either to gauge how others view the situation or to collect as much information as is available.

Assertiveness isn't a fixed personality trait. It's an observable behavior. We are not judging any behavior as more or less desirable. It is simply an effective way to observe and describe how you perceive an individual's behavior—or, for that matter, how they may perceive yours.

Think about each of the professionals in your group. **Can you determine at which end of this assertiveness continuum each might easily fit? You may even want to take out a piece of paper and mark "ask" on the left side with "tell" on the right. Now underneath each, list the names of individuals that you can easily observe falling into either of those two camps.**

We have seen very accomplished people at both ends of this assertiveness continuum. The less assertive professional will quietly and calmly probe a client, by asking question after question, until finally the client perks up and says, "You know, what I think we had better do is X." (To which this professional responds, "Oh, good idea, let us get started on that for you straight away!")

In contrast, the more assertive rainmaker is often in a telling mode, "George, you had better start thinking about what you are going to do with respect to Y. Come on into my office and let's set out a plan for how we get things started."

Each of these styles can be equally effective, since clients themselves have different styles that require complementary approaches. Imagine a more assertive professional trying this same approach with the less assertive client. It may not have such a pleasant outcome.

The other way to observe behavior is by assessing *responsiveness*. Here, you are looking for how your people express themselves and how they react. Some people are more reserved, controlling their emotions, while others "emote" or tend to "let it all hang out."

The more responsive person (someone who is emotive) appears friendly, has an expressive face (smiles, nods, frowns), and uses hand gestures freely. This individual engages easily in small talk, shares personal feelings, recites anecdotes and stories, and has less structured concerns for time.

Alternatively, a more reserved and less responsive person may appear poker-faced, so that you are never quite sure whether he or she is in agreement with what you, or others in the group, are saying. You will find these people disciplined, preoccupied, tackling the job at hand with a deliberate systematic approach, always needing facts and details and with limited time "to visit." You may think that such individuals simply lack feelings or social graces. However, these people may indeed have strong feelings; they are just less likely to display them.

Again, you might want to think about the people in your group and on a separate sheet of paper mark "controlled" at the top and "emotive" at the bottom. Can you now determine which of your people are just naturally more controlled and which express themselves more openly? Where do you fit?

Dr. Merrill tells us—and others' subsequent research bears him out—that we can be highly successful at our profession, irrespective of wherever we happen to be on these two important dimensions of assertiveness and responsiveness.

However, the behavioral habit patterns related to these two dimensions are deeply ingrained by the time we reach adulthood. While it is possible to increase or decrease one's assertiveness or emotional expressiveness given a particular situation or circumstance, we can only maintain that increase or decrease for a relatively short period of time. (We are who we are!)

Suppose you are someone who is most comfortable when you are highly focused on the task at hand and feeling a strong need to get at the facts. Imagine you are speaking with someone who is inclined to want to take the time to explore "the big picture" and discuss the future ramifications of what each decision alternate might portend.

You can choose to plow forward, but if you do, both of you are likely to become polarized and highly irritated. Or you can choose to understand that your colleague is simply flexing his natural style and you need to attempt an accommodation. To accommodate him will require that you modify your style, which is not natural, not easy, and will evoke some level of short-term discomfort. Your level of stress is dependent upon how well you understand these principles of different styles and for how long a period you have to modify your style in order to accomplish the results you want to achieve.

None of this is about manipulation or maneuvering people to do those things you want. It is about understanding how to be an effective communicator.

THE KEY TO UNDERSTANDING YOUR COLLEAGUES' STYLE

Now that we have examined the assertiveness and responsiveness continuums separately, putting the two together will give you an idea of what particular individuals are like, where they may be coming from, their expectations, and how you need to work with them. The styles grid (Figure 7-2) gives a simple frame of reference.

Figure 7-2: *THE STYLES GRID*

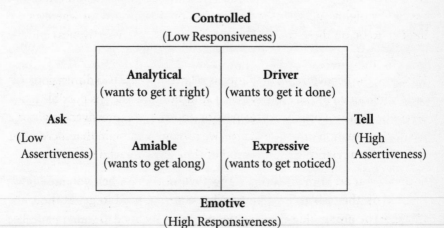

There always exists some concern about attempting to fit people into categories. We all have a natural resistance to anything that suggests putting people in "boxes." We must be careful that, by naming those boxes, we do not focus only on what the particular label might imply, and fail to see the full spectrum of behaviors that characterize that style.

In spite of these cautions, many professional firm managers have made successful uses of profiling techniques. Rob Duboff commented:

> At Mercer Management Consulting we had every partner use a technique like this and encouraged them to use it with their whole team. It was great. It is not touchy-feely, it is quite down-to-earth and illuminates different preferences in communication.
>
> On its simplest level, such an awareness can make you a better leader because you can understand that some people would probably prefer to use and receive voice mail, while others would probably prefer e-mails. By dealing with them differently, you demonstrate that you are dealing with each person as an individual.
>
> In addition, **by adapting your approach based on understanding preferences in styles, you increase the receptivity to whatever you are trying to communicate.** And, of course, your greater understanding of each individual helps you run team meetings better.

The need to understand people's differences, and patterns in these differences, is well understood in global professional enterprises. Joachim Frank is the director of IT Solutions for Hewlett Packard (HP) Consulting's Service Definition and Creation division. He leads a team dedicated to helping companies transform their business through strategy consulting, business integration and technology implementation services. He told us:

> No one wants to be caricatured, or to caricature others, but to be effective you must learn to recognize how to deal with different groups of people. As a German national

now working in the U.S., I had to learn the obvious lessons that Germans do things differently than Americans. Not better or worse, just differently. Along with everyone else, I had to learn how to manage people according to the style that works best for them. Embedded into almost every key training program that HP offers is some aspect of emphasizing and enhancing effectiveness in working across cultures and geographies.

Human behavior is not completely random, and it is possible to obtain clues to the best way of dealing with individuals by observing the styles they tend to exhibit. So, let's see if the styles grid can offer some important insights for you on how you can better work with and coach your colleagues.

(The Drivers among you are thinking, "Can we just get to the point?" The Analyticals are not quite sure if there is yet enough solid data to support this model. The Amiables are completely repulsed by the whole idea of boxes and wondering why we just can't accept people at face value. The Expressives are thinking, "So some of the leading accounting and consulting firms are using this model, are they? I might be impressed if you could give me some specific names!")

YOUR DRIVER COLLEAGUES ("GET IT DONE")

Drivers are people who are perceived as being high in assertiveness, but low in responsiveness. **Drivers are most comfortable when they are in control of themselves, the work environment, and their client transactions.** They want quick action, tangible results, and pride themselves on their bottom-line orientation. Drivers speak in forceful tones and are far more comfortable with verbal than with written communication.

Decisiveness is a salient characteristic of Drivers. They perk up when competing and appear to thrive within a pressure-cooker schedule. This person will squeeze you into her calendar and let you know that her time is limited. A Driver may give in to impatience and rely on educated guesses or hunches rather than facts. You can expect Drivers to be more likely to change their minds and surprise other people with abrupt changes in thinking and sudden shifts of direction. In a Driver's mind, the situation has changed and so too must the response.

It is not unusual for a Driver to call you and, without saying hello, launch directly into the conversation. This individual wants to direct any conversation toward important tasks and goals: "I think we will implement this tomorrow" or "I think this discussion is over." Combine their no-frills conversational style with rapid delivery, a leaning-in posture, forceful gestures, and a gaze that may seem piercing and you have a person that is likely to intimidate the less assertive members of the group.

Your Driver colleague can accomplish a tremendous amount in a short time. However, if she feels bulldozed or depersonalized, there is a danger that the progress will be more illusory than real. Her lack of buy-in or outright resistance may delay or even sabotage the outcome. The Driver's forceful nature may tempt you to assume she has a lack of caring about people. Though a Driver may have a sincere concern for others she may not choose to talk about it, and her body language may not reveal the depth of her concern. Drivers are doers and their feelings are channeled into the language of action.

YOUR ANALYTICAL COLLEAGUES ("GET IT RIGHT")

Next, we have those people for whom details and facts are the most persuasive. These people, Analyticals, are low both on responsiveness and assertiveness. **Analyticals are obsessed with getting information. They crave data, the more the better, often agonizing over decisions, wanting to be certain of making the right choice.**

Analyticals are well organized and can usually be found in their office—with the door probably closed. Their office décor tends to the functional with charts, graphs, credentials, and firm-related pictures. Everything is orderly and in its appropriate place.

Perceived as an individual of few words, an Analytical is more likely to ask pertinent questions than make statements. He tends to be formal and proper, always likes to know where he is going, prefers written communications, may proceed carefully when taking the next step, and enjoys working with complex situations. Analyticals often seem to place a higher priority on the task to be accomplished than on the relationship. They strive for accuracy and expect it in others. They have perfectionist tendencies, set high standards, are often hard on themselves, but are willing to do the time-consuming work needed to achieve or exceed those standards.

These are not "contact" people, preferring to work alone rather than with others. They also prefer formal, businesslike relationships; and may not volunteer much about their personal lives. Despite their solitary nature, they surprise you by being loyal when the going gets rough.

Analyticals favor brief, to-the-point telephone calls, and are inclined to speak in structured, careful speech patterns, weighing their words as they say them. They will typically retain their ground in stressful situations when they can maintain their position with concrete facts or probing questions. They will try to avoid the emotionality related to conflict. When others get carried away by emotion, an Analytical will retreat into his head and become emotionally detached, believing that a rational approach will cool an overheated situation. It often has the opposite effect.

YOUR AMIABLE COLLEAGUES ("GET ALONG")

Amiables are low on assertiveness, but high on responsiveness. Their behavior may suggest little desire to impose their actions and ideas on the group, preferring instead to reserving opinions. **Amiables project sensitivity to others' feelings, exhibit great patience, and believe it important that they take time to establish relationships.**

To a greater degree than others, they are team players—generous with their time, eager to ask questions they hope will get to the core of the matter. Amiables use relationships to achieve results and are skilled at encouraging others to expand on their ideas, good at seeing value in other's contributions, and genuinely more interested in hearing your concerns than expressing their own.

When you enter an Amiable's office you are likely to see group photos, an abundance of family pictures and mementos, and even conservatively framed personal slogans. An Amiable favors arranging her office seating such that she can sit side-by-side with you in a congenial, cooperative manner. She walks casually, acknowledging others, and often get sidetracked in the hallways by chance encounters. An Amiable will express a sincere interest in the point-by-point description of what you did yesterday or the sequential pattern of how to complete a certain transaction. They like to approach their client work in a methodical and sequential order. Amiables are not enamored of goal setting or planning.

Amiables prefer personal interactions to communicating by telephone or memos. They typically express themselves tentatively, defer to the proven way things have always been done, often defer decisions, and feel more comfortable making decisions by conferring with others, rather than by themselves. In conversation, Amiables will reveal personal things about themselves that may have you thinking you know them better than you do others. Often, however, they are surprisingly guarded. Amiables do not communicate many of the thoughts and feelings that are important to them, withholding feelings of anger and critical judgments of others. An Amiable can seem calm on the outside while a storm rages within.

YOUR EXPRESSIVE COLLEAGUES ("GET NOTICED")

Expressive people are high on responsiveness and assertiveness. They are not hesitant about making their presence or feelings known and are generally seen to be very enthusiastic. **Expressives are often highly intuitive and can be highly persuasive when they combine their personal power with emotional display.**

You know when you have entered the working area of an Expressive. Paperwork is probably strewn across his desks, even trailing along the floor. Because they react to visual stimuli, Expressives they like to have everything where they can see it. You may see notes posted and taped all over, apparently at random, but Expressives are apt to tell you that they are organized within their disorganization.

Expressives have a naturally preference for talking, often tending to "think out loud," skipping from topic to topic in a way that defies logic. They are often seen to monopolize discussions and when they talk their whole body joins in. Their varied, emotional vocal inflections and their colorful choice of words may tend toward exaggeration. The telephone can be a favorite toy that enables them to prolong conversations (often with personal stories and anecdotes) and recharge themselves.

Expressives are outgoing, flamboyant, tending toward the dramatic, and enjoy the spotlight. They like glitter, glamour, flash, and excitement. They bristle with energy and are always on the go, enjoy being where the action is, and hate being confined to their desks all day. They prefer to work with others, are great at networking with innumerable contacts who can help them achieve their goals.

In group meetings, Expressives will continually shift about in their chairs and, if bored, will engage in a side conversation. They tend to be highly creative, visionary, and relish examining the "big picture" rather than getting mired in the details. They push others to look beyond the merely mundane and practical.

When you and the others are hard at work with the nitty-gritty of building the castles that your Expressive colleague has dreamed up and sold you on, you may find that he is not working along with you. He is off dreaming of other castles. Expressives are impulsive and have a tendency to act first and think later. Their motto is: "First I dive into the pool and then I look to see if there is any water in it." This impulsiveness often creates problems for them and for others. They prefer to work according to opportunity rather than according to plan. Few are good at time management. And while they are usually good motivators when emotionally high, more than any other style they can often find themselves in the pits.

FURTHER CONSIDERATIONS

In presenting our descriptions of these styles, we are obviously painting them in broad strokes. No one will be completely true to one style. The average person will have most of the characteristics of one of these styles, but not all of them. So when working with any particular person, you need to be alert to the characteristics of their predominant style, but you should also look for behaviors that may be exceptions to the rule.

Don't allow your initial perceptions of anyone to be carved in stone. Continue to absorb new information about each individual's style. Check your hypothesis against specific clues about the style you think someone exhibits. Then test your hypothesis in action. You can do that by reflecting the same characteristics you believe your colleague's exhibits. If doing that seems to make it easier for the person to relate to you, you have probably made an accurate assessment of your colleague's style.

Keep in mind the central point to all of this: No one style is better or worse than any other style, just different. But understanding these differences will help you get results as the group leader.

RESPONDING TO PEOPLE'S DIFFERENCES

If you were to ask each of your colleagues what they were looking for in an ideal practice leader, you would, in all probability, hear a number of very different responses, such as these:

Anthony (the Amiable): "I guess the most important thing is that the group leader be honest and open with me. I always feel awkward when other people have hidden agendas, don't you? I would be most receptive to a group leader who could show concern for me and my situation. I want to know we can work together. "

Dorothy (the Driver): "You have to understand that my kind of practice doesn't run itself. It requires my diligent attention, so my time to spend with anyone who serves as group leader is at a premium. Secondly, I'm not interested in hearing a lot of half-baked ideas, only tangible and practical suggestions are what interest me."

Amy (the Analytical): "Be prepared. I expect that a group leader should know my situation before dispensing advice. Don't play the know-it-all with me. Ask questions and then listen. A group leader needs to show me that they can understand everything about my practice, my clients, my issues, and then give me some options."

Elliott (the Expressive): "I'd like a group leader who is decisive, but that doesn't mean we can't toss ideas around. Just don't wear me out with every little detail. I'd like to see someone who is competent, imaginative—who can catch an image of how to make this group really soar."

Each of your people has his or her special way of behaving and doing things. You can only inspire and move your people forward to the extent that you have built positive relationships with each of them, one by one, and this can only be done when you are prepared to modify your style to accommodate theirs.

It is important to recognize that *you* also fit into one of the four behavioral categories we have outlined. As a result, you will find you share the very same characteristics as some of your people and will have little difficulty in relating to those individuals.

You are also similar on one of the dimensions of behavior (assertiveness and responsiveness) to some people, but different on the other. This will still require you to make some accommodation to your natural "way of doing things" to make the necessary connection. Then, of course, there will be people who are very different in style from you on both dimensions. They will often be very difficult for you to deal with.

To create an effective coaching relationship with any of your people, you will need to adjust (temporarily) your natural approach, as described in the following sections. Before proceeding, you might want to identify one person from your group of each type, and bear them in mind as we make suggestions on how to deal with each kind of person.

To help you do this, we present a summary of each style in Figure 7-3.

WORKING WITH YOUR DRIVER COLLEAGUE

Drivers are outspoken, no-nonsense, take-control types. They usually are (or would like to be) very busy people. They can pick up multiple projects, keep them all in the air at the same time, and juggle them faster than the eye can see. To build your coaching relationship with these people you need to help them maintain control.

COACHING A DRIVER

When meeting with a Driver, give her your complete attention. A positive approach would be to ask what the problems or concerns are. Ask direct fact-finding questions—consistent with your original reason for meeting. Stick to the facts. Draw the person out by talking about the desired results. Focus on tasks more than feelings.

Ask her how she would solve the problem. Be prepared to listen to her suggestions, the course of action she has in mind, and the general results she is considering. Work with Drivers to clarify their priorities. In the interest of saving time, Drivers will usually try to find shortcuts. You need to help them determine the simplest, fastest route to get them to their stated destination.

Figure 7-3: *DISTINGUISHING CHARACTERISTICS OF STYLES*

	AMIABLE	**ANALYTICAL**	**DRIVER**	**EXPRESSIVE**
SEEKS	Acceptance	Accuracy	Control	Recognition
STRENGTHS	Listening, teamwork, follow-through	Planning, systems, orchestration	Administration, leader, pioneer	Persuading, enthusiastic, entertaining
GROWTH AREAS (Weaknesses)	Oversensitive, slow to action, no big picture	Perfectionist, critical, unresponsive	Impatient, insensitive, poor listener	Inattentive to detail, short attention span, poor follow-through
IRRITATED BY	Insensitivity, impatience	Disorganization, impropriety	Inefficiency, indecision	Routines, complexity
UNDER STRESS	Submissive, indecisive	Withdrawn, headstrong	Dictatorial, critical	Sarcastic, superficial
DECISION MAKING	Conferring	Deliberate	Decisive	Spontaneous
FEARS	Sudden change	Criticism of personal efforts	Being taken advantage of	Loss of social recognition
GAINS SECURITY THROUGH	Friendship	Preparation	Control	Playfulness
MEASURES PERSONAL WORTH BY	Compatibility, contribution	Precision, accuracy	Results, impact	Acknowledgment, compliments
INTERNAL MOTIVE	Participation	The process	The win	The show

Drivers like to make up their own minds. They will likely be put off if you simply offer them one course of action. Therefore, present any recommendations with alternatives, together with any documentation or examples that you can offer. Provide solid information that will help them assess the probable outcomes of each alternative. You need to demonstrate that your recommendations are very workable, no-frills ways of getting the results they want. When suggesting a different idea, opinion, or action, be sure to express your desire to identify solutions that will be mutually acceptable. Always respect people's need to maintain their self-esteem.

Drivers are bare-bones planners, but planners nonetheless. They want you to come up with a simple, straightforward, results-oriented guide to action. They take great pride in delivering what they said they would—on standard, on schedule, and on budget. Unless you set up a communications arrangement, you are likely to have trouble keeping track of what is going on. It is prudent to encourage a quick exchange of information at periodic times during the implementation of your action plan.

INSPIRING A DRIVER

Managing Drivers is no easy thing because they want to manage you! Their preference for change and innovation makes them the natural choice for new "frontier" programs or practice development efforts where they can implement new ideas. Winning, more than anything else, motivates Drivers. Make sure they understand the need to check in with the group or they may demonstrate their renegade syndrome.

GIVING A DRIVER RECOGNITION

You need to focus on their achievements and track record. Try to relate some aspect of their personal accomplishments to the group and any group achievement to them personally.

WORKING WITH YOUR ANALYTICAL COLLEAGUE

Analytics thrive on specifics. To build a coaching relationship, you need to be well organized and clear, explain your thoughts systematically, and expect to be asked a lot of questions about the situation or subject at hand. You gain credibility when the Analytic sees that you have chased down every detail. Be prepared to listen to far more than you may want to know, as he explains ideas or project progress in what may seem like overwhelming detail.

COACHING AN ANALYTICAL

Analytics value punctuality. Work hard to be on time with memos, calls, meetings, and everything else. In one-on-one meetings it is usually appropriate for you to spend a little time on openers, but keep it brief, don't make it too personal, and then get right into what you are there to talk about.

Analytics will expect you to be prepared, so don't wing it. Dig up all of the data you might need and anticipate the questions you may be asked. Even for one-on-one meetings, Analytics like to see you having a written agenda. If you do have an agenda, ensure that you get it to this person in advance so that he can think about the topics beforehand.

When communicating with Analytics, rely less on body language. The words that you use are important. Saying "I think" rather than "I feel" can make a difference. Then follow with factual statements. Analytics appreciate the use of such phrases as "I've analyzed the situation," "My objective in suggesting this is . . ." A logical conclusion is . . . ." "Let me get some more information before I give you my opinion on that."

Show him the way to get something done and the Analytic will likely master the format, then modify it to suit his needs, so that it works even more efficiently, as he sees it.

When proposing a course of action, mention the advantages, but identify the downsides as well. The Analytic will respect you for doing that and wants to consider all available alternatives. Analytics particularly dislike change because they view the future as an unknowable variable, where things can go wrong. Allow them to investigate possible repercussions so that they may be more comfortable with possible changes.

You can expect the Analytic to be conservative when it comes to risk, so, where possible, show why the approach you are proposing is a fairly safe bet. Avoid emotional appeals or using someone else's opinion. Hard facts will persuade.

When correcting behavior, specify the exact behavior that needs to be changed and establish agreed-upon checkpoints. Allow Analytics to save face, as they fear being wrong. When you don't agree with something, try an approach like: "I'd just like to play devil's advocate with you for a minute."

When the time is up, depart quickly and graciously. Then cater to the Analytic's preference for written communication. Prepare a well thought out follow-up report together with any support materials. If a decision was reached, include a step-by-step timetable for implementation. Just be sure to deliver what you say you will. An Analytic will get turned off sooner than most if you make a promise and don't deliver.

INSPIRING AN ANALYTICAL

Appeal to his need for accuracy and logic. Keep your approach clear, clean, and documentable. Analytics are complex thinkers, basing their decisions on facts and proven information. "I need to think about it," usually means just that. Supply them with any materials or documents they need, and provide deadlines and parameters so they can build those into their time frames.

GIVING AN ANALYTICAL RECOGNITION

Analyticals will prefer more privately communicated, specific feedback. These people are usually very hard on themselves so keep your feedback simple and concise. Mention their efficiency, thought process, organization, persistence, and accuracy.

WORKING WITH YOUR AMIABLE COLLEAGUE

Amiables are great team players and contribute harmony and stability to the group environment. They are skilled at encouraging others to expand on their ideas, good at seeing value in others' contributions, and genuinely more interested in hearing your concerns than expressing their own. To create an effective coaching relationship, expect to have to project sensitivity for their feelings, exhibit patience, and take time to establish a relationship.

COACHING AN AMIABLE

When coaching Amiables, allow plenty of time to explore their thoughts and feelings. At the outset, touch base personally. Amiables will invite you to talk about yourself, and it will help to let this person know some things that are going on in your life. Be ready to do more talking than listening. Amiables will feel less comfortable when the limelight is focused on them. They are apt to keep their opinions to themselves, and if you don't exercise good listening skills Amiables will clam up even more.

When you are meeting one on one, politely request the Amiable's input and opinions on the topics you want to cover. When explaining your thoughts, you need always to be inviting an Amiable into the conversation. Always test to ensure that she understands and accepts what is being said:

"How does this fit with your thinking?" "I'm interested in getting your views on what I've just covered."

Do not expect an Amiable to verbalize her disagreement. Look for changes in body language as a tip as to how she may be reacting. If you surmise that she has any negative feelings about a proposal, invite her reaction: "Some people seem leery of part of this plan, I'm interested in your thoughts about it."

When a problem arises or a decision is needed, make sure to deal with only one subject or situation at a time, one step at a time. Before moving on to other items, make sure an Amiable is ready, willing and able to do so. Deal with matters calmly and in a relaxed manner. When suggesting a different possibility, encourage her to share her suggestions as to how the eventual decision might be made in a way that is least likely to disrupt things for everyone involved.

When engaging in corrective discussions, recognize that Amiables tend to take things personally. Reassure them that you only want to focus on a specific behavior. Point out in a nonthreatening way what they are doing well or contributing while also emphasizing what needs changing.

INSPIRING AN AMIABLE

Amiables like to feel that their relationships with others will benefit from their completing a project that is within their responsibility. Therefore, appeal to their need to strengthen relationships. Amiables are often the most helpful people. They frequently drop what they are doing to aid someone who is in a pinch. They will appreciate it when you spot an opportunity to give them a hand when they are under pressure.

GIVING AN AMIABLE RECOGNITION

Acknowledge their contributions to encouraging others in the group, their teamwork, and their dependability.

WORKING WITH YOUR EXPRESSIVE COLLEAGUE

With their energy and enthusiasm, Expressives are likely to get involved with many different activities. They may accomplish goals with a flourish. Or, they may show flurries of activity, but not actually accomplish anything. They are concept people who come up with plenty of ideas, but not necessarily with the means of carrying them out. To create an effective coaching relationship, you need to cater to their need to conceptualize, while also helping them fill in the missing pieces.

COACHING AN EXPRESSIVE

When meeting one on one with Expressives, allow enough time for the conversation, recognizing that they are inclined to informality. Take a few minutes to build rapport. You need to show Expressives that you are interested in them as people. Give them an opening to talk about themselves.

Expressives' style requires open and responsive interaction with others. Since Expressives' emotions have a major impact on what they do, it's critical that you stay in touch with what they're feeling. Recognize that, with a tendency to be dramatic, they are likely to exaggerate to make a point.

You may expect that Expressives will want to take a macro view of things. When details are of crucial importance, you need to ensure that they are not glossed over. Meanwhile you may have a lot more topics you want to talk about than an Expressive wants to listen to. Before meeting, prune your list to a few essentials, concentrate on the high priority items and start by giving him an overview of the main points. Make definite statements, avoiding words like try, perhaps, maybe, possibly, and the like.

When coaching, don't give Expressives too much at once or they will become overwhelmed. Frequently, they will want to jump in and try before they are ready, or before they fully understand everything. Help them channel that enthusiasm with tactful reminders and hands-on assistance to help them prioritize and organize. Paradoxically, when tasks become more organized, the anxiety level decreases, despite the fact that your colleague may bristle at the thought of organization.

Expressives are often dreamers, in both the best and worst senses of the word. They will often have a better vision for the group. But if their vision is faulty, or if you can't conscientiously support their proposals, help them inject realism into their suggestions, or be respectful and clear in expressing your opposition. One technique that can be helpful is to highlight the recommendations of those people that you know an Expressive looks up to and respects.

When proposing a course of action, do so enthusiastically. Expressives like an emotional appeal and like to be pumped about the choices they make and the things they do. Expressives see mental pictures first, then convert those pictures to words. They base decisions on their impulses, gut feelings, and others' testimonials. You need to support their ideas and dreams while showing them how they can transfer their talk into actions.

Whenever possible, invite an Expressive's input before a decision is made. If he disagrees with you, he usually comes right out and says so. He will expect the same from you. When problems arise, face them and dispose of them as soon as possible. From an Expressive's point of view, there is no time like the present to resolve a troubled situation.

If you disagree, try not to argue, because Expressives dislike conflict. You might not win an argument with them anyway because their strong suit is feelings and intuition. Try to explore alternate solutions. When you reach an agreement, iron out the specific details concerning what, when, who, and how. Then you must absolutely document the agreement, since Expressives tend to naturally forget such details.

This fast-paced person expects you to do whatever you are doing as quickly as possible, and wants everything done yesterday. You may expect to experience the hurry-up-and-wait phenomenon as that project or action that seemed so urgent yesterday gathers dust today.

INSPIRING AN EXPRESSIVE

Help an Expressive put his personal stamp on whatever he does. He hates doing the same old things the same old ways. Try to find new approaches to the way the two of you work together. Expressives will appreciate little special incentives to inspire them to achievement. They especially like constant rewards along the way and may favor shorter tasks with smaller payoffs.

GIVING AN EXPRESSIVE RECOGNITION

Expressives like recognition, so show appreciation for their contribution. It is even better if the appreciation can be expressed publicly. Try to find ways for them to get the recognition they enjoy, while making sure everyone else in the group gets the credit they deserve.

chapter 8

Help Underperformers

How can you be useful to those
who need assistance?

WHEN SOMEONE IN THE GROUP is not "pulling their weight," the desire to avoid conflict leads many practice leaders to waste a lot of time and personal energy trying to rationalize, rather than correct, the problem. We all face those situations where a performance problem persists in spite of our best efforts to be clear about expectations. We thought that the matter was settled, only to find that the other person's behavior continues to be unacceptable. Many leaders get discouraged when this happens and abandon their efforts to obtain a change or they postpone them for another time. The result is to let the individual off the hook.

However, an effective group leader must have the courage to deal with issues before they turn into real problems. The time to help people is before they are in real trouble. The key to achieving a lasting solution is persistence, sending the message that you are really serious, both in seeking a remedy and in offering your help.

A common mistake in dealing with underperformance is rushing to talk to the underperformer without pausing to consider why he or she is underperforming. At a meeting of group leaders we asked the people there to list the common reasons why their colleagues underperform. Here's their list:

1. Trouble at home or other personal problems (divorce, alcoholism, depression, etc.)

2. "Burnout": No longer finding the work interesting or challenging

3. Lack of competency

4. Fear of failure in trying something new and reaching for career progress

5. Quality of life choice—lack of desire to contribute more energy or time to the business

6. Externally driven reasons such as the loss of a recent client or downturn in their sector

7. Failure to keep up in their field; being less in demand

8. Struggling because of poor time management or other inefficiencies

9. Lack of knowledge about what they should be doing to succeed

10. Being poorly managed

11. Insecurity due to things like firm merger discussions, and being withdrawn into their shell, pending resolution of firm issues

As you review this list, add any other possible causes that you think are missing, and then ask yourself: which of these reasons are the most common in your real world?

When we asked that of our group of leaders, they selected burnout, loss of enthusiasm, quality of life choices, personal/family issues, and externally driven market changes as the major reasons for underperformance in their groups. One of our participants said:

> "It all ties together. The work is so demanding, and it is so hard on you, that the result is that you ultimately say, "I just don't like to do this anymore." That can also spill over into personal and family issues, and it can also make you say you really want a different quality of life."

The reason people are not performing is rarely because they don't know what to do. Nor is it that they don't want to do it. The incentives to do it are probably there. If they aren't doing what they should, it is probably due to something deeply personal in their lives. The only way to find out what it is, and to deal with it, is to talk about it.

We don't know if our unscientific survey is applicable universally. But we found fascinating that this group stressed reasons for lack of performance that were very rarely to do with competence, and everything to do with confidence. (Remember Jack Welch's comment in chapter 4: "Make them feel twelve feet tall.")

If you're going to make a difference, your task of turning an unproductive person around is often to help him or her find some *meaning* in what they (and your group) do. If the issues are loss of enthusiasm for the firm's work, and/or personal issues, then you will need to help the individual rediscover the energy, excitement, passion in the group's work.

Clearly, we don't want you to generalize from our tiny sample. Your task is to figure out for each person, as an individual, which reasons for underperformance exist. You must accomplish that before you can formulate any appropriate counseling response. There is no point in talking about the meaningfulness of your group's work if the problem is family trouble.

Ask first, start responding later. Very often we just rush into assumptions about why people are unproductive. The reason is usually not hard to figure out if you have a track record of ongoing informal conversations with your people. You've got to have a discussion, trying to find out what's going on. Say something like:

> *"I don't want to get things wrong here, but I get the sense that you're not fully engaged with everything here. You don't seem to be showing the normal levels of passion you have shown in the past. Something is going on. I would love to help you if I can. Is there anything I can do?"*

It is important to remember that the goal is to convey a genuine concern ("How can I help you?") while leaving the responsibility for improvement with the individual concerned. No group leader would tell you that this is the easy part of the job. It isn't. The demands of clients, group tasks, and time-consuming projects all combine to make your job of focusing on performance issues an easy one to postpone or procrastinate about. Yet the truly effective group leader succeeds because he doesn't put off the job. Effective group leaders know that the key to improving underperformance is to address it early and proactively, before it becomes a full-blown problem.

Of course, the variations in causes of performance problems are infinite. Some people may not have even recognized their performance deficiency, while others may be unwilling to try to improve. Still others may require time and coaching to move from a declining area of work with encouragement and support to retool for a new area.

A number of important steps can be taken to help a person whose performance needs attention:

1. Set up a meeting to discuss the performance issue that concerns you

2. Reassure the person of your confidence in them and your desire to be supportive

3. Get agreement that a performance issue exists and discuss its causes

4. Identify and discuss any obstacles to performance beyond the individual's control

5. Seek ideas for improvement

6. Mutually agree on specific actions to be taken to solve the performance issue

7. Set a specific follow-up date to review progress

1. Set up a meeting to discuss the performance issue that concerns you

The goal here is to improve performance by stressing your commitment to solving the problem together. You need to be positive, show a degree of personal concern, and make it clear that you want your colleague's ideas in the meeting. Schedule the meeting far enough in advance so that the person will have ample time to consider the performance issue at hand. Try saying:

> "Michael, I'd like to get together with you on Friday to talk about your workload. I have some concerns about your numbers. Since you are a lot closer to it than I am, I would like your ideas on how things could improve. Give some thought to it this week and let's talk on Friday."

2. Reassure the person of your confidence in them and your desire to be supportive

This is important to the individual's dignity and self-esteem. We all want to feel that we have someone on the sidelines pulling for us.

"Michael, I know there are times when work dries up a little for all of us. You're a competent person so I know you can turn this around. I'll do anything I can to help."

The proper role of a group leader, when dealing with thorny performance issues, is to serve as coach, catalyst, and cheerleader. The coach cannot win if the team loses. You have a vested interest in the individual performance of each and every member of your group.

3. Get agreement that a performance issue exists, and discuss causes

Your first, and most important, task is to ensure that the individual recognizes that there actually is a performance issue. You may need to set out (or review) the specific performance expectations for this person. You will almost certainly get a reaction that is defensive, uncooperative, or even slightly hostile. That's only human. Remember that your primary focus is on the problem, issue, or situation, not the individual. Stay positive and listen carefully, because it's important to identify and understand the reasons for the underperformance.

When you get resistance, the smart thing is to ask yourself: what is my goal in this conversation? This question can act like a circuit breaker so that you don't blow a fuse. It keeps you focused on what you want to accomplish so that you don't become frustrated or angry. The key is to stay calm in the face of resistance.

4. Identify and discuss any obstacles to performance beyond the individual's control

Your goal is to improve performance. In some instances there may be perceived obstacles to performance beyond the individual's control. These obstacles may be real (administrative policies, compensation inequities, physical or emotional health, or not feeling fully responsible) or imagined (lack of priorities, convenient excuses).

If the obstacles are legitimate and you are sure that the individual really cannot remove them alone, your role as group leader is to help remove these obstacles. In the event the suggested obstacles are not real, you need to confront the excuses. You might say:

"I understand that you have been feeling rather burned out lately. I think we all go through periods where we need some new stimulus to redirect our focus. The unfortunate reality is that you are accomplishing less and I am concerned for you. Do you have some ideas on how we could help you refocus and what specific first steps you could take to get back on track?"

5. Seek ideas for improvement.

Keep your colleague focused on all the areas in which performance improvement may be possible, and ask for ideas about how they might improve. Say:

"Are you aware that it has been taking you longer to produce things than any of the rest of us? Do you realize how much rework is often necessary on what you do? What do you think we can do to improve this situation?"

6. Agree on specific actions to be taken to solve the performance issue

In most instances you may have a number of constructive ideas that, if acted upon, you believe would help resolve the situation. However, you would be well advised to allow your colleague to come up with his remedial ideas first. It is important to remember that the underperformance issue and whatever action must be taken are the responsibility of that individual. If you shape his remedial action plan for him, you allow him the convenient excuse that this wasn't really his plan, it was yours.

Set out all of the ideas you come up with (together) as an action plan. Allow the person to choose which ones are of the highest priority and capable of being implemented. Make a note of what each idea entails, who's going to take responsibility, the anticipated date for implementation, and expected results.

In some instances you may just get a vague promise to implement some remedial action. If that happens, accept it, but also press for a more specific commitment. If you still don't get a specific undertaking, then ask him to think over the conversation and return to discuss it at a (specified) future date.

It might be useful at this stage to take notes, put your mutual understanding in writing, and ensure that your colleague gets a copy. (Since taking notes in the meeting can come across as authoritarian, you might want to defer this until the meeting is over, but if so, do it straight away!) Say:

> *"I like your ideas about involving another group. Why don't you go ahead and prepare a written summary for the group and I will call their group leader to set up a meeting."*

Coaching someone to success depends upon systematic, quiet repetition. You will need to use frequent (if gentle) reminders. Some coaches might oppose using this approach, believing, "He should know what is expected of him." While that may be true, he may not understand how serious you are about the matter. Repeated and gentle reminders convey your determination.

7. Set a specific follow-up date to review progress

Being consistent (and insistent) is one of the best ways to improve performance. If the person sees this meeting as a one-shot deal, you run the risk of obtaining, at best, only a temporary improvement in performance.

If however, your meeting can be viewed as part of an ongoing coaching intervention, the individual should begin to concentrate on matching performance to expectations. The best way to ensure this is to set a specific follow-up date to review the action plan. Repeating these same key steps will help guide you through your follow-up meeting.

> *"If we can get a meeting with you and the health care group set up for next week, we should have a sense of how things are working by the end of the next month. Let's meet at 4:00 p.m. on the 30th to see how we are doing."*

Acknowledge any achievement, no matter how small, during your follow-up meeting, as soon as possible following any achievements. To position yourself to be able to do this, schedule a series of short review meetings, each a few weeks apart. Your role as group leader is to "praise achievements back to acceptable levels of performance."

DEALING WITH PROTRACTED PERFORMANCE PROBLEMS

Only a few options exist for you as the practice leader to deal with protracted failure to improve performance:

1. You can choose to avoid the problem and let firm management deal with it.

2. You can suggest that the individual may be better served moving to some other practice area.

3. You can warn this person that you are being left in the unfortunate position of recommending a salary reduction.

4. You can lobby the firm to terminate this person.

Here's what Daniel J. Fensin (previously quoted) believes:

> **If somebody is not willing to be part of the culture of the organization, truly has a different value system than the rest of the partners, you know what? They've got to be gone.** It doesn't work. I don't care how much business they bring in. Really! It's not going to work, eventually, for us. It's not going to work for the long-term satisfaction of the firm.
>
> You know, maybe they're going to go off and start their own practice. Let them. They are going to destroy your practice if they stay. We've had the situation. We had a very successful partner. He broke off and went somewhere else. He should live and be well. He wanted things that the rest of us didn't. We were incompatible. It was the right outcome.

chapter 9

Tackle the Prima Donnas

How do you deal with difficult people?

LET'S FACE IT, top professionals are not always the easiest people to lead. Why? Because they are usually creative, talented, and fiercely competitive. Every firm needs prima donnas. They can be the drivers of change, and ask the tough firm questions that most people think but few voice. By having mavericks who provoke a direct and frank dialogue on tough issues, the group is usually better off.

Jim Shaffer, author of *The Leadership Solution* (and a principal at Towers Perrin for twenty years), told us:

> Some of the most brilliant, quirky, eccentric, emotionally zapped people in the world are loved by their clients but they create living hell for everyone who has to work with them and everyone who has to lead them. When a leader tries to use textbook constructive feedback and good performance management techniques, prima donnas are apt to become emotionally distraught, defensive, belligerent, attack-

> ing, and exhibit other defense mechanism behaviors. And because they're so darn smart and usually so darn articulate, they often intimidate the hell out of their manager, leaving him or her speechless.

We all know the type. They are brilliant at what they do, and make outstanding creative and financial contributions to your group's success. They are the first to arrive at the office every morning, put in a stunning amount of productive time, and ensure that services are always delivered to the client's satisfaction. They are major contributors in generating business and reputation.

The only problem is that, in some cases, your firm may be paying dearly simply to retain people like this. Men and women of high achievement can sometimes insist stubbornly on having their own way, and can often be contemptuous of others. In many cases, absolutely no one else wants to work with them.

Too often, they can be obnoxious, arrogant, coarse, and rude to everyone around them. They irritate, criticize, bruise, blunder, push, ridicule, deflate, intimidate, and otherwise generally make pains of themselves. They frequently interrupt conversations that they weren't even involved in, and act as though they were the acknowledged experts in all matters. They can be complainers, loners, backstabbers, rebels, and tyrants. They can push anyone to the limits and they can be immensely irritating.

Almost every group leader is faced with some person who has an attitude problem or is otherwise very difficult to work with. The negative effects of tolerating this behavior can be especially harmful as firms struggle to provide a congenial atmosphere that will foster the retention of their talented people.

If you ignore problem behavior, others in your group may not ignore the fact that you are letting standards be lowered and acquiescing to the idiosyncrasies of one individual, albeit a star performer. It may only be a matter of time before you have a major problem instead of one isolated case.

CONFRONTING PROBLEM BEHAVIOR

If you sometimes find it easier simply to ignore problem behavior, you are not alone. These discussions can be particularly sensitive. But, done with understanding and patience, there are effective ways to deal with difficult people.

Your main concern should be with behavior, not personality. Giving feedback that comments on someone's personality traits is destructive. The individual will only become defensive and subsequently turn off. If it is behavior change that you're after, point out the specific actions in question.

Here are a few steps to take to help resolve these problems:

1. Describe specific situations that illustrate the behavior you are concerned about.

2. Explain why it concerns you and express your desire for change.

3. Seek out and listen to the individual's reasons for this behavior.

4. Help the individual see how improved behavior will improve his or her career.

5. Ask for ideas and commitment to solving the problem.

6. Offer your encouragement and support.

7. Agree on an action plan and set a date to discuss progress.

1. Describe specific situations that illustrate the behavior you are concerned about

If you are dealing with a person who is being difficult, you must act quickly as soon as you sense a problem. The sooner you react to disruptive behavior, the more likely you are to affect it.

You have to tell your colleague what behavior needs to change, clearly and specifically. Try to be as objective as possible. Concrete examples—something you have observed first hand, or a situation that has been brought to your attention—will help the individual understand where the problems lie and show that you are not jumping to conclusions.

2. Explain why it concerns you and express your desire for change

Prima donnas usually have one thing in common: they respond well to candor. Don't be timid. Sometimes people need a mirror held up to them because they don't know how they are being perceived. The person must come away from this discussion understanding completely that there is a problem to be addressed, one way or another.

Again, remember you are concerned with behavior, not personality. Comments like "Others are often offended by your colorful language" get better results than telling someone "You're self-centered and inconsiderate." You must convey that this problem must be solved for the individual's own good, as well as the good of the group, and not just to have him or her toe the line. You are looking for a solution, not a showdown, and if this individual really understands why you're concerned, he or she will be more willing to commit to a solution.

3. Seek out and listen to the individual's reasons for this behavior.

You can't solve the problem if you don't know why this individual is being difficult. Maybe he or she is aggressive with everyone because that is his or her interpersonal style in all relationships. Perhaps deficient training in communications skills or factors outside of the office are causing this behavior. You have got to listen to find out.

Because you are guiding a process through which the eventual solution to the problem must rest with the individual, you should get your colleague to start thinking about the reasons for her behavior. Sometimes just having the issue brought to her attention and having someone to talk to will allow her to analyze the problem and propose remedial action.

Don't get sidetracked in endless discussions. Ignore the prima donna who wants to philosophize, defend, debate, or rant. Ask if he thinks the behavior should change or not. Ask him how he or she thinks others felt when he said or did what you described. Ask if he always gets the results that he wants from other people.

4. Inform the individual how improved behavior will improve his or her career.

If you place the situation in the context of career development, the person is more likely to be responsive. It is important to let prima donnas know what's in it for them if they change their behavior; how they will be more valuable to the firm, acquire more respect from people around them, and even how it may affect their clients. Point out that they run the danger of alienating the people whose cooperation they need. If you come across as being critical, you may get a grudging acknowledgment, but you are not likely to achieve observable or long-term behavior change.

5. Ask for the individual's ideas and commitment to solving the problem

For any solution to have a chance of success, the individual must fully accept that the problem is hers, and not yours or anyone else's; and there must be a commitment to solving it. Any solution you attempt to impose will seldom inspire the needed commitment. By asking for her input, you are placing the responsibility exactly where it belongs—with the individual who needs to solve her problem.

Set small, realistic goals. Micro changes in behavior can be big victories. Change is achieved step by step. Compromise is not necessarily bad. Perfection is not always attainable.

6. Offer your encouragement and support

While you can be sympathetic and display genuine concern, the important thing is to let the individual know that you have his best interests at heart. If, in discussing the problem, you see a workable solution that he doesn't come up with, then do suggest it. In some instances, such as with acute stress, qualified professional assistance may be required. You can offer your support by way of finding out where to get the best qualified help, but he must make the first move.

7. Agree on an action plan and set a date to discuss progress.

You have to go back to your colleagues time and again to make sure that they are on track. If a prima donna needs training or professional counseling, you make sure she gets it. If she needs to improve her listening skills, make sure that you provide the necessary one-on-one coaching to ensure that she keeps asking questions and learns how to listen actively in order to draw other people out.

This step confirms your serious intention to see change. By setting a concrete time and date you establish the parameters within which the problem behavior must be rectified. It may be helpful to have this individual feed back to you exactly what steps she is committing herself to taking.

For very difficult and challenging situations you may want to consider having someone else present for your discussions, ideally someone that this prima donna regards with some respect. Depending on the situation, you may also want to draft a memorandum either during or following the meeting.

ONE FURTHER CHALLENGE

Top performers usually get special treatment. If someone's performance is higher than the norm, his or her abrasive behaviors are all too often toler-ated. In most cases, leaders will go to great lengths to accommodate star performers. However, that same patience does not always extend to the mediocre, or people whose performance has dropped off. A person with mediocre numbers is likely to be treated more roughly than a star producer with an attitude.

Some leaders seem to operate as though they are justified in telling average performers what is expected, and then if these individuals don't like it, they can leave. But talented people are rare, so these same leaders seem more than willing to invest huge amounts of time in making sure they are happy.

Such **double standards are shortsighted, particularly as people are in-creasingly being asked to work in teams. It can be very disruptive to your entire group when one person is being difficult. Indulging that in-dividual can diminish standards and foster resentment.**

Benjamin Haas, of Towers Perrin, had this to say:

> What you do see periodically in professional services firms are the people who are great business developers, great with client relationships, and terrible with people in-ternally. The conclusion I have come to is that they are al-ways going to cause more damage than they are worth. I don't care how effective they are in the marketplace. You've either got to get behavior to change, which in my experi-ence, is pretty tough, or you've got to let them go.

But I would also agree there's a certain core cultural value that I think somebody's got to sign onto. I don't care how good they are. If what they want is something that's fundamentally different, then I think inevitably we should be prepared to walk away from that, just like we're prepared to walk away from some very large clients if we conclude it's a fit that doesn't make sense.

So I am much more comfortable with taking risks around giving up pretty significant chunks of revenue associated with people or clients, if I'm convinced that long term, that's going to be better for the organization. In my experience, the return on that shows up very quickly.

Bad attitudes shouldn't be tolerated in anyone. At some point, even a star performer with attitude isn't worth the effort. If you have to constantly sit down to deal with some prima donna's difficulties, it takes precious time away from helping the team work more effectively.

Handling the 800-pound Gorilla

We have often met group leaders who were beside themselves in frustration:

> How do we get the 800-pound gorilla actively participating in our group when the individual in question will not attend meetings, doesn't want to have anything to do with our group, but has substantive expertise to contribute and would strengthen the team considerably by his or her involvement?

Group leaders faced with this dilemma have two, and only two, options. They either polish their knees and beg this gorilla to play, or they ignore the gorilla.

Ignoring the gorilla consists of informing him that out of courtesy he will be included on the distribution of meeting minutes and highlights. The group recognizes how busy gorillas are, and will not bother the gorilla. The group makes it very clear that it does not expect the gorilla to attend any meetings or to participate in any of the group's activities. However, the gorilla is always welcome to stick its head in, at any time, if only to grab a banana at lunch. The group then sets about its business.

Gorillas hate to be ignored. It is not consistent with how everyone else in the zoo treats them. And it is not in keeping with the begging ritual that they so relish putting everyone through. So, you at least now have them curious as to what you are up to. This is the fundamental basis upon which you can achieve any power shift—what are you up to?

If your group accomplishes nothing meaningful other than to hold a monthly luncheon gathering, then the 800-pound gorilla is fully justified in not wanting to waste his time. However, there is a book title that says it all very well: *Stop Whining and Start Winning*. The essence of our advice to these group leaders: Get busy and start making something happen, quickly!

Develop a time-saving template that everyone in the group can use, invite a key client to speak to your group, host a high-profile seminar. Anything! Just start making some things happen that signal that your group is actually accomplishing something meaningful. Then see how long it takes this gorilla to want to get back into your zoo. How many gorillas do not want to be members of a winning team?

Is this just child psychology? Perhaps, but after all, you are dealing with a large part of the child in most every 800-pound gorilla. And it beats begging! A last thought: Before you let any gorillas in, ensure that they agree to abide by the rules and guidelines that your group has developed. After all, even for reluctant gorillas, there has to be some price of admission.

chapter 10

Build Support for Change

How do you get people to buy into the need for change?

THERE ARE TIMES WHEN you as a group leader identify a need for a radically new idea, a new plan of action, or case for change. This requires communicating your sense of urgency, clearly establishing the benefits of change to your colleagues, and gaining the necessary cooperation to move forward.

Professionals don't like to be told what to do. They like to be part of the decision-making and problem-solving process. However, that absolutely does not mean that your role is merely that of facilitator, devoid of opinions. It means that you must be good at creating feasible alternative options, and good at helping people reason through the options, gently bringing to their attention considerations they may not have taken into account. Don't be a dictator, but don't be a wimp, either!

You need to spend time with one person at a time. Don't hold a group meeting until you have done this. You won't be ready, and you're likely to be drawn into elongated, unresolvable debates. These are, after all, smart, creative professionals who know how to find ten counterexamples for any proposition! They know how to analyze problems, and when you put them together they will go to war for their respective solutions!

It is a myth that people resist change. **People resist what other people make them do, not what they themselves choose to do.** People fight that which fails to take their needs or interests into account and gives them no room to influence decisions. People do not identify their own projects as "change." They are simply acting on their aspirations to get something done that they can shape and mold. That's why groups that innovate successfully year after year seek their own people's ideas, let them initiate new projects, and encourage multiple experiments.

Think about what motivates each person, so that you can match your discussion of the issue to that person's individual interests.

Here are a few steps to take to gain individual support for change:

1. Describe the situation and how it affects both the individual and the group

2. Discuss the stake you both have in addressing the situation and ask the person what he or she thinks you both (together) might do

3. Offer options you see, and ask for comments on the relative merits of the options

4. Ask the person for assistance in addressing any concerns that may arise

5. Ask for the specific support you need and explain what you will do

6. Express your appreciation

1. Describe the situation and how it affects the individual and the group

If you firmly believe this to be an important issue, then to initiate change, you must start by creating a "call to action." A certain degree of zeal needs to accompany the announcement of change as a priority.

> *"I need to talk to you about an issue that I think may have a profound impact on our group and I'd like to get your ideas before our next meeting."*

Be as specific as possible about the effects of the situation, problem, or issue. Describe how it will make or is currently making work for both of you more difficult, more stressful, more costly, less satisfying, more time consuming, such that it lessens your ability to provide for the level of client quality that you would wish. Decide what effects to stress based on your knowledge of the individual you need to influence.

2. Discuss the stake you both have in addressing the situation

This is your opportunity for soliciting the counsel of your colleague, beginning to transform this from being your issue to *our* issue.

> *"I'm thinking of raising the question at next Tuesday's group meeting, but I'm really not sure how the others are going to react. Any suggestions for how you think we should approach this?"*

You may very well have thought this issue through and formed your own opinion as to the best course of action. However, **if your team member gets the impression that you are merely going through the motions in an attempt to persuade her to accept your plan, you diminish your chances of obtaining her support.** Accept that while you may have devoted significant time to this issue, others in your group may offer improvements to the initial thinking, or may even come up with a far better way to approach the issue.

3. Offer options you see, and ask for comments on their relative merits

Briefly explain what you've been thinking, and how the various options might benefit this particular person and how they might benefit the group.

> *"What I thought we might propose is that we at least do a small sampling of client opinion, perhaps only a dozen of our best and closest contacts. I think that would give us all a fair idea of whether we were on the right track. Does that make sense?"*

By thinking in advance about the objections, concerns, or obstacles the person might raise to your ideas, you will be in a better position to address them in a positive way.

4. Ask your colleague for assistance in addressing any concerns that may arise

Make sure the person fully understands the consequences and implications of each possible path of action. Ask for his opinion and reaction to each of the ideas. Probe for any resistance, hesitation, or negative reactions so you can get them out and can deal with them.

> *"I'd like you to help me with drafting the initial questions that we run past the group. That way you can make sure that we're looking at the issues that would be most important to your clients. What do you think of the approach? Do you foresee any of our colleagues being concerned? How could we deal with their concerns?"*

By engaging your colleague's assistance in your efforts, he becomes more of a champion to the cause.

5. Ask for the specific support you need and explain what you will do

Be very specific about what you need (time, funding, approvals, colleague assistance, or certain project parameters) to implement any action plan. Ask for her individual support.

> *"I would like you to talk with Jim to see if you can get him on our side. If you can talk to him, I'll review this with the other two senior colleagues and we can get together before the meeting to compare notes on what kind of reaction we received."*

Explain what *you* will do. People are more likely to give support willingly if they see your own willingness to pitch in.

6. Express your appreciation

> *"Thanks, Kevin. With your help, I think we have a chance of at least testing this idea."*

Convey your appreciation for whatever level of commitment you have received, even if it is not all you had hoped for.

ADDRESSING YOUR PEOPLE'S NEEDS

To achieve commitment, there are some critical personal needs to which you must appeal, in order to influence your colleagues' behavior.

1. The need to feel like a winner
2. The need for respect and approval
3. The need for certainty

1. Help your people to always feel like winners

You may remember an infamous sweepstakes organization that used to promote a slogan claiming: "You can be a winner." It did very well with that slogan for many years, but then suddenly changed its slogan to "You may already be a winner." The new wording brought enormous success, largely because everyone who received an envelope with this slogan on the front immediately became fearful that they might lose something that they already had. **The threat of losing something you already have is far more motivating than the prospect of gaining something new.**

Remind people of what they will be saving themselves from—wasted time and energy, the loss of peer respect, the loss of individual revenue, etc.—rather than what they may gain from taking decisive action.

Avoid creating a win-lose encounter. People respond not only to your ideas but also to the degree of persuasive force you choose to apply. When you push, people's natural reaction is to push back, with equal or greater force.

2. Support your colleagues' need for respect and approval

Everyone wants the approval of his or her peers. Help people see how any new initiative will help them receive the approval of those they care about, internal or external to the group or firm.

3. Address each individual's need for certainty

The need for predictability and certainty is life's glue. It causes us to embrace what has always worked in the past and to be highly skeptical of anything new and different. No matter how exciting or creative you believe your idea is, always remember that these same characteristics can be interpreted by your colleagues to mean risky and unpredictable.

Help the individual see how a revised course of action would be consistent with who she is. Remind her of other things that she has done or accomplished that are in keeping with this current belief or behavior. If she views the new initiative as a continuation of previous experience and thinking and not a departure from it, you will enhance your chances of gaining support.

Of course, not all of your efforts to build support for change will be accomplished through these one-on-one conversations, essential as they are. Group activities (which we shall discuss in the next section of this book) are also required. As Michael Hodges, of the global real estate advisors Jones Lang Lasalle, points out, it is really an iterative process, with carefully planned group activities helping to build individual support, and vice versa. He commented to us:

> We have found that many senior people do not immediately see the need for change. It only becomes apparent that change is an essential step once individuals become aware and accept that their view of the world may not be the same as that of their peers. At this point the need for change becomes an inevitability. It is first important to recognize how dysfunctional our own individual visions of success can be. A group exercise which enables members to compare their own personal view of the challenges facing the company and where the company is going can quickly show that there is little shared perspective. This then creates the context for change.

To Introduce Lasting Change Successfully

You can at any time, in any firm, at any level, make yourself part of an initiative that can begin to make some difference. In *Beyond Knowing,* Patrick and his co-authors set out some basic guidelines for managing your efforts.

If you are just beginning some new initiative or program, it is important that it not be viewed as the latest "flavor of the month." To build credibility, start your efforts quietly with minimal fanfare, taking small steps, and build incrementally.

Avoid being seen as setting high initial expectations. Nothing worthwhile happens overnight, change is often gradual, and it always takes longer than we planned to realize those first signs of progress.

Expect varying degrees of commitment as people's reactions to any new direction will be mixed. Work with those considered the informal group leaders at all levels within the firm to try to get them on board early, or at least neutral to the proposed change.

Get people at all levels involved. Find ways to encourage teamwork with the effort being undertaken. Experience shows that people do not believe in or support any initiative that they have not had some part in formulating.

Momentum is your best friend. Every leader faces the challenge associated with creating and then sustaining change. Momentum is one of the key factors that separates winning initiatives from those that fall by the wayside. Often, it is the only difference.

In a typical basketball game, when the opposing team scores a lot of unanswered points and starts to develop too much momentum, a good coach will call a time-out. The coach knows that if the other team's momentum gets too strong, his team is likely to lose.

So as a leader, you can't afford to let down your guard or turn your attention to other matters once a project is launched. You can't delegate (or abdicate) an important initiative. Your hand must *always* be (and be seen to be) on the throttle. When there is the momentum for accomplishing something important, professionals are motivated to perform at ever higher levels. Lose that momentum and it looks like just another passing fad that inevitably undermines your next attempts.

To Introduce Lasting Change Successfully *(Cont.)*

Every new undertaking looks like a failure in the middle. Understanding this principle can make a huge difference. Predictable problems arise in the middle of every attempt to do something new, whether launching a new service offering, opening an international office, altering the people' compensation plan, instituting a small merger, or installing new technology. The more different it is from what's been done before, the more problems emerge. Give up at the first sign of trouble, and by definition the effort (and you?) will be a loser.

A little-known fact is that the Apollo moon missions were on course less than 1 percent of the time. The mission involved almost constant midcourse corrections. That's also true of most new endeavors.

In the "middle," you can overspend both time and money because forecasts are always overly optimistic. You should expect to have the unexpected pop up that no one knew was there. After all, no one has been down this path before. Momentum slows down due to fatigue—everyone likes the promise of beginnings, but middles are hard work. Or professional turnover in the middle of the endeavor means that valuable knowledge is lost, and the implementation team starts stumbling. And the middle is when the critics attack. Opponents start to notice and offer favorable comments about the project only when it looks like it might be a winner.

The lesson is clear: Success belongs to those who persevere. To convert imagination into useful results, leaders need patience, flexibility, and persistence. Leaders have the enduring task of inspiring and motivating people to put aside any small differences in the interest of larger causes.

That's not a fad; it's a permanent job description.

PART THREE

COACHING THE TEAM

WE NOW TURN TO MANAGING YOUR GROUP as a group. Not only must you be able to understand and influence individual people, but you must understand and influence a significant number of them simultaneously.

11. Clarify Group Goals
    Does your group have specific, clearly articulated, shared objectives?

12. Develop Your Group's Rules of Membership
    What do members of your group owe to each other?

13. Build Team Trust
    What gets group members to trust each other?

14. Throw Down a Challenge
    Has your group selected an exciting challenge?

15. Energize Your Meetings
    What are good meeting disciplines?

16. Give Recognition
    How do you acknowledge accomplishments?

17. Resolve Interpersonal Conflicts
    What do you do when team members fall out?

18. Deal with Your Crises
    How do you respond to dramatic events?

chapter 11

Clarify Group Goals

Does your group have specific, clearly articulated, shared objectives?

AS A GROUP LEADER, your initial organizing task is to help educate and guide your people in a direction that is in the best interests of their personal careers as well as your group's future. Loosely organized individuals accountable only for their own performance are less likely to succeed than would a well-managed team engaging in collective activities with collective responsibilities.

Before you can make your group work, you need to determine (collectively), and to share *explicit*, clearly articulated answers to three questions:

1. Why does our group exist?
   (*What specific benefits can your group expect to obtain from acting as a coordinated team?*);

2. How will working together as a group help us compete?
   (*What might the benefits be to each member and to the firm from investing some amount of each individual's discretionary non-billable time in pursuit of building a strong practice team?*)

3. What's in it for each of us?
   (*What might each individual member want to get out of working as a group for their respective career satisfaction?*)

It is surprising to learn how many groups in all professions (and professional departments within corporations) still have not thought this through.

1 | WHY DOES OUR GROUP EXIST?

To obtain the benefits of coordinated groups, everyone, including the people in the group, firm management, and the group leader needs to have a clear, unambiguous understanding of what the group is seeking to accomplish.

In some firms there is a general understanding of the group's purpose, but this is insufficient. All too often group members sit around asking, "What are we supposed to be doing at this meeting? Why are we here?" This is, of course, a disastrous waste of everybody's time. The goals, and specific target benefits, of each group must be discussed, resolved, and written down.

We suggest that you pose the following question to your group:

> "What benefits should we expect to get [not: are we getting] from practicing with a group of like-minded individuals, pursuing a common purpose that we could not get if we were each practicing on our own? Let's make our list together and see what it suggests."

The most common responses that people are likely to give include:

1. Improving value to clients by delivering to them the collective wisdom and skills, and accumulated knowledge, of the group

2. Making business development efforts more effective through pooling and coordination of individual efforts

3. Better utilization and development of junior professionals through collective decisions on staffing of client work, allocation of resources, and mentoring

4. Collective development of tools, templates, databases, and other practice aids to benefit everyone

5. More rapid and effective dissemination of expertise and skills among the group

6. Better client service through greater ability to put the right people on the right job

7. Better market image through development of a collective reputation, not just the sum of individual reputations

8. The comfort of belonging to a small group rather than being lost as one of a very large number of people (applies both to the successful retention of senior as well as junior people)

9. Informal coaching on a one-on-one basis acting as a source of help for personal growth, rather than relying on firm-wide, annual, bureaucratic performance appraisals

10. Improved profitability from focusing as a group on ways to enhance performance

11. Creation of a critical mass of time and resources to develop innovative service offerings, which no individual could afford to do alone

This list is not intended to be exhaustive. But responses like these encourage your people to think through and identify the benefits of working together. After adding your own objectives, you might want to examine this list by asking the members of your group:

1. Which of these benefits will be easiest to obtain? Hardest?

2. Which will be the quickest to obtain? The slowest?

3. Which disrupts your culture least? Most?

4. Which represents the biggest impact on your success? The smallest?

5. Which requires the most change in behavior? The least?

6. Which requires the most activist role for the leader? The least?

Your answers will determine the ground rules under which you will operate and the kind of group you want to be. Consider, for example, a group whose defining purpose is to set common service standards. This may require only a modest amount of joint commitment and coordinated action among group members (as long as everyone meets the common standards) and only a limited set of activities by the group leader.

Compare this to a group that wants to take a collective approach to improving the development and utilization of junior people. This probably will require that the group engage in team consultation on how all projects (above a certain size) are to be staffed. It would mean a great deal more intrusion into the autonomy of the individual group member, probably taking away that person's freedom to staff his or her own jobs. It will also require much more attention and intervention by the group leader.

There is no point aiming for a group benefit or goal if the group has not thought through, or is not willing to do, the things necessary to achieve that benefit or goal. Accordingly, as you consider the various benefits your group might reach for, you need to discuss (explicitly) how the group would need to operate (the minimum ground rules) in order to get there. If the group will not accept the new operating procedures, then they must acknowledge that they are unlikely to achieve the benefit.

One thing is clear. The worst position to be in is *pretending*—that is, asserting that your group is pursuing a goal or benefit when it will not accept the discipline necessary to pull it off. Hence the need for an up-front *explicit* discussion of what the group is really trying to achieve through its collective action, and *precisely* what this would mean for how you operate together.

2   HOW WILL WORKING TOGETHER AS A GROUP HELP US COMPETE?

As the group leader, you must find ways to communicate clearly how the development of a strong practice team can impact your collective fortunes in terms of building competitive superiority in the two most critical areas—the competition for clients and the competition for talent.

The stronger (and more focused) the group, the more likely it is going to be active in the marketplace and the more widespread will be its ultimate reputation and profile. Obviously the group with twenty people practicing in a specific area is likely to be better equipped to handle a client's problems than the firm with just a few. Its very size indicates a degree of success. The client who retains the services of one or two people who are part of a larger group expects to get the benefit of the shared expertise of the group. After all, no one person is likely to possess all of the necessary experience to handle many of today's more complex matters.

Winning the war for talent (recruitment and retention) may ultimately determine marketplace success. We were intrigued to learn recently from one major Los Angeles law firm how significant the cost attached to losing talent really was. According to their calculations, it cost each and every principal approximately $23,000 a year in lost income for each and every departing junior person that the firm did not want to lose.

We once asked a firm leader, "Do you sense that you are losing your best young talent from those groups that you would consider your best organized, or from those groups that are slightly dysfunctional?" This person paused for all of two seconds, looked at us and said, "You know, I think you're onto something there!" We have since posed that same question to at least fifty firm leaders in different professions around the world and without exception have elicited a very similar response. Their reactions suggest that having dysfunctional groups is costing firms large amounts of money.

What develops is a virtuous circle. A firm develops a strong group and, as a direct result, that group gains a market profile, that profile attracts the better client work, and the better client work then attracts the more talented players in the market.

3 WHAT'S IN IT FOR EACH OF US?

Finally, to help your group determine what it wants to achieve, you must help each individual to determine his or her career objectives. You should have a general discussion with the members of your group about personal objectives. Start by going around the table and asking each person, "Please tell us, what specifically do you want to get out of being a member of this group? Be honest! What can our group collectively do to help you be even more successful?"

Here are some topics for discussion:

1. Are we prepared to create a supportive environment? What would it look like?

2. Are we prepared to work at getting the benefit of joint intellectual exchange?

3. Are we prepared to cooperate in developing common tools and methodologies that we might all share?

4. Are we prepared to invest in developing superior support staff, internal systems, and technologies to provide for the effective conduct of our practice?

5. Are we prepared to effectively engage in joint marketing activities?

6. Are we prepared to devote non-billable time to helping each other when facing sensitive client issues?

It is also important to learn what your people want and need from one another, what they prefer, how they differ, and how to value and use those differences. Spend some time addressing as a group some of the more common unspoken, personal questions that exist within the minds of all members:

1. Why was I asked to participate in this group?

2. Who are the other members and what are their strengths?

3. How am I going to find out what they are good at, and also let them know what my capabilities and interests are?

4. What are they likely to expect of me?

A group becomes a team only when people help each other out, when assistance, cooperation, support, and mutual encouragement are readily forthcoming.

Here is how Karl Kristoff, of Hodgson Russ, described this task:

> It's not published, but we had a meeting using the tried and true butcher-block paper approach, and we scoped out what this group ought to look like and what its mission ought to be. There's certainly a firm understanding amongst the people who are involved in the project. Ultimately, as we continue to mature as a group, we'll probably see a more formal statement because, as new people join us, they will need something beyond an oral history of what we've done.

chapter 12

Develop Your Group's Rules of Membership

*What do members of your group
owe to each other?*

ONE OF THE MAJOR PROBLEMS of groups is that they often have no explicit, shared agreement on what it means to be a group. They have not discussed, let alone reached a consensus on, what responsibilities they owe to each other, nor on what principles their group will operate. Many so-called groups are really just collections of people who, in subtle ways, are each simply pushing their own special interests. Members avoid dealing directly with each other when performance is lagging or when individuals behave annoyingly and obstruct progress.

Because professionals jealously guard their autonomy, reserving the right to work as they see fit, professional groups have a greater-than-average tendency to become ill-disciplined.

Take an all-too-typical group meeting: At 4:00 p.m., the scheduled start time, people begin to enter the boardroom and drop their papers off at their favorite seating place while quickly scanning the room to see if anyone more powerful or senior than themselves is already there. Seeing none, and with their papers now signifying that they were on time, they rush back to their offices on the pretext of making "just one quick client call."

Then there is that insecure person who brings his work into the meeting to impress upon everyone just how busy he really is. And, of course, there is the person who accepted responsibility for an important project at the last meeting, but who quickly reveals that she has no specific action to report (which doesn't prevent her from talking aimlessly and at length to try to cover up that fact).

In the face of such behavior, members are quick to blame the group leader for being unable or unwilling to deal quickly and decisively with self-serving or noncontributing members. These people say things like:

> *"This is George's group. We're there to lend a hand and provide some ideas when he asks for them, but when things get off track or people are wasting time, it's his responsibility to set things straight. If someone else in the group isn't delivering the goods then, as long as it doesn't negatively impact my client work, that's the group leader's concern. If I'm asked my opinion, I'll give it; but there's no sense in ruffling anyone's feathers to make your point."*

What is needed is an approach that will create a more inspiring system that provides for higher levels of shared enthusiasm, decision making, performance, participation, and morale. This can be done by basing your group on three fundamental principles:

1. Mutual accountability. All group members must hold one another accountable for individual and for group performance.

2. Shared contribution. All group members must have an opportunity and obligation to contribute.

3. Shared values. All group members must adhere strictly to the values, principles and standards established by the group.

SETTING LEVELS OF MUTUAL ACCOUNTABILITY

The group leader must ensure that group members primarily feel a sense of accountability to each other, not to the leader (that's being the boss). Group members must have high expectations of each other. They must expect that everyone will contribute to the extent that each is capable. They must feel unhappy and frustrated when certain members or the group it-self is not performing well. There is no better way to achieve this than to clarify the rules and principles upon which the group will operate.

A basis for every championship team, in every endeavor, is having hard-and-fast, non-negotiable "ground rules" that everyone agrees to abide by. Great groups formulate and commit to writing a set of ground rules for how their team will work together and how they will manage themselves, thus bringing about constructive peer pressure.

For example, is it acceptable for group members to confront those who don't complete the projects that they have accepted responsibility for? Those who place their personal agenda ahead of the group's goals? Is the group leader to be the only individual responsible for the group's collective performance or should individual group members be expected to be re-sponsible for each other?

It is wise to discuss and establish (explicitly) some very basic ground rules for your group. They will serve as a group conscience, having a positive im-pact upon your group's performance.

Sensible issues that the rules could cover include:

1. Mutual respect and cooperation

2. Interpersonal communications and expression of ideas

3. Making of decisions and resolving of conflicts

4. Support for personal risk taking

5. Frequency and format of group meetings

6. Meeting attendance and punctuality

7. Participation in group business development efforts and sharing of clients

8. Completion of individual projects

9. Client service and handling of complaints

10. Learning and sharing knowledge

11. Supervision, training, delegating, and staffing of engagements

12. Constructive feedback and performance evaluations

Some of the practical and important ground rules we have seen include:

1. Meetings of the group and prompt attendance are a priority. Unless there is a client emergency, everyone is required to attend—on time.

2. Honor commitments. If you say you'll do something, do it. If you can't accomplish a task, don't say you can. If you have committed to doing something and a problem arises that will prevent you from following through, let us know in advance.

3. Be receptive to all new ideas. Don't tell us about someone who's tried this before and failed or why it won't work, until you have constructively addressed "how we can make this work."

4. Don't point fingers or assign blame. Every success is a group success, and every failure is an opportunity for the group to self-correct, to learn something new, and to constantly improve.

5. Maintain confidentiality. The group's dysfunctional processes are the group's business. Don't bad-mouth our team or any individual members, or discuss contentious issues outside of our group.

In great groups, the players police themselves. People hold themselves, and each other, accountable. Discipline boils down to several basics. Do that which one commits to doing. Live within the agreed-upon rules. Stick to standards.

Deborah P. Koeffler of Mitchell Silberberg & Knupp had this to say:

> Our written commitments from our group members came about as the natural conclusion of brainstorming on managing our practice and ourselves after the death of our departmental chair. We met for a full day and talked about clients, contacts, and business development opportunities.
>
> Sixty pages of notes emerged from that meeting, which I distilled into a concise statement of group goals. These included setting billable expectations as well as mundane, but important, things like setting up lunches to encourage cross-fertilization of client business or integrating more practice members into the work. We included a commitment to training, and creating more community awareness of our capabilities. Practice development targets were quite specific by business name, contacts, and substantive area.

> I asked each person to draw up and sign a statement of personal commitments, consistent with the fact that each of them had varying strengths as finders and as minders. Each one of them drew up his separate agenda of what he would undertake to advance the group's goals and committed to them. Lawyers take written commitments very seriously and each group member was very thoughtful.
>
> The idea of getting every person to write a commitment statement arose out of a discussion at our retreat on the subject: "What Do People Owe Each Other?" It was an extremely good session. In fact, after we got back to the office, several people left voice mails reaffirming some of the points about mutual commitment and pride in the their relationships.

Basic ground rules foster trust and openness and establish common expectations for members' behavior. They provide a guide for how your team will operate on a day-by-day basis.

The best ground rules are:

1. Behaviorally defined
2. Agreed upon by all members
3. Always kept visible
4. Consistently observed
5. Specific as to consequences

1. Behaviorally defined

Behavior is observable. A ground rule like, "Show respect for your fellow group members" may sound good, but isn't likely to work if it's not behavior-specific. One thing you would likely see or hear if you were showing respect for one another would be group members having their say without interruption from colleagues. The ground rule might be: "We agree that only one person should speak at a time; therefore we must allow people to complete their statement before responding, and we will refrain from having side conversations during our meetings."

2. Agreed upon by all members

Majority rule does not build accountability. Total consensus is what makes the rules come alive. Everyone must agree to participate in developing the group's rules, actively support them, and be confronted if his or her behavior contravenes any of the agreed-upon rules.

Great groups will also go to great effort to ensure that new members agree to the existing ground rules as a condition of joining, or as an expression of their commitment to the group.

3. Always kept visible

People give more credibility and pay closer attention to that which is committed to writing and kept in sight. Great groups ensure that every member has a copy of the ground rules and may even refer to them at the beginning of potentially contentious items on any meeting agenda.

4. Consistently observed

Among the best performing teams there is an understanding that any member may stop the play by calling a time-out if someone's behavior is inconsistent with (or overtly contravenes) the rules. If someone does something inconsistent with the defined standards, anyone in the group can and is encouraged to say: "Excuse me, didn't we all agree that . . ."

5. Specific as to consequences

Effective group leaders make sure that **the group defines what the consequences will be if any of the group's ground rules are violated. If there are no consequences, there probably are no rules.**

Consequences are usually designed not to be overly punitive, but simply to serve as a gentle reminder that the standards are important. There might be a two-dollar sanction that gets contributed to funding the group's beer bash, or sent to a favorite charity. Or, the rule might be that the last person into the meeting is obligated to take the minutes.

The essential principle is that the group collectively sets and manages the ground rules, and the ground rules then manage the group.

SETTING LEVELS OF SHARED CONTRIBUTION

Being a member of any group of truly committed, exceptional people can have a motivating impact on each individual. To that end, high-performance groups demand some price, some requirement, and some commitment for membership. This approach incorporates one of the most fundamental motivators throughout human history: pride in belonging. Accordingly, **the first question that must be addressed is: "What is the price of membership in our group?"**

When you establish a level of shared contribution in advance, you increase the likelihood that everyone will freely cooperate, contribute, and be committed to achieving reciprocal benefits from working together.

A good place to start is to ask how much "investment" time each person is willing to commit, beyond their normal production or client-serving workload, to further the group's objectives. While most firms are obsessed with revenue production of their people, very little attention is given to the (usually substantial) amount of non-reimbursed time that people spend at work. Yet it is precisely through the wise use of nonproduction time (i.e., investments in the future) that effective groups achieve new things. We recommend the following process:

1. Define how many investment hours each member is prepared to commit to the group

2. Agree on how those investment hours are to be used

I. Define How Many Investment Hours Each Member Is Prepared to Commit to the Group

Begin by determining how many hours in a week the average person devotes to your firm and its clients, including all activities. Suppose this comes to approximately 55 hours a week. Accounting for holidays, sick time, and vacation periods, we can conservatively project a work year of 45 weeks, that would result in each person spending approximately 2,475 hours annually at the office. (Your numbers may differ: Work with your numbers, not ours.)

Next, deduct from this the number of production, billable (or fee-earning or client-service) hours that each person is expected to work. Let's assume this number is 1,800 hours (higher for some professions, lower for others). Third, deduct from this an allowance for personal time (call the kids, fill in time sheets, go to the bathroom). Let's say that is 175 hours per year. That would leave 500 nonproduction hours remaining as each group member's available "investment" time.

The next question becomes: "How many of these very precious, discretionary, non-billable hours are you prepared to invest as your contribution to being a member of this group?" The group leader goes around the table and solicits each member's individual commitment.

Now imagine that your people agreed to devoting a conservative 30 percent (150 or so) of those available hours to efforts on behalf of the group, leaving 70 percent of their investment time to be allocated to their own individual pursuits. (Again, your percentage may be different than our guess: use yours.) That 150 hours per person per year (or 12.5 hours per month) would provide ample time to attend one monthly meeting, and also allow for an investment of at least one day every month to the implementation of some preselected activity that would advance the common interests of the group.

Note that this is only a modest beginning. **In firms where groups have functioned for a long time, and true team play is the norm, it would be typical for people to contribute 80 percent or more of their available investment time to the group effort, retaining only 20 percent for purely individual initiatives.** But you've got to start somewhere!

If each member of the group realizes that every other individual has also signed on to provide a relatively equal commitment, most people will then be prepared to do their part. They will want their colleagues to think of them as team players.

2. Agree on How Those Investment Hours Are to Be Used

The next challenge is to ensure that people appreciate that the investment time contributed to the group is for projects and activities that will benefit the group as a whole. It is not merely to be spent in the pursuit of their own personal aspirations, or projects that will only benefit their own personal agendas. (That's what the remaining individual investment time is for.)

You must ensure that everyone understands this distinction and agrees to abide by that understanding. As specific activities are proposed, someone must ask, "How specifically is the activity that you are proposing to undertake intended to benefit our group?"

A skilled coach would ensure that there was an absolute minimum of "assigning" tasks to people. We can all remember the meeting where someone in the group stuck George with the most forbidding project, since George wasn't able to attend that particular meeting. Now there's a surefire recipe for motivating one of your colleagues! The skillful group leader relies as much as possible on people volunteering for tasks about which they are enthusiastic.

It is also sometimes necessary for the coach to manage down the size or scope of a task that someone wants to take on. Since the important principle that you must keep your promises is established, the coach would never accept an undertaking to "Try to get this done." As the character Yoda said in the film *The Empire Strikes Back:* "Do, or do not: there is no try!"

You can use collective management of investment time to develop a group strategy. Here's how it's done. You give each member of the team four sheets of paper, each headed with one of four key objectives:

1. Raise client satisfaction
2. Increase skill building and the dissemination of skills
3. Improve productivity and efficiency (not just production)
4. Get "better" work (not just more work)

Beneath the objective listed on each page are five columns:

1. What actions are proposed?
2. Which individual will take responsibility for each action?
3. How much time will be spent on each action?
4. By when will each be done?
5. How will we know each action's been done?

You tell each team that you, the group leader, will meet with them to discuss what actions they are prepared to commit to do over the next three months to make progress toward the four objectives.

Let them know that only *actions* will be accepted, not goals. Thus, it is not permissible to write, "Raise our market awareness." That's a goal. Instead, they must choose something like "Put on three seminars on topics X, Y, Z." "Train juniors better" is also too vague. They must decide on something like "Hold weekly discussion sessions with staff, including presentations by senior partners on their respective specialties."

Each action must be the responsibility of a specific person. This is not meant to discourage teamwork (different actions may be part of an integrated plan), but is required to ensure a specific focus of responsibility. Many people may be involved in putting on a seminar: but some specific someone must be "on the hook" for ensuring that it all comes together and takes place.

During the discussion of the action plan, you "test" the feasibility of the plan. Will the proposed actions really make a difference? Has enough time been budgeted to complete each action properly? Is there enough investment time available to do it all? Is the team leaning too much on a few individuals? Are there other people who have some time who could be brought into the effort?

You should alternate between encouraging ambition ("Couldn't you accomplish a little more in three months? Can't we put a bit more stretch into this plan?") and dampening excessive enthusiasms ("Let's take it a step at a time. I recommend you limit yourselves to what you really think you can get done. Remember, we're asking for solid commitments."). If necessary, you might offer some suggestions (not instructions) for possible actions. Try to guide the team (gently) to actions that create the early successes that breed optimism and enthusiasm. This raises the morale and commitment to do more, to try it again.

At the end of this session, the surviving plan becomes a "contract" between you and the team or more correctly, between each team member and every other team member. Before the meeting concludes, a specific, ironclad meeting date is chosen approximately three months hence to review the execution of the plan and its impact: what worked, what didn't, what proved easy to pull off, what is more complicated than it first looked. At that meeting, in addition to the look-back review, a new action plan covering the next three months (using the same planning forms) will be discussed and agreed to. And so on, until the process becomes a routine part of your group's operation.

This approach is not a budgeting process, but is meant to complement financial budgeting. Budgets describe what firms aim to accomplish with their reimbursed (production) time. This process provides a framework for groups to make wise use of their investment time. What a group does with its production time determines its income for the year. What it does with its investment time determines its future.

The group leader plays a key role in this process not by telling people what to do, but by encouraging each and every one of them to take responsibility for the group's success. You must make the process work by giving as much attention and seriousness to reviewing the investment action plans as you do to the monthly financials.

One part of this system is critical: follow up. What will make the whole process work is that you, the group leader, will be coming around to see how things have worked out. Not a year from now, but in three short months. The short cycle is essential to breed the sense of urgency that leads to action. Of course, even though the planning is done in three-month cycles, there should be more frequent formal or informal monitoring of actions and commitments than that. Monthly reporting of actions and progress would be sensible.

Here's what Jack Newman, recently retired from Morgan, Lewis & Bockius, told us he believes about planning:

> Any danger in overplanning is minor compared to not having a formal business plan at all, and hoping that things will just naturally happen. We have reviews every four to six weeks to assess the group's progress in meeting the plan, and to determine if changes are necessary.

ESTABLISH YOUR SHARED VALUES

According to Jon Katzenbach (co-author of *The Wisdom of Teams*):

> Pride is a more effective motivator of professional talent than money. And you can motivate that talent with pride in

more than just belonging. There is pride in the specific work product that you deliver to clients, pride in the kinds of clients that you serve, pride in the expertise that you can apply, pride in the values of your firm.

Excitement, energy, and pride (and thus the accomplishment that drives financial success) can be created by building agreement that the group will conduct its affairs to higher standards than the group's competitors. The group voluntarily accepts greater discipline in monitoring and enforcing excellence, never settling for competence.

John Graham, of Fleishman-Hillard, noted:

> The first key to a culture of success is that the organization must be inspirational, and intolerant at the same time. A culture of success appeals to employees' aspirations to do the best work, to be the best in their profession, to set the standard. Everyone wants to be associated with excellence and we want the challenge of gaining that exclusive reputation. But hand in hand with inspiration is a level of intolerance that the organization must assert to be credible. You cannot tell a person that the company is committed to being the best without underscoring the things the company cannot allow. The management challenge therefore is twofold: to hire people who are motivated to achieve excellence, and to make sure that personal motivation is not diminished.

To create this form of compelling challenge, the group must decide, in advance, what standards of excellence it is willing to see enforced. Among the most common "nonnegotiable minimum standards" are:

a. Only truly superior work will be accepted.

b. There will be no room for mere competence in client satisfaction. We will operate as our clients' trusted advisors, not their technical experts.

c. Every person must have, and be working on, a personal development plan: no cruising is allowed.

d. No one will work on things that could be delegated to a more junior person. If it can be delegated, it must be.

e. Everyone must treat all others with respect at all times.

f. Anyone in charge of a client assignment will be required to supervise all the work on that assignment to a high level, since we owe a duty of due care to our clients to manage the affairs that they have entrusted to us.

Any group that adhered strictly to these standards would not only flourish commercially, but would create an enjoyable and fulfilling work environment. The group leader must ensure that everyone in the group deals with each other according to a common set of values and principles. What standards of minimum behavior would your group accept?

In order to create a productive culture, in which the members can take pride, the group leader must influence how people in the group treat each other. According to the results of *Practice What You Preach*, the group leader must be absolutely, 100 percent intolerant of the following behaviors by anyone in the group:

1. Abuse of power or position

2. Any disrespect shown by anyone to anyone else

3. Back stabbing

4. Betraying secrets

5. Bullying

6. Cruising

7. Dealing in blame

8. Gossiping, whining, complaining

9. Hiding from accountability

10. Lack of teamwork

11. Intimidation

12. Noncompliance with standards

13. Making one's own rules

14. Unreliability and failure to keep promises

15. Shirking or dumping responsibility

16. Being political

17. Delegating by "throwing work on the desk and walking away"

We suggest sharing this list with your group and seeing if they, too, will agree that your group should show zero tolerance for these things. If they delete or add items to the list, all to the good. At least you will then have "nagging rights" to enforce a culture that they have agreed to.

In the same spirit, there are certain things (as demonstrated in *Practice What You Preach*) that financially successful groups *require:*

1. An attitude of "We don't care how it happened, let's just get it fixed"
2. Continual skill and career development for everyone
3. Diplomacy, courtesy, professionalism
4. Team play from everyone
5. Approachability
6. Self-motivation
7. Consultation (everyone's voice must be heard and valued)
8. Working together for the overall success of the group, not just themselves
9. An acceptance that, if you take something on, then you must deliver
10. Trust, respect, and integrity at all times

If people agree to these standards, then it becomes your job to be the "culture cop." Deal with noncompliance gently, at first, but be prepared to escalate. In the long run, you will need to be intolerant and enforce your values.

We stress that our advice is that you and your team develop your own values, which does not necessarily mean adopting those listed here. There's no virtue in being a "copycat." Adopt the values that you and your group truly believe in, and not just those you think you should!

chapter 13

Build Team Trust

What gets group members to trust each other?

THE EXISTENCE OF A PROBLEM in the functioning of a group can show up in many ways. Some of the more common symptoms of group problems include:

1. A lack of cohesiveness as discussions occur between differing coalitions within the group

2. Members of the group openly complaining and finding fault with one another

3. Combative behavior displayed in the name of "playing devil's advocate"

4. Subjecting of even minor decisions to protracted debate and excessive time

5. Frequently debating or changing decisions reached by the group after they have been made.

These everyday frustrations soon result in energy lost to suspicion, unresolved issues, forgotten commitments, unclear agreements, missed deadlines. In turn, these cause blame, gossip, resentment, and frustration.

Many of these symptoms derive from a common cause: a lack of trust between and among the team members. When we are in an environment of trust we feel reinforced, validated, and supported, even when our ideas are not always accepted. As a result, we are far more likely to plunge in, to be creative and generous with our talents. When trust is lacking, people reveal only what they feel is safe, and that is usually only a small part of their potential contribution. The group leader is left trying to conduct a symphony with one-stringed instruments.

Everybody endorses trust, yet it remains hard to define and even harder to measure. Trust is too often an unspoken issue. However, it is so critically important to the team's performance that it needs some group time and attention. As one managing partner commented: "If you don't have trust, people won't cooperate, won't be committed, and won't know where they stand."

It is important to recognize that **failure in building trust is rarely a result of poor ethics or bad intentions. Rather, trust is too often destroyed by thoughtless behaviors:** not getting back to people, failing to consult people who have a stake in an issue, overly focusing on your own duties and not being considerate of others. Since professionals lead demanding, busy lives often with great pressures and short deadlines from their clients, it is all too common to see them acting in trust-diminishing ways. Professionals are not less trustworthy than other people, but they may, in general, be more neglectful of trust-building activities.

TRUST-BUILDING INITIATIVES

Most of us tend to reserve our greatest trust for our more intimate relationships, such as our family, our long-term friends, and our social circles, those who have proven themselves over time to be worthy of our confidence. We often have reservations about people we work with. We are often not sure how they might act or react in any given situation. As a group leader, you can help your people establish a level of trust among themselves by helping them understand the behaviors that build trust. It won't happen overnight, but a big difference can be made. To begin, you might want to try this exercise at one of your next meetings.

Step 1: Identify the specific elements that constitute a trusting relationship.

Step 2: Develop shared guidelines for personal conduct.

Step 1: Identify specific elements in a trusting relationship.

Ask your people, as a group, to complete the following sentence: "I trust people when. . . . " Ask them to use words that describe specific behaviors and observable actions. They are likely to complete the sentence as follows:

"I trust people when . . .

1. they keep me informed on things that may have an impact on me personally, my practice, or my client relationships.

2. they share their views and expertise, and even admit their shortcomings and mistakes.

3. they follow through when they make a commitment to do something either for me or for the group.

4. they tell me up front if it is not possible for them to do something that I have asked.

5. they let me know in advance if they are going to miss a deadline that we have agreed to, so that I can readjust my expectations; or we can work out an alternative arrangement.

6. they ask for my input concerning a decision they are contemplating and then either follow my guidance or let me know why they are taking an alternate course of action.

7. if they don't know the answer to a question, they say so, rather than trying to bluff their way through.

8. they let me know when they don't agree with something that is being said, but do so with respect and offer an alternate suggestion or solution;

9. they let me know to my face that something I have said or done is upsetting them so that we can discuss it and resolve it, and I don't have to hear about it later from someone else.

You will note that the question was not posed as "I *can't* trust people when" since that might serve as a catalyst for some people to engage in nonproductive finger pointing. The goal is to get trust-building behaviors out on the table without being negative about the past performance of anyone in the group.

Encourage your group to understand that it is within their power to increase or decrease their credibility with others. **The strength of their interpersonal relationships depends on whether they deliver on their promises, are considerate of others' schedules, deal in a straightforward manner, and respond promptly to requests** even if they don't know the other member very well. They also need to understand how the group will benefit when each member reaches out to help another.

Step 2: Develop shared guidelines for personal conduct.

After you have identified some of the elements inherent in trust relationships, your next step is to brainstorm ideas with your group to establish specific guidelines that encourage the trust behaviors you have listed and that prohibit trust-eroding actions. Help people understand that trust takes time to establish, and seconds to destroy. To trust requires us to be vulnerable and to take risks, giving away control of a situation.

It is not the group leader's job to set or enforce trust-building guidelines. They must become self-imposed standards if each person expects to win the support and credibility of other members of the team. This second step helps everyone understand what others may expect of them and how they can conduct themselves in a trust-building manner.

ELEMENTS OF TRUST

Here we consider some of the trust elements, and what you can do about them.

1. Sharing

2. Following through on commitments

3. Letting people know if you can't do something

4. Keeping people informed after asking for advice

1 SHARING

Consider conducting this exercise: Give each member of the group a card to write upon. Ask each to list on the card:

1. A particular attribute, talent, or skill that they possess

2. A unique experience or accomplishment of theirs that other members probably would not know about

3. A personal quirk, idiosyncrasy, or shortcoming that they wish they could remedy or are currently working on rectifying

These need not all be professionally related.

Ask people to initial the backs of their cards. At the appropriate time collect the cards, reshuffle them, distribute one card to each member, and ask each in turn to read the card aloud. Ask the group to try to identify the individual who listed the articulated attributes. If necessary, use the initials on the card to reveal the owner.

The valuable part of this exercise is in helping team members learn more about each other. Trust involves the personal risk of disclosing something intimate about ourselves, both positive and not so positive. But by taking these risks, we move to a deeper level of trust. Trust needs to be earned.

Trust is the emotional glue that holds the practice team together, and in using glue one cannot avoid potentially sticky situations. One such situation may be having to admit that you made a mistake, screwed up, or failed in some way. How will you set trust-building guidelines for dealing with failure that don't involve some member having to wear a permanent badge of shame?

One way to reduce perceived vulnerability is to collectively agree to openly celebrate failure for the learning that it brings. The great groups we have worked with operate according to a declared philosophy that "a success is everyone's achievement, while a failure is no one's fault." Thus if people are not worried about the repercussions arising from a well-intentioned failure, their perceived vulnerability declines and their trust in their fellow group members increases, as will (not surprisingly) the level of the group's willingness to innovate.

2 | FOLLOWING THROUGH ON COMMITMENTS

When people agree to do something, it is not uncommon for them to ask themselves: "Can I really get this done, and done on time?" Doubt also exists in the minds of those being given the commitment: "Is this person really likely to deliver on what he says?" That's natural and even healthy. It makes us hesitate for a moment before accepting responsibility for an undertaking.

What is not healthy is saying "yes" to a commitment without the pure intention or strong desire to produce the final outcome, or produce it on time.

Failure to deliver on a commitment may be passed off in several ways:

a. As a memory lapse ("I'm not sure that's what I said.")

b. As an inconvenience ("I didn't realize that it was going to take so much time.")

c. As an interruption ("You wouldn't believe the intensity of my client demands over this past month")

d. As a change of heart ("After thinking about this project, I'm not so sure that it really is the right thing for us to do.")

The reactions of the other group members may range from irritation—at having to revisit the same topic and establish a new commitment—to there being absolute hell to pay. Failure to deliver also demoralizes others and compromises future commitments by others. If you weren't on time, why should I be?

Unfulfilled promises bleed away your team's energy. What offending members of your group must understand is that when others don't get the desired result, they are far less likely to trust that person the next time he or she promises anything. In a group that winks at commitments, people stop believing what others tell them.

Many problems with commitment come more in the making than in the executing:

a. Preventing memory lapse

Set up a guideline where someone in the group (on a rotational basis) documents each commitment that was undertaken and circulates the list of commitments to all members within twenty-four hours following the discussions.

b. Preventing the commitment becoming an inconvenience

Set a guideline for a conservative and modest investment of time that will be devoted to any project. In other words, better to approach any under-taking incrementally, with small steps, getting at least the first parts of it ac-complished, than allowing too much to be put on someone's plate.

c. Coping with an interruption

In people's busy lives, there will be times when emergencies upset the best-laid plans. Make contingency arrangements so that someone who has com-mitted to taking on a project has someone else serving as a back-up resource. If each person agrees to serve as a back-up resource for some other team member, then, if and when a client emergency arises, someone can be called in to help on the execution of the promised commitment.

d. Avoiding a change of heart

A change of heart usually comes about when people feel that a project was forced upon them. To avoid this, make sure that you allow group members to take only those assignments that they have voluntarily agreed to imple-ment. How many of us have attended a meeting where someone said: "There's a great project for Betty. Let's assign it to her. That'll teach her to miss one of our meetings." This seemingly innocuous gesture not only serves to diminish Betty's trust in the group, but also allows her to feel jus-tified in not following through.

3 | Letting people know if you can't do something

Consider the following scenario: You are sitting in your office and Jonathan sticks his head in the door. Seizing the moment, you ask, "Jon, if you've got a moment later today, could you take a look and see if you can find that report we were discussing?"

Jonathan disappears without comment. Now it begins. You start wonder-ing: Did he really hear me? Has he gone to look for the file? When should I expect to be able to review it? Is he upset that I asked him in the first place? Does he remember that I did him a favor, or did he forget?

The fact that Jonathan did not respond leaves you with strong feelings of doubt. Doubt that he heard you, doubt that you might have offended by asking for the favor, doubt that he will do anything to help. That doubt does not build trust.

Had Jonathan simply said, "I'll do what I can," it would have reassured you to know he heard you and was willing to help. But there is still room for doubt as there is no specific agreement about what will be done. He is still not communicating to build trust.

Jonathan might have said, "I'll get you the report." And some time later, you would be thinking to yourself "yeah, when?" **It is easy to see how failing to confirm agreement specifics breeds uncertainty, hesitation, doubt, wasted time and energy, resentment, and lack of trust.**

The act of confirming specifics involves being crystal clear in your communications and then seeking an acknowledged agreement about what will be done, by whom, and with a specific time or date for completion. You don't leave anything to chance.

When a group agrees to communications guidelines that always include confirming specifics, they are acknowledging the need to ask each other to be clear about detail and time for taking action. The goal is to have 100 percent confirmed specifics on all communications, big and small.

4 Keep people informed after asking for advice

One of your people wanders into your office with a question about a topic for your group's newsletter. Since it involves your area of expertise, she values your opinion. You discuss the options and offer to prepare a brief synopsis on the new development. You draft a one-page summary and forward it to her. A week later the next newsletter comes out but there is no sign of the summary you submitted.

That afternoon, you catch up with your colleague in the hall. You casually ask if she received the summary that you drafted. She tells you that she did, but after speaking with a few others decided to defer including the piece until further developments concerning the issue were forthcoming from the regulatory authorities.

You are now left to contemplate how many others she had to talk to before making her decision? Who may have had more influence than you? Why you were not informed in advance of the newsletter coming out?

It is virtually impossible to build trust if people lack integrity in their behavior, if they favor one person over others, or if they lack fairness in their handling of situations. Do your people believe that they are being treated fairly, without prejudice, or do some of them feel excluded from the decision making process?

5 | Constructive disagreement

One of the most common reactions in any discussion or meeting, when someone is presenting an idea is for another person to comment, "Yes, that's a good approach, but . . ."

Professionals all live and work among very intelligent people. They quickly become annoyed by what they perceive to be patronizing agreement to something they have said, and which concludes with a "but." The "but" really constitutes disagreement with the entire statement that precedes it. Yet we all still do it, all the time!

Group members must set guidelines for how their team should behave. **Is it acceptable to challenge people in a team meeting? Accepting that honorable people need not always agree, how should group members disagree with one another and still demonstrate respect for each other?**

Many groups have developed some simple accepted procedures for dealing with these situations. The procedures themselves are not what are important here. The thought and discussions that are part of developing these procedures are important.

Here are a few examples:

1. You must conduct yourself in such a manner as to avoid using the term "but" in response to any comment made by a colleague. All buts are out and fines will be imposed for those who light up group discussions using them.

2. If you hear an idea from a group member that you disagree with, you cannot offer a contrary view until you have restated the initial idea and

then proposed one supporting or embellishing thought to improve upon that original idea.

3. If any idea is viewed as so contentious as to require a vote of the members, the vote will be deferred until the next meeting to allow group members to give the idea further thought.

Daniel J. Fensin (of Blackman, Kallick, Bartelstein) told us:

> You have to be very, very open with people. You need to tell them what you're going to be doing and then do it. If you say you're going to do something and suddenly something else comes up, call the people that you told. Say, "You know what? I'm not going to be able to do that. Let me tell you what happened." Don't just let it go by the wayside. We can actively, actively engender trust, but to do it, you've got to be open with people. They've got to know that you always keep your word.

What happens when some member of the group continues to behave in a manner inconsistent with the group's guidelines and begins to create a toxic environment for others?

Obviously, people have more trust in others who conduct themselves with integrity. It is therefore difficult to understand why generally good group leaders are reluctant to remove weak team members. This reluctance could be the product of personal loyalty, a fear of conflict, or the belief that the individual can eventually be coached back to a level of acceptable performance.

The job of the group leader is to encourage people to earn the trust of others in their group, and then show them how it can translate into greater commitment, greater creativity, greater professional satisfaction, and better performance.

Bonding the Group Together

People find it easier to trust other people that they know and have interacted with. The more you can find ways to help your people get to know each other as individuals, the more likely they are to trust each other. Jon Katzenbach, the recognized expert on teams, elaborated this point when he told us:

> Trust and mutual respect are not necessarily synonymous. Mutual respect is an added dimension that can be as important as trust, particularly in the early stages of group work before personal trust has time to develop. On the one hand, it highlights the importance of "competence" in professional service work. You can have respect for someone that you do not necessarily like—and you can work effectively with them. On the other hand, you can also trust someone whom you do not necessarily "respect" in terms of their competence. One of the best ways for two people to develop trust is to do "real work" together.

There are many ways to give your people the experience of working together, on or off the "real" work. Here are a few community-building tactics uncovered in *Practice What You Preach:*

1. Create "task forces" for all projected changes in the group.

2. Discuss all financials (except salaries) with everyone.

3. Have a bulletin board where you list everything anyone wants to celebrate—for themselves or for someone else.

4. Make sure everyone knows why a decision is made.

5. Every Friday afternoon, get everybody together and review the week.

6. Encourage people to eat lunch together (with no agenda).

7. Give regular "State of the Union" addresses to the entire group.

Bonding the Group Together (Cont.)

8. Have a very active program of cross-functional information sharing, using briefs, e-mails, lunches, whatever.

9. Make a lot of use of cross-boundary teams.

10. Take the time to interact socially, even if just in the hallway.

Remember, these are not just arbitrary rules of good people management. These are the practices of the most profitable offices in a global database!

Next, there is solid evidence to show that the most money is made when people feel like they have fun at work in addition to being challenged. The challenging part is common. The fun is not. As John Feinstein of Vanasse Hangen Brustlin, Inc., one of the top 100 U.S. engineering firms, put it:

> Through experience we found that creating an atmosphere where people not only worked hard but also were able to socialize and "party" was very important. I will never forget when I first joined VHB from an old-line conservative engineering firm. We won a major job at VHB and the receptionist announced over the loudspeaker that it was time to "Celebrate." Cases of beer and pizza rolled in and the entire staff was united in a victory party. I sat back in amazement at how the unity and camaraderie was exhibited. In my prior firm this would never have happened.
>
> At VHB we now have in most of the departments and offices Committees for Fun. It allows many of the junior and middle managers to plan monthly fun activities—ballgames, pool nights, movies, etc.—to be scheduled. We also urge that departments conduct these together so that people from various disciplines can get to know each other and really socialize. This is an important component of the success of integrated service because when people become "true colleagues" instead of working partners they have a different sense of dedication and discipline than is ordinarily exhibited.

Bonding the Group Together *(Cont.)*

Here are a few (real world) tactics employed by successful professional groups to bring fun into the workplace (and build a sense of belonging, and hence trust, to the group):

1. Arrange a series of group days out of the office.

2. Eat lunch together every day as a group.

3. Hold a Spring Break party.

4. Have a charity day where the firm pledges one day per employee to a group of local charities.

5. Have ad hoc events like firmwide parties and open days.

6. Offer free massages, shoeshines, book clubs, exercise classes, language lessons, surprise ice cream sundaes, pinball machines, Mother's Day gifts, and so on.

7. Arrange group outings to film premieres, gigs, and shows.

8. Announce the top ten mistakes of the year.

9. Hold a parents' day: Let people bring their kids to work.

10. Fund client entertainment liberally.

chapter 14

Throw Down
a Challenge

Has your group selected an exciting challenge?

C OMMON WISDOM SUGGESTS that offering generous extrinsic rewards (money) gets people to increase their performance. But is money really the whole story? Well, maybe. A few more dollars in the retirement account can't hurt. However, at the upper reaches of most senior people's prosperity curve, money no longer matters quite as much. Except, as Bunker Hunt once put it, "as a way of keeping score." As a group, professionals earn high incomes, and are more likely to seek additional rewards from their work lives.

People have other important needs, such as learning, self worth, pride, competence, and serving others. If people gain *only* financial rewards from their work, they will never contribute more than the minimum. They will also feel alienated and will leave at the first suggestion of a more financially rewarding offer made by some competing firm. Alfie Kohn, in his book *Punished by Rewards,* showed convincingly that monetary rewards can actually decrease a person's desire to perform.

In 1975, a group of University of Chicago psychologists published a study that explored activities that contain rewards within themselves. They studied such leisure activities as rock climbing, dance, and chess; and work activities including music, medical surgery, and teaching. They wanted to know what made these activities enjoyable. They found that the primary reason the people studied or participated in their chosen activity was for the enjoyment of the experience and to make use of their skills. And what is it about the structure of these activities that produces intrinsic motivation?

The Chicago study found a surprisingly consistent answer. "Whatever the specific activity, it seems that the most basic requirement is to provide a clear set of challenges." The challenges that ranked highest in this study were "designing and discovering something new," "exploring a strange place," and "solving a complex problem." These suggest that the key to intrinsic motivation is getting involved in something that requires us to become challenged: physically, mentally, or emotionally.

Whether it is doing our best as practicing professionals or enjoying the clients that we have the privilege of working with, answering the summons of a new adventure lifts our spirits. There is something inspiring about being invited to do better than we have ever done before that compels us to reach way down inside of ourselves and bring forth the champion within. The lessons for group leadership are clear.

First, as we have already stressed, you must devote the time necessary to get to know what each member of your group would really like to accomplish, what each may find personally challenging. **You must uncover the dreams, desires, and aspirations of your people and find the proper balance between the action opportunities that are available and the individual skill capabilities of your people.**

DEVELOPING YOUR CHALLENGE

Helen Keller once said, "Life is either a daring adventure, or it is nothing." Stop dreaming and you die! Too often, without something to shoot for, only a major crisis gets our attention.

We need to wake up our potential for higher achievement. But how? We usually do not wake up by ourselves. That is where a talented group leader can help—someone who understands that satisfaction always leads to dissatisfaction. A work life without challenge and difficulty leads to a sparse and shallow existence. Nothing shapes our lives as much as the questions we ask, or refuse to ask, about our career directions.

Think about the last time in your work life when you were really inspired. What was the source of that inspiration? A new intellectual provocation to master, an especially difficult client problem to overcome? What was that special possibility that captured your imagination? Has there ever been a time when you were pushed far beyond what you felt were your limits and found that you could do more than you thought you could?

Building on this same theme, what you as the group leader need to ask, and assess in each of your people, is:

1. Who are we and what are we capable of?

2. What common goal might people be prepared to rally around?

The one attribute that stands above all others in distinguishing a great group is that they seem to develop and radiate a "shoot-the-lights-out" attitude where the group has collectively found some greater, compelling challenge to conquer. The pursuit of some compelling challenge is what creates truly interdependent teams capable of delivering a signature performance.

Group leaders should not only help each member of the group become more successful but should look for ways to invigorate the group as a whole toward accomplishing goals they might not otherwise focus upon.

An important part of this is helping people find the drama and meaning in their work. Liza Bailey, co-head of the consumer products group in the investment banking division at Credit Suisse First Boston, says:

> It's really important for everyone on the team, from the analyst crunching the numbers to the more senior people, to approach our client from a very broad point of view. I like to ask people to think about "what's keeping our client's CEO up at night? What are the client's issues and anxieties?" I want people to rise above the minutiae and understand what's really up with the client and what's really important. All of the issues the team needs to address fall below this broader sense of what's important and it helps us to identify the right business model. This also changes everything in terms of how the analyst, who is revising a discounted cash flow statement at eleven o'clock at night for the fifth time,

is able to look at her work and connect it to how we are adding value. We are improving a company's balance sheet or helping them to expand their business in Asia versus just getting a new deal to do.

In *Beyond Knowing*, Patrick and his co-authors expressed it this way:

What motivational lever are you employing to engage the hearts and minds of your people? What is your group's reason for being?

What significant contribution does your group make to the firm, the industry you serve, or the profession you belong to? These questions are intended to have each of us think not only about what we do, but why we do it and what would challenge us to go beyond the ordinary, the mundane, the conventional.

What, if anything, is our compelling challenge to want to achieve something insanely great?

Having a compelling challenge is having an expressed image of a desired state of affairs that inspires action. Groups need a sense of urgency or significance. When a group has too many competing goals, it dilutes the effort and an individual's goals soon take priority over team goals.

Great groups manage conflict by having their people abandoning individual egos to the pursuit of some compelling challenge. **Having some understood and shared challenge is the single most important building block in enabling a group of unlikely collaborators to come together.** That challenge can be a powerful antidote for people to overcome their natural tendency to spend time pursuing one's own agenda or defending one's turf. People are inspired to collaborate when they sense a challenge that is deeply meaningful for them and they recognize that they can't accomplish it alone.

The group leader needs to ask:

1. What breakthrough goal would we like to achieve?

2. What complex problem would we like to solve?

3. What would we like to create that never existed before?

4. Which competitor would we like to vanquish?

5. Do we have a deep energy and passion to accomplish something extraordinary?"

The answers you are most likely to hear include some variation on:

a. A specific high-profile "project" where the group is playing for high stakes and perhaps even racing toward completing a task or achieving a goal within a predetermined deadline (a high-stakes, time-sensitive target)

b. A perceived cause or crusade where the group members are committed to effect change (explore a positive course of action) or arrest an economic condition (divert a negative course of action)

c. The perception (real or created) of an enemy to be vilified or a competitor to be vanquished (to attain a position of superiority over a rival)

d. A sense of viewing themselves as the "winning underdogs," a feisty collection of mavericks with fresh ideas, or a spunky little group of upstarts determined to set new directions (rebellious revolutionaries with something to prove)

e. A dream that members of the group share of creating something new, exploring new precedents or solving some tough problems, and achieving some sense of recognition (aiming to accomplish something that redefines the very essence of their practice)

It's all about striving, and struggling, for something noble, uplifting, and inspiring. Work with your group to articulate your compelling challenge, realistic or crazy, and pursue it. Be outrageous. Be the group everyone talks about.

Next, create a case for taking immediate action and get a voluntary commitment from every member of the group. Instead of reducing the magnitude of your challenge or trying to address the question of how it will be achieved, you need to create a powerful and urgent reason to achieve the goal. The thing to focus on is why achieving this challenge is important to the group. You can do this by building a case for action that is based on facts and real business needs. Try the following process:

1. Ask the members of your group to articulate what's in it for them

2. Give everyone the opportunity to stand up and declare his or her personal commitment

3. Focus first on what you can do now, with existing resources

4. Encourage experimentation

5. Build for an early success to continue the momentum

6. Search continually for opportunities for people to create or outdo themselves

7. Set unreasonable expectations

8. Focus on the excitement of the endeavor

1   Ask the Members of Your Group to Articulate What's in It for Them

Start by asking each person in the group to define why reaching the destination is important to his or her individual practice and career direction. Have a discussion about how each person feels about the challenge, as well as the opportunities in it for each of them. This helps generate a sense of urgency about the effort. They must all feel that their skills and talents will be used in a meaningful way. Going through this process allows the members of your group to articulate the reasons why it is worthwhile for them personally to invest the effort and make this a real focus.

2   Give Everyone the Opportunity to Stand Up and Declare His or Her Personal Commitment

Keep in mind that everyone in your group is ultimately a volunteer. At some point, each person must choose to be either in or out.

In order for people to go for a goal, they have to have a hunger, a thirst, a yearning. No one is going to overcome the stresses and endure the effort of pursuing some compelling challenge without that hunger. People are motivated by who they aspire to be, and by what they judge to be important.

Everyone, particularly those who have chosen professional careers, wants to have the opportunity to be significant, to make a difference, and to have an impact.

Recognize that there are different and growing levels of commitment. At first some people may be in agreement intellectually, but not in alignment emotionally. Later those same people may be ready to take action, but they will only be capable of sustaining that action in the presence of the group leader or with group support.

The highest level of commitment is when people can self-sustain action toward a breakthrough goal independent of the group leader or group, and in the absence of immediate results. At this point, the level of a person's commitment is usually connected to his or her noblest aspirations and is deeply purposeful.

3 | Focus First on What You Can Do Now, with Existing Resources

Ensure that people do not become overwhelmed or discouraged by the complexity or enormity of the challenge. There is a risk of getting stuck in the discussion, planning, and analysis and never achieving anything meaningful.

Instead of getting paralyzed by an overwhelming challenge that calls for becoming the leading group in the country in your particular area of expertise, why not pick one area to aim for and then take the necessary actions to increase your performance in the coming quarter?

The idea is that by producing some tangible results in the short term, the group will build momentum, as well as learn something that might create an opening for further progress.

4 | Encourage Experimentation

Can you point to a half-dozen small experiments going on within your group that you believe could provide fundamentally new value for clients, yield new revenue streams, take the group into new markets, or create new knowledge? The more experimentation, the faster your group can understand precisely which strategies are likely to work.

5 Build for an Early Success to Continue the Momentum

Remind the team of what's at stake. Once we are captured by a challenge, our molecules get rearranged and one of the greatest forces in our human arsenal is activated—determination. Never doubt the capacity of the people you lead to accomplish whatever they truly desire. The lesson is that most ambitious people do *not* want to join a firm or some group. They want to join a movement! Something that has a larger meaning, makes us feel that we have made a difference, and gives us the opportunity to leave our mark.

6 Search Continually for Opportunities for People to Create or Outdo Themselves

As a leader you must find ways for people to solve problems, make discoveries, explore new ground, reach a difficult goal, or figure out how to deal with an external challenge. And you must endeavor to make it fun.

7 Set Unreasonable Expectations

When you have objectives that are outlandish, you are forced to think differently about your opportunities. What would be a reasonable expectation for revenue growth this year? Groups rarely outperform their aspirations, since these set an upper limit on what people think is possible. A bold aspiration won't suddenly by itself produce a multitude of nonconformist strategies. But its absence always yields bland, me-too strategies.

8 Focus on the Excitement of the Endeavor

Market leaders in every profession become preeminent by repeatedly making, breaking, and changing the rules of the game. They do this either by developing totally new practices or by completely reinventing their ways of serving existing markets.

We have come to think of the influence and expectations of leaders and the articulation of some compelling challenge as the "Fish Tank Factor." Goldfish will grow larger or stay smaller according to the size of the fish tank or pond they are placed in. Doctors can affect the success of medical treatment by their expectations of their patients. Teachers' expectations of students have a dramatic impact not only on their grades, but on their IQ scores as well. People in your group will grow large or remain small according to the environment that is created for them.

chapter 15

Energize Your Meetings

What are good meeting disciplines?

WHEN PEOPLE SAY that they despise meetings, what they are really expressing is their frustration with having to sit through protracted and unproductive meetings. People despise meetings where "minutes are taken, but hours are wasted," where nothing meaningful is ever accomplished.

Most meetings among professional groups are disorganized. People rarely seem to speak to the topic at hand, time is wasted on trivial items not on the agenda, and a specific course of action is rarely agreed on. As one of our clients observed:

> Our meetings are like television soap operas. You can leave the group for three months and return to pick up exactly where you left off in the discussions, with no new progress ever having been made.

Here are some warning signs that something is not right in your meeting structure and procedures:

1. Group meetings continually start and/or finish late.

2. Group members don't come to meetings or arrive later and later each time.

3. No agenda exists, or the agenda, materials, and reports are not distributed in advance.

4. The agenda lists more items than can reasonably be dealt with or acted upon.

5. The group leader is not prepared.

6. Some people are allowed to monopolize discussions.

7. Only a few members speak; others withdraw nonverbally.

8. Members interrupt each other or "cross-talk" (excluding others).

9. There are long-drawn-out discussions, but conclusions are rarely reached.

10. The meeting concludes with no clear agreement about who will accomplish what, by when.

11. Specific projects are not completed on time.

12. There are no consequences for nonperformance or challenging behavior.

MEETING GOALS

You cannot afford to invest time in gathering numerous people together if doing so does not advance the accomplishment of your group's goals. To tackle this situation, **it is useful to discuss "meeting rules" with your group. We suggest you begin by asking your group to debate: "What benefits should we expect to get out of meeting together as a group?"**

At this point, you're not really interested in determining when or how often the meetings should occur, or even who should attend. You just want people to think through whether there is any point at all in having meetings. Several reasons are commonly identified:

1. We could learn a bit more about the client assignments that other people in our group are working on and the specific issues they are facing.

2. Members of the group can take turns making a substantive presentation to the group on some area in which they are developing

expertise, especially if they have recently attended outside courses or seminars.

3. The meeting can serve as a forum to orient our juniors, review work assignments, give them feedback, instill some pride, and help them feel like they are part of an important practice team.

4. We could invite clients, the group leaders from other related groups, or even outside experts to come and tell us about the issues and projects they are working on.

5. We could work together on some joint projects, especially if it helps make our group more attractive to clients or helps each of us to be more proficient at developing business.

This list (like all of our lists) is not intended to be comprehensive. If you try this with the members of your practice team, you will find that there are essentially two different types of meetings: one type involves spending time sharing information and acquiring knowledge, while the other involves working together on mutually important projects to accomplish something together as a team.

MEETING RULES

Next, the group needs to (collectively) identify and agree upon some basic procedural parameters for how the group's meetings are to function:

1. Do we want to meet on a regular basis?

2. What specific benefits would each of us have to realize to make such meetings a worthwhile investment of our personal time?

3. How could we better serve our clients by sharing knowledge, enhancing our collective efforts, and engaging in some joint action planning activities?

The group should identify (in writing) the specific benefits that each member expects to achieve as a result of their meetings. They should then review periodically whether everyone is receiving the benefits they expected, and if not, should take remedial action to modify the meeting format or content in order to make meetings more valuable.

The group should determine how much time they are prepared to commit to each meeting. Larger groups may have difficulty with only an hour, but in situations where people are not used to meeting at all, an hour is at least a reasonable start.

In addition, you should establish people's preferred schedules for meeting: "When should our meetings occur? Which day of the week and when—early morning, during lunch, at the end of the day, on the week-end?"

Great groups seem to schedule their meetings well ahead, on a consistent day and time (such as the second Tuesday of the month at noon), so that everyone is able to reserve that time. (If, as David's business manager, Julie MacDonald O'Leary, points out, this is so basic that they teach it in secretarial classes, we plead in our defense only that so many groups still fail to do this!)

Cliff Farrah commented to us:

> Even the best business schools fail to teach how to run an effective meeting. The only time you learn it is if you are lucky enough to be hired by a firm that has it as a standard, when you are taught by an effective manager, or when you buy a book like this one. I always plan and run my meetings jointly with my administrative assistant, who is detail-oriented and who makes sure the key issues are covered. I will only send out an agenda once she has reviewed it. At firmwide meetings, the best administrative staff ask the hardest and most probing questions.

As part of your deliberations, your group should also establish some agreements governing whether everyone is committed to:

1. Being at the meeting

2. Starting the meeting on time with everyone in attendance

3. Submitting their action reports to everyone in writing a few days in advance of the meeting

4. Keeping commitments previously made to implement a specific task (Yes, this looks unnecessary. But it's essential to get it out on the table.)

After the group has determined its own acceptable guidelines, the leader should circulate them to everyone in writing. He or she should also periodically remind members of their mutual agreements, and take a moment at the conclusion of some meetings to assess whether the meeting functioned to everyone's satisfaction and was consistent with the guidelines.

Because of time pressures (and depending on the size of your group) it is wise to have with you an able assistant, secretary, or other staff person who can help out. A deputy can do a lot to help you keep minutes at the meeting. He or she can also be helpful between meetings, monitoring activity and keeping you informed as to which projects are on track and which may need your personal attention.

THE KNOWLEDGE-SHARING AND SKILL-BUILDING MEETING

One of the best ways to satisfy the diverse interests of your group is to devote one meeting to sharing knowledge and building skills, while reserving the agenda of the next meeting for an action-planning issue of importance to determine the group's future direction and/or incremental improvement.

While it is important to share substantive and technical information, a small caution is necessary. Some people seem to think that the true purpose of every group meeting is to provide a forum for their long-winded exposition on what they have been up to lately.

Keep in mind that information can be shared with group members in countless ways: memos, electronic bulletin boards, intranets, e-mail, written progress reports, and even informal word-of-mouth communications during social or office corridor gatherings. Valuable meeting time can be spent tapping into the collective genius of all the minds present but only as it contributes to moving the group forward.

The highest priority for this type of meeting is to have an agenda that encourages substantive learning and skill development. **The very best use of the group's time is to review specific lessons and new developments acquired while serving clients, dealing with client problems, or gleaned by researching new and emerging issues that may impact the group's practice.**

Daniel J. Fensin uses this simple technique:

> We put out something we call consulting capsules. What we do is we ask each of the consultants to abstract for us

> something that they've done in the last month. They write it
> out for us and we distribute it to everyone. It makes every-
> one, in all departments, very aware of what the consultants
> do. That, in and of itself, is critical.

And Jack Newman of Morgan Lewis & Bockius had this to say:

> We want to make sure that all group work products are
> disseminated to everyone in the group. That's not as easy as
> it sounds. Say a lawyer has done an outline for a client pre-
> sentation. Without discipline, it might be perfectly natural
> for him to put it in his desk drawer. But we need to make
> sure others benefit from his work. Maybe it's just an outline,
> but seeing it might encourage another member of the group
> to make a similar presentation. Or, the information in the
> outline itself might prove valuable to other group members,
> especially since most of our clients are similarly situated. In
> other words, these meetings underscore the point that vir-
> tually anything done in the group is important to everyone.

It is one thing to hear people talk (in general terms) about a task they have
been working on. However, it is much more valuable to find out what that
person learned (specifically) from the work that might be of use to others
in the group.

All too often, when the meeting finally does start, the group leader starts a
round-robin session that begins: "So, Ivan, tell us what you've been up to
lately?" This gives no concrete direction to the group's discussions, often allows some individual member to pontificate at great length on subjects of
little interest to the entire group, and manages to consume an hour long
before you have even gone around the table. Meanwhile others have either
quietly left the room or are engaging in side discussions on topics that are
of more interest to them.

A better question might be: **"What have you learned during this past
month that may be of value to the rest of us?"** Productive time is then
spent hearing from each individual, in turn, about new knowledge they
have acquired.

Groups might also find it valuable to devote some time to hearing from a client directly, perhaps by inviting a client to address the entire group on issues facing their particular industry. Many groups also make it a habit to have each of their members take turns preparing a brief presentation designed to enhance the skills of everyone involved. Examples of productive presentations include:

1. Demonstrating the effective use of a new technology that everyone could benefit from being more familiar with

2. Briefing the group on a development that will have impact on the problems facing clients

3. Role-playing by having a couple of the more accomplished rainmakers show how they actually handled a particularly difficult client interaction

The best groups videotape these sessions for their archives and to capture their collective knowledge.

If your group were prepared to meet monthly for one hour, you might want to schedule a knowledge-sharing and skill-building agenda for every second meeting. Your intervening meetings could then be dedicated to more specific joint activities.

THE ACTION-PLANNING MEETING

This is perhaps the more difficult type of meeting to handle effectively. The group leader should adhere to eight interrelated principles that together will help energize these meetings and make them far more effective.

1. Set a singular focus

2. "Brainstorm" ideas

3. Ensure ideas are actionable

4. Get "voluntary" commitments

5. Keep commitments small

6. Establish your "contracts for action"

7. Follow up between meetings

8. Celebrate successes

1 SET A SINGULAR FOCUS

Each meeting should be devoted to only one action-planning issue of importance to your group. You may need to have some housekeeping, administrative, or residual follow-up items also on the agenda; but the majority of the time available should be highly focused.

Consider the following topics and you can well imagine the numerous ideas that might be generated by your team:

1. What is our group's strategy for being more profitable over the next year?

2. In what ways can we improve our overall efficiency and get our client assignments accomplished at a lower cost to us?

3. What kind and amount of training may be necessary to have each of us performing at a higher level of efficiency?

4. What actions can we take to improve the fees clients will pay for our services?

5. Which of our most recent client engagements would we consider to have been our most profitable and what do we need to do to get more of those?

6. What could we be doing to ensure a higher degree of morale, motivation and enthusiasm, so that we might better retain our talented people?

7. What do we need to do to better understand our existing clients, figure out what is keeping them awake nights, and actually be more valuable to them?

8. What kinds of services might existing or prospective clients want that no one else has yet offered them?

9. What do we need to do to get our existing clients to refer others to use our group's services?

You should now have enough agenda items to stimulate your group for the next year!

2 "BRAINSTORM" IDEAS

Whoever in your group is responsible for facilitating discussions at your meeting (most often the group leader) should engage the group in a "brainstorming" exercise. The idea is to elicit individual action ideas that, if implemented, could serve to advance the group toward its objectives.

If all agree to be highly disciplined about concentrating on potential action ideas and avoiding lengthy discussions and debates, you can devote about forty minutes to this process. Of course, professionals' natural propensity is to enjoy engaging in lengthy discussions, so it is helpful to have your group agree on some basic rules at the start. The accepted rules for this brainstorming activity are usually some variation on the following:

1. Say everything that comes to mind

Yes, we know that you were taught to think before you open your mouth. This is going to take a bit of an adjustment.

2. No discussion

Many people have a tendency to put everything they say into a discussion sandwich: first they present the general concept, then they give you the idea, then they explain why that was a good idea! We need to encourage them to be succinct.

3. Make no value judgment comments—positive or negative

It is often helpful to remind your people of the three questions that successful entrepreneurs ask when confronting a new idea: How do I make this work? What's the worst that could happen? Where is my back door (exit) if the worst that could happen actually happens? Then remind them of the usual response among professionals to a new idea: Not a second passes before we hear thirteen reasons why that isn't going to work.

4. **Record all comments quickly so that they can be seen and get down lots of ideas**

> *Your objective here is quantity, not quality. And if Janice gives you an idea and you write it down, and then Chuck gives you an idea and you don't record it, Chuck is probably thinking either "I guess my idea wasn't good enough" or "What kind of jerk is this?"*

5. **Encourage participation and build on each other's ideas**

> *One of the great myths associated with brainstorming is that people will recognize a good idea when they see it. The truth is that it is extremely rare that a breakthrough new idea is recognized for its brilliance when first uttered. New ideas almost always are flawed in some way when they first appear. As Albert Einstein once said, "If at first a new idea doesn't seem totally absurd, there is no hope for it."*

Once having agreed to these rules, the group can begin the exercise. One technique that helps is to go methodically around the table asking each member to contribute one idea. Another method is to have everyone write down one idea (anonymously) and hand it up to the facilitator, who then records it on a flip chart for all to see. The advantage to using a paper flip chart is that you can mount the charts for everyone to see and retain them for transcribing a permanent record of the group's contributions.

The role of the facilitator is to get everyone's ideas out and recorded. It helps to number each idea as you write it down. Sometimes, in the verbal flurry of ideas, it is easy to either miss hearing someone's idea or record it in terms that do not adequately capture the intent. It always helps to ask members of the group to assist you to ensure that all ideas are captured and recorded accurately. Try to capture a few of the words actually used rather than summarizing or paraphrasing.

Ensure that an assistant is there to take notes. If left up to team members, it won't happen. She or he should be the same person who draws up the chart or action list (mentioned above) and oversees it for progress and accountability. As Julie MacDonald O'Leary, points out, assistants can often be more effective than the group leader in following up. When an assistant drops by to say, "I have been given the task of compiling everyone's promised work product. When might I be able to get yours?" this is often received as more gentle "nagging" than when the group leader does it. In addition, a person struggling, they might be less intimidated about revealing why to an assistant.

3 ENSURE IDEAS ARE ACTIONABLE

Once all the ideas are listed (without judgment), the coach must now ensure that the ideas expressed are specific, doable, and can be implemented. Sounds easy, but it's not. In our experience, this is the most difficult part of the brainstorming process. We are all prone to expressing concepts or goals, and often find it difficult to transform those concepts into actions.

For example, one common concept is "I think that we should always make a point of visiting our clients at their place of business to learn more about them." The concept is a good one. The only small hurdle is "how?" How will you ensure that everyone does this? How will you know that it is happening?

As the facilitator, you must always ask, as these ideas surface: "Is this proposed idea specific, tangible, and quantitative enough (or is it merely a goal, concept, or objective)?" A test of this is to ask whether you could delegate this idea to a junior for implementation, and have that junior know exactly what action should be taken.

It also helps to think in terms of the tangible outcome (or "deliverable") that will be presented at the next meeting to evidence the execution of this idea. Will this involve doing some research (a report); developing a policy, procedure, checklist, or template; or taking some specific action that can be shown to have happened?

Where ideas do not measure up to these criteria, you might want to gently encourage more specifics, without discussion. For example, you might say to the individual:

> "Janice, that idea would no doubt be very helpful to you and the group. Could you help us determine how we could ensure that everyone in our group was doing this consistently and how we would know that it was happening?"

Take a moment to explore with Janice (asking other group members to contribute) how you could do this. By gently probing for more specifics, you may elicit something like:

> *"Well, we could develop a wall chart that would display a list of our top twenty clients down the vertical column and the members of our group along the horizontal. We could then initiate a system whereby each of us took responsibility to visit one client over the next quarter and note on the chart the date that client was visited and submit a one-paragraph report to the group on our findings."*

Now you have something specific. The group will be able to assess for itself, at any point, how far along with this action plan they have progressed. Have the top twenty clients been identified? Has the wall-chart been developed? Has a visitation plan been drafted? Have client visits been made and reports submitted? The facilitator's job is to ensure that he or she has helped the group generate a good list of very specific, tangible, quantitative, and implementable ideas for moving toward their objectives.

Is this basic? Yes. Does it work? Yes. Do all groups do it? No! (Does yours?)

 GET VOLUNTARY COMMITMENTS

To simply engage in discussion may be informative, perhaps even entertaining, but it accomplishes nothing—except perhaps to frustrate those who yearn to see the group accomplish something meaningful. **Action-planning group meetings should conclude with each member taking responsibility for a specific action task.**

Some group leaders arbitrarily delegate various items to members of the group as assignments for the next meeting. That is not the most effective way to get meaningful action. It might be necessary in an emergency, or for a very junior person who simply needs to be given some tasks at first, but will not be effective as the standard operating mode with the group.

As the meeting facilitator, you should reserve the final fifteen minutes to determine which of the ideas that were generated are sufficiently appealing to members of the group that they might be moved to volunteer to invest a modest amount of their discretionary non-reimbursed time.

You might say to the group:

> *"We're going to take a moment to review all of the ideas we generated. Then, I want to hear from each of you in turn. Is there one idea on our list that you feel sufficiently motivated by, that you would be prepared to invest a few hours of your time over the next month to get started on? Please understand, this is to be totally voluntary: no obligations, no recrimination.*
>
> *"If you don't see an idea that you're prepared to work on, then you may simply 'pass' when I get to you. No explanations are necessary. However, if you do see an idea that you find motivating, then I want to hear which one it is."*

Your role, at this point, is to:

1. Ensure that the idea is not completely contrary to the goals of the group

2. Confer with each individual on what modest amount of non-billable time they have to work on implementing this idea over the next month

3. Determine precisely what the first actions might be to moving this idea forward

4. Have members describe precisely what they will bring back to the next meeting as evidence that something has been accomplished.

The essence of success is not picking the best, most strategically important ideas. That can wait until your group has had some experience and successes with productive meetings. Rather, **your goal is to stimulate members of the group to take some modest amount of constructive action,** thereby building momentum.

5 KEEP COMMITMENTS SMALL

Each specific task must be small and doable. When people get caught up in the process of generating good ideas or are stimulated by an idea that they like (often the very one that they themselves offered), they immediately want to volunteer to "change the world." This person returns to her office with the very best of intentions, but is soon sidetracked by numerous client fires that must be put out.

She finds herself at the next month's meeting with nothing substantial to report. She and her colleagues then enter a demoralizing cycle where some members "promise big, deliver nothing, and get forgiven" (since we all, really, are so very busy) while others think to themselves "Why am I doing all the work?" or "Why do we bother?"

It is important to temper people's enthusiasm by reminding them that their regular revenue-producing work must also be done. You must determine with them what they think they can actually, realistically accomplish in the designated time period.

Benjamin Haas, of Towers Perrin, observed:

> I think we have a lot of people who overcommit. Part of the issue is really pushing back on people to say, you know, don't make commitments that you're not going to deliver on. In a lot of cases, that's the biggest reason that we don't get the results.

 ESTABLISH YOUR "CONTRACTS FOR ACTION"

You must ensure that each task is carefully defined ("What can we all expect to get from you by the next meeting?") and completely capable of being accomplished. Before you adjourn your meeting, you need to help each person define specifically what the group should expect to see from him or her by the next meeting with regard to the execution of each particular assignment.

Will your group get a report on some research that has been undertaken, evidence that the initial steps to completion are under way, a summary of the completed project with the outcomes achieved, or a tangible product that can be distributed amongst the members? The task and tangible outcome expected need to be outlined in specifics.

The underlying philosophy becomes one of not letting the team down. **In one great firm we know, the rule is, "There's nothing you must do, but what you say you'll do, you must!"**

 FOLLOW-UP BETWEEN MEETINGS

Since expectations are naturally high following a good group meeting, any lack of progressive action by the next meeting is extremely detrimental to group morale. This is the most frustrating problem for busy group leaders.

This is also the one area where a true group leader can have the greatest impact and really display good coaching abilities. It is essential that you schedule some time to wander about and offer to help various members of your group with their specific projects.

To achieve continuous action requires frequent interaction. What you might expect to hear from an effective group leader is:

> *"Hey, Tom. I remember that you took on the project of helping us initiate our client visitation efforts. How can I help? Do you think we might schedule a half hour together later this week and I could work with you to develop our list of the top clients and a visitation schedule for our next meeting?"*

According to Daniel Fensin:

> It starts with making it clear to people what your expectation of them is. I'll go to the partner and say, look, here's what the assignment means to the firm. Here's the importance of it. You need to complete it. You need to stay in touch with me. I need to know how well you're doing on this assignment.
>
> If you think you're not going to be able to manage this assignment for one reason or another, you've got to tell me as soon as possible. What you say to them is the last thing in the world you want to do is embarrass either one of us. So stay with me on this. If you have a problem, you come to me and you let me know what that problem is and then we'll see what we can do.
>
> People want to do what they say they're going to do. They sometimes let things get in the way, and think it's okay to let things get in the way. So tell them, don't let things get in the way. If they do—let me solve that problem for you. Somebody says, well, something comes up, I have no choice. I have to do it. Come to me. I'll help resolve that problem for you. And I can.

It is disconcerting to see how much time is invested in making good plans and how little effort is spent in follow-up to ensure that actions are being taken consistent with those plans. **The single highest value-added use of a group leader's time is following up, one on one, with members of the team, to help them succeed.** By pitching in and lending a hand to complete projects, you will be able to demonstrate an interest in the individual and make a meaningful contribution to the morale and results that a group can achieve.

8 CELEBRATE SUCCESSES

The best groups always take time to acknowledge a specific accomplishment and improvement in reaching a personal or group goal. The outcome of present actions plays a major role in determining future actions. At the personal level, if people work especially hard and devote long hours to a project that eventually goes unnoticed, they will soon minimize or abandon their efforts. At the group level, if expectations are exceeded but there is no means of expressing pride in those achievements, it becomes a hollow victory.

Here's Dan again:

> I try to spread good news around the firm. I meet with every one of my partners once a month. It's a huge commitment of time for me. Everybody knows when they are scheduled to meet with me. I talk to them all about what they're doing and I try to let them know about what positive things are happening in the firm. I tell them to talk to their staff when they're out on the job or at lunch, and to tell the staff what's going on that's positive in the firm.
>
> When somebody does something worthy, we do an e-mail, press the "Everyone" button, and everyone finds out: "Here's somebody that's done something." We always try to make it clear that people have done something well. I ask partners to tell me about staff that do things well. I'll make it my business to bump into them in the hall and say, hey, you know what? Larry told me you did a really good job on this. I want you to know I appreciate it.

Just as there is a time value to money, there is a time value to enthusiasm. The earlier you stimulate that enthusiasm, the sooner you can leverage it into real momentum. People like winners. And they like to be part of winning teams. Early wins and clear evidence of early momentum translates into early enthusiasm.

chapter 16

Give Recognition

How do you acknowledge accomplishments?

CONTRIBUTIONS TO THE GROUP effort may be less visible than individual achievements, but they must be highlighted and recognized. Such contributions can often be neglected as people focus on their own individual achievements.

There often appears to be an absence of any meaningful acknowledgment of people's contributions to the team. For example, a junior investment banker returned to her office after a night spent at a financial printer and ran into a group of people, who joked that they thought she looked a little ragged, but did not comment on her contribution. Six months later the incident is still the subject of jokes, but not one of them ever congratulated her for her efforts in helping complete the documents overnight.

A longtime support staff member at a major accounting firm confesses that morale is so bad within the offices that the support staff retaliate against those people who are seen to be the cause. For example, they see to it that critical fax communications received from key clients "just don't seem to make it to the desk of the person in question."

What is missing from many people's work lives is any kind of personal appreciation or recognition. This is as true of senior people as it is of juniors. Managers often fall into the trap of looking for problems to be fixed rather than seeing successes that can be multiplied. This results in everyone being risk averse and cautious. It does little to encourage the vital task of regularly finding new ways to do the job better.

Think back to the last time someone took the time to tell you how much he or she admired your expertise, respected your decisions, or had confidence in the way you handled something. How did that recognition affect you on an emotional level? Your answer may be all the argument you need to appreciate the importance of giving recognition.

So, what stops us from expressing recognition? Some people think that it's actually unprofessional or too "touchy-feely" to express appreciation. There is often a fear of intimacy, a fear of getting too close. Expressing recognition makes a lot of people feel embarrassed, both in the giving and in the receiving. What should we do? Here are a few suggestions:

1. Decide what actions are worthy of recognition

2. Do it only when appropriate

3. Determine the appropriate method and form for extending your recognition

4. Deal with each individual in a manner that fits his or her personal style

5. Institute an "Awards Program" within your group

6. Prepare an "Accomplishments" report for your group

1 DECIDE WHAT ACTIONS ARE WORTHY OF RECOGNITION

Be alert for opportunities to provide recognition to a member of the team who:

1. Provides extraordinary service to a client

2. Supports the efforts of some other member of the group

3. Learns a new skill

4. Invests time to research new developments affecting a specific industry or group of clients

5. Shares information and knowledge with others in a clear and timely manner

6. Analyzes workflow processes to simplify them, cut costs, or eliminate repetition.

7. Takes initiative to solve a problem

8. Accomplishes more than he or she promised

2 DO IT ONLY WHEN APPROPRIATE

Telling people that you really appreciate the way they handled a specific activity or transaction is not something that has to be done too frequently. In fact, if you do it too often, it can lose its potency. It can seem insincere or even manipulative. So just do it when you feel the circumstances warrant.

3 DETERMINE THE APPROPRIATE METHOD AND FORM FOR EXTENDING YOUR RECOGNITION

Are there any non-financial incentives available for recognizing and celebrating performance and achievement, both professionally and personally? Consider the following list:

1. Approval

2. Gratitude

3. Autonomy

4. Participation / involvement

5. Personal interest / support

6. Public recognition

7. Visibility (inside and outside the office)

8. Contacts

9. Access to information ("being an insider")

10. Access to additional resources

11. Rapid response (access to the manager)

12. Task support

13. Titles (official and unofficial)

14. Special roles or assignments

15. Challenge

16. Meaning

Each of these items represents a nonfinancial currency that the group leader can influence, and use to provide rewards. There is, of course, danger here, in that the group leader must not be seen to be acting politically or playing favorites. However, the list reveals that the leader has more than a few arrows in his or her quiver to reward and acknowledge contributions. Great group leaders have learned how to use all of these currencies, adapting each to the personality of the individual.

Peter Friedes, the former CEO of Hewitt Associates, cautions that **individual recognition and rewards must be used delicately and with discretion, in case they destroy teamwork by singling out individuals for what was, in fact, a team effort.** He points out that the mere existence of individual rewards might create an internal competitiveness for individual recognition, rather than collaboration. Jeremy Silverman, now a general partner of Frontenac Company, a Chicago-based private equity investment firm, worked at Bain & Co. (the eminent strategy consulting firm) for twelve years. He recalls:

> Bain's culture always stressed the importance of team, rather than individual, performance. Indeed the mission statement referred to the firm as a "community of extraordinary teams." I remember an offsite event where, following some business meetings, several teams competed in a series of outdoor sports. At the end of the day, to the contestants' surprise, the prizes were awarded to the losing team: I still treasure the crystal paperweight recognizing me as a member of the "Least Extraordinary Team" that day. I thought the prizes were a brilliant idea on the part of the senior partner

responsible for organizing the event. Even if you're unsuccessful at softball or Ultimate Frisbee, he was suggesting, the team esprit is what's critical to success.

We recognize the importance of Friedes' concern and Silverman's example, but believe that, appropriately handled, individual rewards can play an important role. Here are a few no-cost to low-cost ideas and examples from those firms where common sense has been transformed into common practice:

Visit individuals in their office to thank them for some specific contribution or post a thank-you note on a colleague's office door.

Send an e-mail message to everyone in the group advising of someone's personal contribution to your own accomplishment.

Organize a number of your group to take a specific staff member out for lunch on their birthday or arrange to send a card home signed by everyone on the team.

Present a stuffed "Energizer bunny" to that group member who keeps going and going, or a stuffed roadrunner to those who manage to complete a particular rush client project in record time.

Arrange with firm management to rename one of your firm's meeting rooms (on a rotating basis) each year after the person who has made the most notable contribution to the team during the previous twelve months.

Present each new person joining the group with a specially printed T-shirt displaying his or her name above the name of the group and the firm.

Initiate your own internal one-page monthly newsletter. Arrange a "Bravo" column to salute personal and professional activities or a "Good Tries" column to recognize and offer encouragement to those whose innovations did not achieve their full potential.

Allow new people and staff to rent, from a local art gallery, a work of art of their choice for their office or work area.

Encourage and support people in developing their own recognition programs.

Create a "Hall Of Fame" wall with photos of outstanding achievements, both professional and personal.

Create an annual report, yearbook, or photo album containing memorabilia and photographs of every group member along with their best achievements of the year.

Acquire some luncheon certificates from a nearby restaurant to hand out on the spot to support staff observed to be putting in effort above and beyond expectations.

Acquire a tabletop-sized Japanese daruma doll, color in one eye signifying a goal, and after achieving that goal, color in the other eye and have everyone sign the doll and put it on display.

Give an employee a day off with pay if he or she recommends a person who is hired and makes it past a ninety-day probation period.

Buy a local billboard to celebrate a person's professional, political, or civic honor.

Host a surprise picnic for the entire practice team in the parking lot or parking garage.

Designate days when anyone who makes a negative comment forks over a dollar, and use the proceeds to fund a social event or external charity.

Send flowers to the spouse of any person or staff member who has to be away from home for an extended period on client business, to show appreciation for the sacrifice.

Phil Gott, the UK consultant to the professions, points out that **regardless of their effect in providing recognition, activities such as birthday celebrations, a hall of fame, or a yearbook serve to bond the team together.** They might be worth doing on a regular basis even if your primary purpose is not recognition. He tells a wonderful story:

> Several years ago one of my clients had set itself some very ambitious goals for the year and at the end of the year, it had fallen a little short. Nonetheless the leadership still wanted to recognize people's contributions, and it decided to hold what it called a "half-pint party." This said "thank you

for everything that you did even though we recognize that we did fall somewhat short." People could, of course, drink as much as they liked but every glass was handed over half full. It sent a very strong message and was one of those events that went down in the company's folklore.

4 DEAL WITH EACH INDIVIDUAL IN A MANNER THAT FITS HIS OR HER PERSONAL STYLE.

Observe the people you work with and consider what would motivate each of them.

a. Will he or she respond well to your giving them recognition in front of the others—or would a one-on-one conversation, a voice-mail message, or memo make them more comfortable?

b. Will your verbal recognition be enough—or should you also provide some more tangible and alternative form of (nonmonetary) appreciation?

c. What other methods and forms of (nonmonetary) recognition do you have at your disposal—considering the specific individual's interests, leisure pursuits, and career development needs?

The form of recognition you offer may be as simple (and cost-free) as a thank-you note placed on an individual's office desk or as modest as a gift certificate for dinner. If you have done your homework you will be able to offer something that appeals to the individual you are recognizing.

5 INSTITUTE AN "AWARDS PROGRAM" WITHIN YOUR GROUP.

Awards in different categories could be given out to a number of group members, and members of your group could be encouraged to submit the names of individuals they feel most worthy of receiving recognition:

Service Quality Awards: Nominations should be made for those individuals who consistently complete client work in a timely fashion with very high quality and who make the effort to produce excellence.

Practice Development Awards: Nominate individuals who have put forward the most consistent effort in working together as a team to help build the practice.

Streamliner Awards: Nominate individuals who come up with the best suggestions for improving the efficiency and effectiveness of the group.

Administrative Support Awards: Nominate the individual who provides the most helpful support to you.

Golden Rule Awards: This award recognizes that person who always treats you kindly and fairly, who recognizes his or her responsibility to be part of the team, and knows that by helping you succeed, the whole group benefits.

Best Suggestion to Clients Awards: Nominate someone who saved your client money, increased your profitability, found errors which could have resulted in embarrassment or penalties, reduced paperwork, or increased a client employee's productivity.

Mentors of the Year Award: Nominate someone who caused you to perform at your best, helped you develop to your true potential, or provided a supportive environment that allows you to take risks and accept challenges.

 6 **PREPARE A REGULAR "ACCOMPLISHMENTS" REPORT FOR YOUR GROUP.**

A compilation of all of the positive changes and improvements of the past period throughout the group could include statistical summaries, war stories, improvement charts, lessons learned, specific accomplishments, client testimonials, and the like. It could very well become a source of enormous energy, pride, and surprise to everyone in your group.

Performance is determined by what we finish, not by what we start. Failing to take the time to review and assess progress is one of the major reasons why so many improvement efforts lose their way. When the essential component of celebration is lacking, individual learning, energy, and momentum dwindle.

chapter 17

Resolve Interpersonal Conflicts

What do you do when team members fall out?

THE SEQUENCE GOES something like this: A member of your group does or says something that causes some other member to have strong negative feelings: anger, frustration, annoyance, embarrassment, humiliation, or disappointment. The offended individual stays upset, perhaps for a day or longer. She replays whatever happened over and over again in her mind. Perhaps she even talks about what happened with other members of the group. Eventually, she begins to calm down and the intensity of the initial bitterness begins to subside. However, the offended individual does not talk to the offending person about what happened. The feelings about what happened subside, but they never disappear completely.

Conflicts among group members can take several forms:

1. "Chronic bickering" between two members of the team

2. Verbal abuse or a harmful "put-down" remark that diminishes or demeans other individuals, their opinions or ideas

3. "Finding fault," publicly, with the work, performance, attitude, or almost anything another colleague does

4. An icy coolness between a couple of group members such that they eliminate all but the most formal of interactions, ignore each other when speaking, and give each other the cold shoulder or "silent treatment"

When two (or more) people are in conflict the initial anger can soon lead to stronger feelings of resentment if the underlying issues are not confronted. If you, as the group leader, don't intervene to help your people talk out their problems, these negative feelings may intensify to the point of seeking release, the psychological equivalent of a toxic spill. This can be damaging not only to the individuals involved, but also to other group members and to the overall spirit of the team.

Conflicts are unavoidable when any group that works together comprises differing personalities and impassioned views. Some can actually provoke periods of great creativity and an intensity that fosters team spirit. *Healthy* conflict can result in better ideas and more innovative solutions.

However, *unhealthy* dysfunctional behavior so often results, usually due to chronic reluctance to air the issues. **We all are prone to chronic avoidance in our important relationships. We know that we should resolve an unhealthy personal conflict when it first arises, but we don't.** It is easier to avoid the potential confrontation, even if it makes things worse tomorrow. After all, we think, we have a hard enough time getting through today to worry about tomorrow.

The prospect of confronting a colleague about a touchy subject is unpleasant. We worry that a confrontation might cause even more serious problems. We are afraid of how the other person may react ("I could alienate someone here today who can make life far more miserable for me in the future"). We may feel that the chances of having a constructive interaction are slim to none. So we say to ourselves, "It's not worth the hassle."

The most effective response to dealing with unhealthy conflict is one of negotiation: The group leader listens to both sides, identifies the common areas of interest and agreement, and builds on these areas of agreement so that each individual can understand the other's point of view. The advice from Roger Fisher and William Ury, the authors of *Getting to Yes,* is also worth bearing in mind: To help resolve disputes, you should help people focus on their respective long-run interests, not on their short-term "bargaining" positions. A mediator is never more valuable than when reminding the contentious parties of their long-run interest in having a relationship, rather than focusing on the immediate points of contention.

Here are some steps to resolve conflict:

1. Describe the conflict and the nonproductive behavior you are observing.

2. Ask each person to comment on the cause of the disagreement.

3. Have each person, in turn, summarize what he or she heard the other person say.

4. Ask each person, in turn, to identify points of agreement and disagreement.

5. Invite your colleagues to suggest ways to proceed.

1 DESCRIBE THE CONFLICT AND THE NONPRODUCTIVE BEHAVIOR YOU ARE OBSERVING

"It appears to me that neither of you seems to be listening to the other, and obviously each of you has some very strong views on how you want to approach this project."

Differences in needs, goals, values, or competition for scarce resources are all potential triggers for conflict. A group leader who hopes to resolve an interpersonal conflict must take the initiative to bring the disagreement to the surface as soon as it is apparent and help the people involved to analyze their differing points of view. By bringing the conflict out into the open, stating it in nonjudgmental terms, and offering it up as a mutual problem, you acknowledged it as "ours." Until then it will be very difficult to progress to a cooperative resolution.

The first step to moving forward is getting your two colleagues to take the time to look objectively at how they are interacting with each other. Your main focus should be on the interpersonal process, not on the content or topic of contention. What must be addressed are the specific behaviors that seem to be preventing these people from interacting effectively.

2 ASK EACH PERSON TO COMMENT ON THE CAUSES OF THE DISAGREEMENT

"Can I suggest that we take a few minutes and may I ask each of you in turn to comment on what you see going on between you? What is the problem here as you perceive it? What does Wayne do that contributes to the problem? And what are you doing that contributes to the problem?"

To resolve interpersonal differences between people the group leader must exercise active listening and be able to hear the emotional aspects of what is being said.

Calmly invite each of them to describe what they think is the reason for their apparent conflict. Don't try to solve the problem. Simply invite your colleagues to discuss the underlying cause of their differences. Many conflicts can have several or ambiguous causes.

Jean Lebedum in *Managing Workplace Conflict* tells us that there are four basic categories of conflict:

1. Over facts and data. A basic misunderstanding or misinformation is the easiest type of conflict to resolve.

2. Over process or methods. Your people may have the same goals but differ on how to achieve those goals, a situation where compromise is often possible.

3. Over purpose. Your people may have different goals or agendas, which sometimes can be merged.

4. Over values. Your people may have differences in basic beliefs or principles. These create the most difficult conflicts, and sometimes people must agree to disagree.

Sometimes one person may try to focus blame on the other instead of stating their views objectively. There is some merit to allowing someone the opportunity to vent and get any hurt feelings off his or her chest. Should that happen, calmly ask the person to state "what" not "who" is keeping things from moving forward. You need to help both parties see that they each need to take some small responsibility for the situation.

HAVE EACH PERSON SUMMARIZE WHAT THE OTHER PERSON SAID

"Wayne, for purposes of just making absolutely sure that we are all understanding each other, can you briefly tell us both what you just heard Marie say is the core issue that's upsetting her?"

Now ask each person to repeat back what the other person said. By having each one paraphrase the other's main points, you are encouraging them to listen to and acknowledge each other's views.

Then ask each person to confirm, clarify, or correct the summary that was repeated back. If you are not sure about what one of your people was saying, ask for clarification.

Maintain a position of neutrality. If you offer a critique of one person's position, you will appear to be taking sides. Again, don't try to solve the conflict. Your role is simply to gather information.

4 ASK EACH PERSON, IN TURN, TO IDENTIFY POINTS OF AGREEMENT AND DISAGREEMENT

"Can we identify the points where the two of you obviously agree? You both seem to be saying that you want to work together on (X). Now, without losing sight of that, let's identify the points of contention between the two of you on how you each want to approach this differently."

With the conflicting views now calmly and clearly expressed, your two colleagues may be surprised as to how much they actually agree. First ask each to first identify the points of agreement in their two respective positions. Then do the same for areas of disagreement.

Should either person just want to rehash where they disagree, ask questions to help them see where they agree. But **don't pretend that differences don't exist. Your coaching role is to lay the groundwork for future cooperation by clarifying the various points of view. To successfully rechannel conflict, you as the group leader must withhold judgment.**

An interpersonal conflict is most likely to be productively resolved if both parties can see that they stand to gain something from the resolution. Your task is to highlight what is in their mutual best interests, or where they need each other to accomplish more than either of them could on their own.

 ## INVITE YOUR COLLEAGUES TO SUGGEST WAYS TO PROCEED

"How would you suggest we move forward? Are either of you willing to compromise slightly in the interests of achieving what you both have agreed that you want, and ease the tension here a bit?"

Conflict resolution poses the most gain and the least pain when the parties are able to take a cooperative rather than an adversarial approach to working out differences. For this to happen, both of your colleagues need to own the problem and recognize that they have a stake in solving it.

Ask them to suggest actions that address the points of agreement and disagreement they've just reviewed. Your task is to have them reach agreement on the steps that are needed to resolve the situation. Such agreement is usually most effective when it involves some small quid pro quo between the two people.

Be practical about any suggestions. As they propose possible actions, ask questions to help them clarify how their ideas might unfold. Look for workable suggestions and small initial action steps. Sometimes the only viable suggestion may be simply to let the dust settle and set a date for another meeting between the two.

Any agreements and actions that do result from your discussions should be put in writing to prevent any further problems from arising and reduce the chances of any misunderstanding at some later point.

The key to this process is to expose destructive differences as early as possible. The longer unhealthy conflict persists, the more difficult it is to resolve; and once conflict has erupted into open warfare the effects can have serious repercussions throughout your entire team as others feel obligated to take sides.

chapter 18

Deal with Your Crises

How do you respond to dramatic events?

WILL YOU BE PREPARED when that major-panic, drop-everything, what-are-we-going-to-do disaster occurs? Not likely. After all, it wouldn't be a crisis if you were prepared, would it? But it *will* occur. Something always does.

Crises can be precipitated by events such as the following:

1. A significant person decides to leave the firm

2. Someone in your group behaves in an inappropriate manner or is perceived to be unethical

3. The group loses a major client

4. Economic conditions necessitate the release of some people

5. A valued member of the group dies

SOME KEY PRINCIPLES TO KEEP IN MIND

Managing a crisis is a finely tuned blend of art and science. We recommend the following steps:

1. Calmly attempt to get at the facts

2. Identify the real problem

3. Decide who should handle the crisis

4. Involve everyone where possible

5. Remember that, in a crisis, everything (emotions, results, etc.) is magnified.

1 CALMLY ATTEMPT TO GET AT THE FACTS

The inevitable challenge with any crisis is to avoid making a bad situation even worse. Your biggest dilemma may be determining whether you have the right information. Often, you don't know what you don't know. There may be too little information with a lot of conjecture and rumor, or there may be too much information with no way to sift out what is factually relevant and what is not.

It's easy to overreact when you see your colleagues getting concerned about what they perceive the situation to be, but a measured, thoughtful approach to getting at the facts during any crisis is the best strategy.

2 IDENTIFY THE REAL PROBLEM

The most pressing task in a crisis is identifying the real problem. When your practice team loses a major client you might think the problem would be blatantly obvious—a loss of a significant chunk of revenues and perhaps a blow to your group's morale. However, these may not be the real problems.

The actually disaster may lie more in the effects of the incident:

1. A distinct possibility exists that some senior professional may abandon your group to join the competitor now getting the work.

2. Other clients may learn of this client defecting, and it may impact their ongoing confidence.

3. This client loss may be an indication of much deeper quality or service problems that have remained hidden.

4. Some of the junior group members, who were dependent upon this client's work, may have to be let go.

If you don't take the time to identify the real issues, you are vulnerable to putting your energies and resources into addressing the wrong crisis.

3 DECIDE WHO SHOULD HANDLE THE CRISIS

Sometimes you are not the best person to be in charge of dealing with the crisis. Consider the situation where your group learns that a major client has decided to move all or a major portion of its work to a competitor. An internal marketing professional (or your firm's leader) may be better suited to visit with the client to ascertain what the central problem is (and whether anything can be done to appease this client). Or perhaps one of your senior professionals has been accused of an action that borders on sexual harassment. Perhaps an experienced, external professional would have a better grasp of what steps should be taken to correct and contain the damage.

Your most important job may very well be to decide who is best equipped to handle the particular crisis. That doesn't mean you should abdicate your leadership responsibility. You need to remain on top of the situation.

4 INVOLVE EVERYONE WHERE POSSIBLE.

Sometimes your crisis needs only the attention of a few key professionals and it is quickly resolved. In other instances it may take some concerted effort on the part of a much larger group of people. There may be times when you need to ask your entire team to stay late or work through an entire weekend. A crisis is an opportunity to bring out the hidden talents in members of your group. **Find ways to make everyone feel that they played some role in helping save the day.**

5 REMEMBER THAT, IN A CRISIS, EVERYTHING IS MAGNIFIED.

Regardless of what kind of loss or crisis you face, you need to understand how the others in your group are going to perceive the situation. Often, it isn't the precipitating event itself, but rather the perception of the other members of the group and their subsequent actions that can really cause a crisis.

As Daniel J. Fensin commented:

> I don't want to say mine is the kind of position where you can't ever let them see you sweat, but if I worry a lot about something and really get concerned about it, it's like chaos in the corridors. It's, like, "Oh, my God, if he's worried about this, it's got to be really, really bad." To a certain extent, you have to maintain a level of calmness to allow the team to really do what they do best.

A Few Rules of Crisis Communication

Handled badly, any crisis can harm the respect and loyalty you enjoy with your group. Handled well, it can boost your team's enthusiasm.

Here are some basic guidelines for effectively handling your communications with the group.

1. Keep every member of your group fully informed

2. Involve your group members in key decisions

3. Be accessible to your people

4. Don't lose your sense of humor

1. Keep every member of your group fully informed

No one wants to have a negative situation exposed publicly. But during a crisis, trying to keep whatever details might be available hidden from your fellow group members is usually fruitless. If it's really a crisis that affects your group or people's careers or client retention, the story will eventually get out, no matter what you do. And the story that gets out will be rife with misinformation and probably far more damaging than the facts and the story you would have wanted to communicate.

A Few Rules of Crisis Communication *(Cont.)*

2. Involve your group members in key decisions

Obviously, when you are responsible for a large group of professionals in geographically dispersed offices, you can't start organizing group meetings to gain consensus on the best solution to take. But you do need to go as far as you can to involve your group. It is important to remember that to the extent that people are involved, they will feel far more committed to the ultimate decision and responsible for making it work.

3. Be accessible to your people

To the extent that any crisis becomes emotionally charged, it is a safe bet that many of your people will be anxious, aggravated, frustrated, or even enraged. Should people feel that you are too busy for them, they are likely to feel alienated and demoralized.

Make time for them to express their concerns, share their feelings, seek your advice, or offer their views. Make sure your colleagues feel that your highest priority is attending to their best interests.

Most real crises have an important and central communications challenge, whether dealing with external audiences or internal. But a crisis is not likely to be solely a communications challenge. Communications professionals often wind up managing a crisis because no one else wants to do it. In fact, communications is only one aspect of true crisis management.

4. Don't lose your sense of humor

It is an old cliché, but laughter really is the best medicine, especially when you need to take the pressure off or need to reduce people's stress. Cliff Farrah told us that he purchased fireman's helmets for his key team members and handed them out at a crisis meeting, telling everyone to keep them mounted on the wall. When he needed to rally the troops around a problem, he called them and said "better put on your helmet."

ADVICE ON SPECIFIC TYPES OF CRISIS

Let's look at the common crises (listed above) to examine what action you might want to take next.

1 A KEY PLAYER IS DEFECTING

You have just received word that one of the key players in your group is leaving and, even worse, leaving to join a competitor. Your own most natural reaction would be a sense of extreme disappointment, anger, even a feeling of betrayal. But you must also think of others. How is this going to affect the morale of the group? Are others also likely to defect? What void will this person's going leave in the group's client service capability?

You will probably be tempted to speculate about why this person has chosen to leave, what his motivations and future plans are, and whether it is likely to be a friendly departure. You may even react in anger, giving others in the group either a verbal or nonverbal indication that you knew the departure was imminent and are happy to see this individual go.

Whether or not there is any validity to your feelings, such a communication will run the danger of having others in your group begin to question their own value and what might be said about them if they ever decide to leave.

Your first step should be to have a talk with this person. Perhaps his decision isn't irrevocable. Maybe he doesn't truly want to leave but is looking for an indication that your group and the firm really value his contribution. He may be upset about something that was really a misunderstanding or miscommunication that can be resolved. Perhaps it's as simple as the person defecting because he has been offered a more lucrative compensation package. You need to discover, firsthand, what is motivating his move.

There is an inherent danger in trying to appease an individual who doesn't feel valued. This person may discern that your eagerness to keep him gives him the power to influence future situations to his personal best interests. So it is important that you do not overreact or make promises that will come back to haunt you. But you certainly have everything to gain and little to lose by speaking with this person face to face— and doing so before the word gets out that he is leaving, and before you have to address the reality with your team members.

Ask what his intentions are. Ascertain what each of you should do to make that departure come about in the most amicable manner. Discuss how the internal and external communications should be handled so as to pose the least amount of disruption to the group. Collaborate on drafting a memo to all members of the group explaining what is happening and wishing him the best in his new undertaking. Develop a joint communication to clients.

Breaking the news to your group won't be a pleasant task, so you need to be as positive as possible. Tell them the reasons why the decision has been made. Follow the bad news by presenting them with a challenge that they can get their energy into, preferably something you are confident will work out well. Drive out suspicion and build trust. Remove as much uncertainty as possible by being clear and positive about how the group will go forward.

2 SOMEBODY MADE A MISTAKE

You find out that two married members of your group are having an affair. One of your colleagues has just discovered that she is being sued for professional malpractice. One of your people made an inappropriate gesture to someone in the firm of the opposite sex. Perhaps you have just been confronted with the evidence of poor judgment. How do you respond, and what do you do about it?

Your best response, in some cases, is to do absolutely nothing! You must distinguish between what may be immoral and what is a crisis. Something should be viewed as a crisis only if it interferes with the other members of your group or affects their work on behalf of clients.

If you are caught having erred, show that you are repentant. Don't try to hide it or cover it up. Most people are willing to forget and forgive if there are sincere expressions of error and repentance. During and after a crisis, leaders are judged not so much by the original negative actions, but by how they handle them. Nixon's crime was not the burglary at Watergate, it was the cover-up. The public can forgive a politician's infidelity, but not the act of lying outright.

People are capable of forgiving those who make mistakes, even fairly major blunders, if they are honest about the mistake, indicate that they have learned from it and will not repeat the error, and are truly concerned for how it may reflect on the group and on the firm.

If the behavior in question was something unlawful or contravened the code of ethics of your profession, then your situation is far more critical. Your course of action is usually apparent and spelled out clearly by that body governing your profession. In those instances, decisiveness is critical and tough decisions have to be made fast. Your problem will never improve with age. Speed is of the essence. This crisis will not wait.

3 WE LOST A CLIENT

It is always preferable to err on the side of disclosure. Often you may have to face your people with less than full information as to why the client was lost, because in many cases we may never really know. In those instances it is best to state clearly that you don't know all the facts. Then promptly share the facts that you do know.

The bottom line is to tell the truth and tell it fast. Your established level of trust with the group is at stake. **Whether your people will believe you when you badly need them to do so will depend on how much confidence you have established with them before the crisis occurs.** If after the crisis, you try to snow them in any way or not disclose all of the facts, your trust will be irreparably harmed.

1. Face the reality of the lost client, instead of denying it.

2. Do what you can do; do something instead of being fatalistic.

3. Hold a session with the group to analyze the mistakes or weaknesses. But avoid the "blame-throwing" syndrome. Instead, look at the problem and search for answers.

4. Count your blessings, your other clients, and resolve to serve them even better.

5. Remember the old army maxim: "There are no bad soldiers, only bad officers." Your group needs to know that you are with them and that you aren't putting the blame on them when you talk to others outside of the group.

4 WE HAVE TO LET SOME PEOPLE GO

We all know that at times economic conditions can make it necessary for a firm to downsize. Perhaps some senior people are not performing up to standard. Perhaps some staff have become redundant.

When this crisis strikes, keep everyone in your group informed from the earliest possible stage. People always get wind of these things through the office grapevine and, when they do, their imaginations are likely to create a situation far more grave than it actually is.

Here's how to deal with cutbacks:

a. Don't give your group your best guess and don't speculate. Find out the facts and communicate whatever the group wants to know.

b. Don't stay quiet. That will not protect them.

c. After a downsizing, talk collectively to the members of your group that remain. Tell them that you regret what has happened and help them face the reality of the economic facts.

d. Recognize that many of your team may feel threatened, expecting the other shoe to drop—and the next time it could be them. Assure all of the remaining group members of how valuable they are and how each has an important contribution to make in helping the group get through the economic storm.

e. Get up and move on again. Fight self-pity.

f. Ask for help from a professional. You don't have to face it alone.

g. As you sense the crisis is passing be sure to give the members of your group credit for handling the unpleasant situation well.

5 A VALUED COLLEAGUE DIES

The worst possible thing has just occurred. A member of your group, your "family," has passed away. Some members of your group will feel this loss far more personally and far more deeply then you might ever imagine. These situations always have us reflect upon our own mortality.

A person who comforts can be a tremendous help to those who are left grieving, either fellow team members or direct family members. Your support as the practice leader will help those grieving heal a little faster. However, there are some do's and don'ts to remember.

DO'S

1. When you hear the news of a death, call the whole group together and tell them all at once.

2. Be prepared for some colleagues to be extremely upset—prearrange to have a professional counselor available.

3. Cancel any scheduled meetings or presentations. Don't allow any of your group to think that you put work before people.

4. Give your fellow team members time to go to the funeral.

5. Make sure to send flowers on behalf of the group, independent from anything individual members decide to do on their own.

6. Give individual members of your team plenty of time to get back to normal.

7. Let people feel that they can talk about their loss. Speak naturally of the person who has died. Be empathetic. Don't allow it to be a taboo subject.

8. Make a phone call or send a card to the surviving spouse or family, especially on anniversaries because anniversaries can be the hardest.

9. Tell the surviving spouse or family member to feel free to phone or visit you at any time (and mean it).

DON'TS

1. Don't assume you know it all or that you have all the answers and don't use textbook advice that is formal and rigid.

2. Don't rush a grieving person through the need to talk about it. Give the person the gift of listening.

3. Don't use anyone's grief to express your own grief. Avoid the temptation to talk about yourself, thereby stealing the conversation.

4. Don't use cliches like, "I know how you are feeling."

5. Don't compare the person's grief to someone else's experience. No two experiences are the same.

6. Don't impose if your attention is not welcome.

7. Don't intrude in the person's life. Give the person space and permission to be himself or herself.

8. Don't break confidences.

9. Don't expect too much, too soon, from any of the closest members on your team. Be prepared for mood swings.

CONCLUSION

No one wants to be involved in a crisis. Crises can cost money to resolve. They require time spent in remedial action. They keep you from your client work. A big one can undermine your group's morale.

But crises can also be exhilarating. They require an intensity of effort and a focus that is not normally needed. They create strong relationships among group members. **Tempers may flare, but if the crisis is handled well, your group's commitment and focus can emerge even stronger.** Helen Ostrowski, managing partner of U.S. Public Relations operations at Porter Novelli, tells the following story:

> Along with everyone else in our industry, we have had to deal with the issue of layoffs. We planned the process down to the last detail. We carefully figured out who would be spoken to, and by whom, covering those who had to be asked to leave and those remaining. We brought in an outplacement firm to train our top executive team in how to deliver the message, and I wrote the key messages myself, crafting every word. It was a tense day, but it all went off as planned, with good feedback about how compassionate and respectful we'd been.
>
> At the end of the day, the executive team all got together to discuss how the day went, and, at that moment, I just lost it. I poured out my emotions in front of my top team, breaking every rule I had ever heard about maintaining an even keel. To my astonishment, rather than destroying my credibility, I received e-mails the next day from virtually everyone thanking me for my guidance through the process

and asking if there was anything they could do to help me. It actually bonded us together. In retrospect, it was critical that I was cool, calm and collected while we dealt with the crisis, but it was also, to my surprise, probably a good thing that I allowed myself (and everyone else) the emotional release when it was over.

PART FOUR

BUILDING FOR THE FUTURE

19. Nurture Your Juniors
How do you deal with your junior staff?

20. Integrate New People
How do you integrate new hires?

21. Control Your Group's Size
How do you respond to the problems of size?

22. Measure Group Results
How do you measure your group's success?

23. Why Bother?
Why would you want to do all this?

chapter 19

Nurture Your Juniors

How do you deal with your junior staff?

IN SMALL GROUPS, the group leader has the opportunity to interact regularly, on and off client projects, with all members of the group, senior and junior. However, as the group gets larger, most of the leader's time will be spent with senior colleagues, and it will be these people who must motivate, energize, supervise, and develop the junior staff. It becomes the group leader's job to ensure that this happens.

Junior staff, by definition, are at the early stages of a career, and need one thing above all: the chance to develop and build their skills. Without this, their career (and their livelihood) is at risk. How well skills are built depends upon two key processes. The first is the work assignment system that decides what projects they get to work on (and for what part of the project they are given responsibility). The second is the quality of supervision that they receive while working on these assigned projects.

While the practice leader must ensure that these two processes are working properly, firms differ greatly in how formal these processes are, and on how formal a role the group leader plays.

THE WORK ASSIGNMENT SYSTEM

In some firms, each senior person has the freedom to staff his or her own job from a general pool of junior professionals, while in others, junior professionals tend to work for the same senior people all of the time, becoming either officially or unofficially "their" juniors.

A better model, in our view, is one where all the senior people get together regularly and jointly allocate junior staff to projects, thereby sharing the responsibility to act like a group. They can consider together the trade-offs between keeping people busy, providing the best resources to key clients, providing developmental work experiences, achieving efficiency, and keeping motivation and morale high.

Even where there is no formal authoritative role for the group leader in work scheduling, there is an important informal role of monitoring the pattern of work assignments that juniors are getting. By knowing what is going on, the group leader can have an influence by dropping in on senior colleagues from time to time and saying things like:

> "I see you're using Jimmy for the sixth time on this kind of transaction, which makes a lot of economic sense since he's so much up to speed. However, I know Jimmy's keen to learn some new things, and I wondered if, next time you have a transaction like this, you might consider using Mary instead.

> "I know she's dying to work with you and would be really committed, since she would be exposed to new things. She would be eager to look good in your eyes. If you'd be willing to agree, you'd really being contributing a lot to the group, since we'd reduce the risk that both Jimmy and Mary might quit to get the work opportunities they're after. Would you be willing to help me out on this?"

Done with enough style and grace, the group leader can have a significant impact on the pattern of work assignments, and hence on motivation, morale, and retention.

THE WORK SUPERVISION SYSTEM

Ensuring excellence in work supervision can be a harder topic for the group leader, since many groups do not have a prior agreement on what constitutes appropriate standards of supervising work. In many firms, this is an area left for each senior person's autonomy, with project leaders free to manage in the style they prefer.

We believe that **the quality of work supervision is so critical that it deserves special attention.** In *Practice What You Preach*, it was shown, in a global statistical study, to be one of the prime determinants of financial success.

As always, we think that it is wise to engage your senior colleagues in establishing standards, rather than trying to impose standards upon them. You should ask what standards of work supervision they think they ought to be accountable for. Note that we do not suggest that you establish standards you will "try for," because "agreeing to try" leaves a lot of loopholes. ("I didn't agree to do this, I agreed to try, but I got busy. Sorry!")

Here are some standards we would propose. We think it reasonable that the junior people on a transaction are entitled to certain expectations:

1. When tasks and projects are assigned to them, they understand thoroughly what is expected of them.

2. They understand how their assigned tasks fit into the overall objectives for the engagement.

3. Help is available when they need to have questions answered.

4. They receive prompt feedback, good or bad.

5. When they are corrected for something they did or failed to do, it is done in a constructive way.

6. They receive good coaching to help improve their performance.

7. They are kept informed about the things they need to know to do their job properly.

8. They have the freedom to make the necessary decisions to do their work properly.

9. They are actively encouraged to volunteer new ideas and make suggestions for improvement.

10. Team meetings are conducted in a way that builds trust and mutual respect.

11. In each engagement very high standards for performance are set and enforced.

12. They feel like a member of a well-functioning team.

13. Their work makes good use of their knowledge and ability.

14. Their projects help them learn and grow.

15. Their work is interesting and challenging.

If you have difficulty getting your senior colleagues to accept these accountabilities, ask them to cast their minds back to when they were junior people. Ask them how they wished to be treated when they were juniors! (Not how they *were* treated, but how they wish they had been treated!)

You will probably end your discussion with a different list (and maybe a shorter one) than ours, but that's OK. What you will have accomplished is raising your people's sensitivity and awareness to the fact that there are *some* standards of behavior in work supervision that must be considered and enforced.

After this discussion the group leader should monitor performance in this area, formally or informally. The formal approach might involve a questionnaire completed by all the staff on each project, rating their work experience, with the forms going back to the practice leader.

According to Karl Kristoff, of Hodgson Russ:

> The desire amongst our younger professionals for the kind of structure and leadership that creates those kinds of feedback programs for them is quite significant. Sometimes even some of my more skeptical partners have been pleasantly surprised during meetings which have been preceded by anonymous questionnaires and other devices designed to bring out the views of our young people in a nonthreatening way. Associates (junior professionals) want to be part of an organization that is interested in their training.

However, such formality might not be needed if the group leader is prepared to walk the halls, hang out in the coffee room, or chat by the watercooler. **It is usually not difficult for an activist group leader to find out which senior colleagues are doing this well, and which are not. The key is the group leader's willingness to act on the information.** For example, he or she could drop by a senior colleague's office, close the door, and say something like:

> "Richard, this is just between us, but I wanted to pass on some things I'm hearing. I've been talking to our juniors and, to put it bluntly, you're not their favorite person to work for. They say they don't get enough guidance from you as to what you want them to do, and you don't give a lot of feedback.

> "I've no idea if this is true, but it might get to the point where our best juniors avoid your projects. This would be tragic, because you've got a lot to offer and your clients deserve to be served by the best we've got. Can you tell me what's going on from your perspective? Is there anything at all I can do to help?"

Naturally, this approach won't work every time. But if the group leader is diligent in having such conversations every time they are needed, people will eventually get the message that the standards are real. The group leader does not need to act like a bully, or a cop, but it can be remarkably effective to be the conscience of the group, continually reminding people of the standards you (collectively) set for yourselves.

"Inculcate the right values in the partnership in terms of how they practice in the team context. Every one of our partners does some supervising," says Bevan Ashford's Nick Jarrett-Kerr. "It's part of what being a partner means at this firm."

MENTORS

It is a good idea to establish a system whereby everyone in your group has a mentor. You will play the mentoring role to your senior colleagues, but, in turn, each of them must be a mentor to at least one (and probably a few) junior professional. The mentor role is not to be an advocate for those they are mentoring, but to be a sounding board, to provide career guidance, and to be someone to turn to when there are difficulties.

One of the most respected and admired group heads at Credit Suisse First Boston is Bayo Ogunlesi, who is the head of the Energy and Power group in their investment banking division. Eileen Urban, who is the chief operating officer in the group, tells this story:

Ogunlesi established a system of assignments for mentors that paired (senior) managing directors with (more junior) vice presidents who are outside of their reporting line. The mentors are expected to develop a relationship of trust and great communication. One of Ogunlesi's unusual rules is that the mentor is fined (actual cash out of his or her own pocket) if the mentee resigns and he was not forewarned. The issue isn't the resignation itself but the lack of communication. If the communication is not enough for the mentor to understand and help the person act on issues that are troubling to them, then they must not be doing the role as they are expected to.

The system has been a great success. The mentoring has turned into a way of differentiating our group, and even some of our "unbelievers" have turned into stars at it. We believe that everybody has the ability to mentor someone; the secret is in the match.

The virtues of a good mentoring system (which combines two rules: "everyone must be a mentor" and "everyone must have a designated mentor") are many. Naturally, your junior staff will benefit, because they will have someone to turn to. Second, your time will be freed up. A formal mentoring system will mean that you will not have to do *all* the coaching yourself. Third, the practice your colleagues will get in being a mentor will help them develop interpersonal, social, and emotional skills that will help them in their professional work. Last, but not least, a mentoring program will help you identify those who are particularly skilled and help you groom either your successor, or new subgroup leaders that will be needed when your group gets to large to manage.

Francine Popoli Edelman, President of I2i Communications, told us:

A former mentor of mine was a brilliant, caring human, with high professional standards and impeccable integrity. While he treated employees with fairness and generosity he failed to inspire loyalty. There was no communication and therefore no emotional connection. So when an employee got a better or different offer they had no reservations about leaving the company. I spend at least twenty minutes or more each day talking to my staff; not just about business, but about them; how they are doing, how their kids are, what their plans are for the weekend. They know me, my family, even my dog. But more importantly, I know them; their interests, hopes, aspirations and expectations.

The results are clearly instructive. We continue to have one of the lowest attrition rates in our industry. In my judgment, that makes for a more stable, cohesive, and collaborative work environment.

Embedded within Ms. Edelman's story is the lesson that **mentoring is not just a job for the group leader. With appropriate role modeling, the group leader can raise the level of mentoring throughout the group—with obvious benefits.**

HIRING

Since professional firms have nothing to sell but their people, it is wise for group leaders to be significantly involved in all new hires (senior or junior) to the group. This doesn't mean that the group leader has to do it alone, just that he or she plays a significant role.

The most important hiring lesson to remember is that you should hire for attitude, and train for skills. Skills you can build. Attitude, and character, are harder to change. You need to have a sense of who is and who is not your firm's kind of person, and hire to fit the culture. You should look for people with enthusiasm, excitement, sparks, energy, spirit, a sharing style, personality, and compatibility. Try to hire people who have all this innate in their personality.

It is wise to involve your whole team in hiring, including both junior and senior people. They are the ones who will have to work most closely with the new person, and their judgment is crucial. Never hire just to fill a capacity need: Remember always that you are entering into a multiyear relationship with this person. Ask, "Do I really want to live with this person, day in and day out?"

The problem of hiring people for professional careers is that there is an overwhelming tendency to focus on qualifications, grades, and techni-

cal accomplishments. Yet, as we have argued repeatedly, professional life is not about technical matters alone: whether one is talking about dealing with clients, colleagues, superiors, or subordinates, success in professional life is also about (perhaps, ultimately, even more about) the ability to deal with other human beings.

How do you identify attitudes and personality characteristics in the hiring process? Interviews help, of course, particularly if you pay attention to the non-work-related things that people have done with their lives. There used to be a maxim that having organized a scout troop when you were young to help old people cross the road would count more toward getting admitted to the Harvard Business School than a few extra points in your school record. This may not be literally accurate, but it reflects a great truth that those who have already shown initiative, drive, and organizing ability in their personal lives will probably show it in their work lives.

On similar grounds, it is worth paying attention to the previous jobs someone has held. Has this person ever had to deal directly with any form of clients or customers? Has she ever held a job that required her to deal with the public? The specifics don't matter, but the experience and practice such jobs give in developing interpersonal, social, and emotional skills can be invaluable. Past experience (no matter how brief, nor how long ago) in some form of retail sales, we have observed, is an immensely useful background.

It is possible to go beyond interviews to screen for attitudes and personality. Two firms in our experience were creative about their interviewing process. The first, a law firm asked all candidates at their final interview to say which had been their favorite course in law school. After giving the candidate a half-hour to think about it, they asked him to explain the content of the course to a secretary. The secretary, in essence, had the final say on whether the person was hired. It was not enough, this firm believed, to know your stuff. Before you were hired, you had to demonstrate the ability to explain it to an intelligent layperson.

The second firm, accountants, brought all their final candidates together, and put them in a room with a two-way mirror. The candidates were told they would be observed, and were asked to do a joint exercise (equivalent to building a house out of playing cards). The resulting behavior was fascinating to watch. Thinking that they were suppose to be demonstrating leadership, many candidates competed to "take charge" of their group. In fact, the accounting firm was looking for people who felt comfortable being part of a team without the ego need to be its leader, and made offers only to those who did not try to dominate.

If your purpose in recruiting is to try and discover the truth about each candidate's character, the equivalent is also true in reverse. Candidates want to know what it really is like to work for your group. **It is foolhardy in the interview process to misrepresent in any way what your group has to offer in terms of work environment, client challenges, degree of collaboration and teamwork.** If someone joins you because they bought into a "pitch" that turns out to be false, or even slightly exaggerated, they will discover the deception in the first week. Recruiting interviews are about trying to uncover a true compatibility, so that both sides can work together with energy and passion. Tell the truth, warts and all.

chapter 20

Integrate New People

How do you ensure the success of new hires?

"**T**HE GREATEST HAVOC comes when a firm is unable to integrate new people into the culture of the firm," claims Robert M. Dell, leader of the law firm Latham & Watkins. It can be disruptive to introduce new capabilities and personalities into an established and well functioning group. With each addition, the group's requirements for communication grow exponentially. The addition of even one new member requires that the entire team regroup and rebond, finding new ways of working and ultimately recreating their dynamics and working style.

It takes time and effort to integrate a new team member. Without it, the new member may (and indeed, often does) flounder, become isolated, create conflict, or worse. While some firms may try (even in this day and age) to rationalize a sink-or-swim philosophy with junior people, most firms cannot afford the internal and external impact (not to mention the costs) of people coming and going with frequency.

Each group is, of course, special, having its own unique culture, systems, strategies, and ways of doing things. People take pride in the fact that their group is different and often go out of their way to convey that difference in discussions with any new addition to the group. As good talent becomes harder to find (and increasingly harder to retain) your internal processes for orientation and integration (how you welcome these valuable new-comers to your group) become absolutely critical.

After all, **you're not just hiring a warm body. In most cases you're adopt-ing a new colleague, or someone you expect has the potential to become a colleague, into your family.** With a little thought and attention you can take steps to ensure that these new hires don't take a good look behind the curtains and head back onto the open market.

Search consultants Major, Hagen & Africa conducted a survey of 1,200 lat-erally hired people at 253 law firms nationwide. They codified the factors that make laterals (senior hires) satisfied with their new firms, and asked these laterals to rank how effectively their new firms worked to integrate them into the culture. Alarmingly, of the six firms cited as examples of "where new laterals felt best integrated," people at only two of the six rated their firms a 4 on a 5 (very effective) point scale. The remaining four firms scored only a 3 out of 5. One wonders what the remaining firms are doing (or frankly, not doing) to rate such a dismal performance score.

There are, of course, places where this integration is done superbly. Listen to Eric Vautour, managing director of the Washington, D.C. office of exec-utive recruiters Russell Reynolds Associates, who told us this:

> I believe that having a systematic way to integrate new people is essential. Three or four times a year I invite a cou-ple of recent hires and a couple of senior people, together with their spouses, to my home in Vermont for a weekend of social activities. I work to make sure that there is a mix of ages, specialities, background, and so on. We spend the weekend enjoying ourselves and getting to know each other.
>
> The benefits from this have been numerous. The new people get to hear war stories, of successes and failures, and become "part of the firm" very quickly. Our culture and val-ues are imparted informally but firmly. Real bonds form be-tween new and experienced people such that a new person feels comfortable, once back in the office, to reach out to the senior person and ask for guidance or help, something that doesn't normally happen. We benefit from much higher degrees of collaboration, and getting people up to speed

quickly in functioning as a real team player. I can't imagine not doing this.

INITIATIVES TO INTEGRATE NEW ADDITIONS

Here are some steps to integrate new additions:

1. Manage first impressions
2. Give them support—before they ask
3. Make them feel valued
4. Provide an immersion experience.
5. Communicate, communicate, communicate.

1 MANAGE FIRST IMPRESSIONS

First impressions are critical. Design an orientation program that provides information to people as soon they arrive. Remember to introduce your group to the new person and the new person to the group.

One practice team greets new people by having their photos taken and affixed to a large sheet of flip-chart paper that also displays the personal answers to two questions in the new people's own words: my most gratifying personal achievement and my most important transaction. The sheet is then posted on the boardroom wall at the group's next regularly scheduled meeting.

One public relations firm insists that new people in each office travel to the other offices of the firm within their first month in order to meet, get to know, and develop collaborative working relationships with their fellow team members working in the same area.

A simple memo from the group leader (distributed on the day of their arrival) welcoming new people and sharing pertinent details (where they came from, what they do, their credentials, new office location, secretarial assignment, etc.) can do wonders. Suddenly everyone in the group knows enough to say "hello" and "welcome."

2 GIVE THEM SUPPORT—BEFORE THEY ASK.

New people require a clear understanding of their group's expectations. They also need introductions to specific people that can support their aspirations, training on the equipment and systems they may need, and a tour of the facilities. Someone must invest the time necessary to make them feel welcome. It is up to the group leader to organize this.

The executive director at one consulting firm invested in a staff coordinator whose task was to spend one-on-one time with new additions during their first days in the office. She trains them on the telephone system, explains firm resources, shows them how to access the computer network, makes introductions to staff members with whom the person will interact, talks through office kitchen protocol, and answers the myriad of seemingly trivial questions no one would wish to ask the person in the next office.

3 MAKE THEM FEEL VALUED

High-quality internal training programs not only give people the skills they need, but also send the clear message that you care about people's career development and are willing to invest in them as individuals. According to one group leader, "It is the quality of the client assignments and the quality of the people in our team that often tips the balance between whether a person stays or leaves."

This leader reports that his group holds a special meeting on the very first morning of the lateral's arrival at the office. This gives the entire group a chance to strategize with the newcomer about which of their existing client matters the newcomer will get involved in, and which of the firm's clients might benefit from an introduction to the new person. Any discussion as to which of the lateral's clients could be cross-sold is held in abeyance until this new person develops some sense of trust from having become integrated into the work with existing clients of the group.

One group leader makes it a habit to conduct a two-hour interview with every new addition, following their initial month with the group. She asks for their observations of what they have seen or experienced that could be improved. Since new hires have often worked somewhere else, they bring with them knowledge and experience that can benefit their new team.

Sometimes new hires bring experience that can be immediately applied. Don't wait. Include them in the group's joint marketing projects or in the delivery of substantive internal training efforts, if they have the interest. Their experiences in a different environment and with different clients can often provide a shot of new energy for your team.

Experiencing an early success helps newcomers establish their own confidence and place in the firm and gives their co-workers confidence in them.

 PROVIDE AN IMMERSION EXPERIENCE

Orientation systems that steep newcomers in the personalities and culture of their new group build career-long relationships that support success in their new environment. Think bonding. Think teamwork.

One practice team goes so far as to run a special program welcoming the spouses of those they have just hired. As one lateral tells it,

> Loyalty is a funny thing. It never comes in the same envelope as my draw check. But it can be nurtured to the extent that you take an active interest in the members of my family. So, if you are truly interested in building my loyalty, help me make my "significant other" feel part of the family.
>
> Have you involved them in any firm or group functions, helped them get integrated into any important community networks, found a way to promote their individual business or career interests? Remember, how my spouse feels about the firm has a profound impact on how encouraging he is toward enduring my long hours, and ultimately how I feel about becoming a member of your team.

Who will take responsibility for organizing lunches and dinners for the new lateral hire? Don't leave it to individual initiative. Someone (preferably the group leader) should take it upon herself to create regular social occasions for the new person to develop personal as well as professional ties with your team members.

5 COMMUNICATE, COMMUNICATE, COMMUNICATE

Those groups that take internal communications seriously tend to do a far better job of retention. One group conducts an annual internal survey of its people (including junior people and support staff) to give them a voice and let them share their feelings, offer constructive ideas, or vent concerns. The results are shared with absolutely everyone.

The group leader conducts a two-way feedback process to assess the results, celebrate strengths, and get constructive suggestions for remedial action. He reports that the real value of the survey is that because it is annual it allows the group to monitor their progress. Surveys can be used to promote constructive change.

Is your group lucky enough to have a group leader with a dose of infectious enthusiasm? One midwestern group leader begins each week with a "good-morning" voice-mail message, broadcast to the entire group, introducing new people, announcing special achievements, and discussing client news and developments. E-mail and internal newsletters are full of wonderful cultural tips for the new arrival (and are a great "refresher" tool for everyone else).

IT'S YOUR INVESTMENT TO MANAGE

If you believe that what your group earns its living from its talent and skill, then making people want to stay is a very good business strategy. It makes sense to bring in good people, help them succeed, and invest some time in making them part of the fabric of the group. Too often, when a new person fails to make it in a group, it's because the group failed the person.

Newcomers deserve your support. It only works to your advantage to have them settled in and thriving as soon as possible. Help them understand how they can best contribute to your group's success and then make sure everyone is contributing to theirs. It only makes sense, having made the initial investment, that you work hard to guard the long-term success of this, your greatest strategic asset.

chapter 21

Control Your Group's Size

How do you respond to the problems of size?

BIGGER DOES NOT ALWAYS MEAN BETTER, and nowhere is that more evident than when it comes to measuring group effectiveness. One of the surest ways to ensure failure is to allow membership to grow beyond a small, solid working group. Firms seem to allow leaders to build large groups, because these leaders mistakenly believe that if they have a big group with a big budget, then their role as group leader must be important.

Moreover, many firms seem to demonstrate their seriousness about group structure by attaching every single person to a number of different groups within the firm. The result is that groups have grown in size but decreased in effectiveness. Group members feel no real sense of attachment or personal commitment beyond having their names included in group brochures and they find that they are spending too many nonproductive hours in multiple group meetings.

While some may see larger groups as a means to bring more minds to bear on the growth and development of a practice, it soon becomes evident that not all of those minds actually have any significant contributions to bear. As the group size increases, an individual person's opportunity and ability to participate effectively decreases dramatically.

As the number of group members increases, participation, trust, and accountability also decrease. **The more people in a group, the less commitment any one person shows to following through on individual projects, and the less buy-in any individual has for the group's success or failure.** Members sense that there are other people around to pick up the slack. However, when people believe that their individual performance is important to the group's cumulative efforts, and that their progress is visible to their peers, they are more likely to be concerned about how their peers view them.

The larger the group, the more likely it is that a few power people or strong personalities will dominate the group's agenda, meeting discussions, and the decision making process. Others may choose to remain passive, hesitant to voice their ideas and opinions for fear of criticism, unwilling to disagree with the leader or give each other honest feedback, and not fully confident that they can depend on each other. Therefore, the level of interpersonal trust, always an important issue within the firm, can be damaged as the group size increases.

There is simply no getting around the fact that small groups work best. As Peter McKelvey of L.E.K., the strategy consulting firm, puts it:

> The rule of thumb that I use is that if I can't tell you the name of everyone's spouse (or significant other) in the group and what that person does for a living, the group has become too large. This rule of thumb accounts for the fact that certain individuals are more capable of leading larger groups than others.

What to do? Here are some options for you to consider:

1. Downsize your groups

2. Use a "resource member" approach

3. Create splinter groups

1 DOWNSIZE YOUR GROUPS

When new groups are formed, insist that they include fewer than a dozen people to start. Nick Jarrett-Kerr of Bevan Ashford notes:

> We never have more than twelve fee earners on a team. Sometimes, blessedly, we'll have just three or four. Tight, coherent teams—it doesn't sound like a profound or revolutionary idea, and, like much practice management, it is not, in fact, complicated. But actually being able to do it, making the commitment and finding ways to staff an ideal sized team, that is very challenging.

Reorganize existing groups into smaller units. It may not be easy to remove some people from some groups, but the long-term impacts on productivity makes this effort critical.

2 USE A "RESOURCE MEMBER" APPROACH

A core group should consist of only those whose full-time efforts are involved in the specialized area. The core group meets regularly and makes decisions on the direction for the practice and with respect to the group's business development efforts. Concurrently, group leaders remain free to invite others to assist and participate as substantive experts on specific client projects or to "help get stuff done" as the need may arise.

Each person must choose one core group to belong to. After making that choice, they may choose to serve as resource members for other groups that they wish to accommodate their personal interest or because of their occasional client work in the area.

As resource members, they are always welcome to sit in and to receive the minutes from any of the group's meetings. If and when they do attend meetings, they are welcome to contribute suggestions and involve themselves in brainstorming sessions. They are simply not expected to volunteer for projects unless a specific task or project might involve or benefit some of their individual clients

3 Create splinter groups

One obvious tactic may be to break up your larger teams into smaller practice-specific splinter groups, usually defined by the distinctive clients the group seeks to serve. In this model, the high-technology industry group might split into the computer technology group, the e-commerce group, and the biotechnology group. Not only will these focused groups be smaller, but they will have more in common and will be more likely to function as an integrated team.

Groups seem to be particularly prone to the temptation to grow in size in an effort to become more effective. We seem to do this even when common sense suggests that smaller is better. But then common sense is not always common practice.

SHALL WE CONTINUE AT ALL?

Jeremy Silverman, of Frontenac, the private equity firm, noted:

> Helping the team figure out when it has outlived its mission is also part of the leader's role. Our firm is organized around industry-focused teams, each of which addresses a different area of investment opportunity. As markets ebb and flow, we tend to group and regroup on about a three-year cycle. Acknowledging that an industry has lost its investment appeal is sometimes painful, but leading the group to that realization (and ensuring the rapid redeployment of the team's professionals to other pursuits) is essential to our long-term performance.

chapter 22

Measure Group Results

How do you measure your group's success?

WHATEVER INDICATORS ARE USED to measure your group's performance must be agreed upon with senior management at either the time of the group's formation or at the point the manager assumes responsibility. They must be in alignment with compensation as well as the firm's stated strategy or objectives for the time period. They must be clearly communicated to each team member both in terms of their impact on the firm as a whole and on them as individuals. Do not lead a team unless you know at the start how you (and the group) will be measured!

In assessing (and discussing) your group's performance, we recommend that you monitor, report, and debate a "balanced scorecard" of performance measures, mixing quantitative and nonquantitative measures and indicators that allow you to judge financial health, quality, market success and people development. Here's a comment from John Harris, regional CEO of BKD, LLP, a large accounting firm:

> We don't necessarily have precise dollar quotas, but the group leaders are evaluated against four measurable criteria.

The first measure is practice expansion, measurable in revenue and benchmarked against past performance and what the other groups are doing.

The second is people development: recruiting, turnover, training. It's not just growth numbers or attrition numbers that allow us to evaluate industry directors on this score. We also do 360-degree surveys on all our people, so we get a good picture of how their co-workers, from senior people to secretaries, feel they manage the human infrastructure.

Third are economic indicators, like realization. That's obviously measurable.

The fourth is client service. We use frequent formal client surveys for concrete data on how someone's doing. Of course, losing a big client will have a direct impact on a director's total performance evaluation as well.

We have a "key client program" that requires the firm managers as well as the regional firm leaders and the industry group directors to meet with clients. These aren't just goodwill tours. Every time I go to one of these meetings, I come away with ideas for new products and services.

Like all living things, your group is constantly changing and evolving. A periodic self-evaluation can help the group grow in the right direction.

Conducting a progress check can help identify strengths and obstacles to performance. It can also assist your efforts as the practice leader in knowing where to direct some of your coaching, training, feedback, and resources. This self-evaluation can be especially helpful when the group is having difficulty staying on schedule or appears stressed out for some other reason.

CONDUCTING A GROUP SELF-EVALUATION

A specific meeting dedicated to self-evaluating the team's progress is especially useful for celebrating accomplishments and developing an improvement plan. Before the meeting, you may want to distribute some questions to get members thinking about how the group is performing. These questions can help you guide your colleagues in an objective discussion of any sensitive group issues.

Here are the steps you should follow:

1. Explain that this is a time to improve teamwork, not to fix blame

2. Identify areas where the group members respond favorably and celebrate the group's performance

3. Ask which items the group feels a need to improve and why

4. Solicit ideas for improving weak areas

5. Develop an action plan to resolve those issues of highest priority

1. Explain that this is a time to improve teamwork, not to fix blame.

Recent research on motivation has verified at least two important facts: Performance tends to rise to the expected level of performance; and praise produces better results.

2. Identify areas where the group members respond favorably and celebrate the group's performance.

In the crush of day-to-day client priorities, a group can lose sight of how much progress it is actually making. One remedy is finding the means of identifying what is going well.

One further method of accomplishing this is to have each member describe one good thing that the team (or a specific group member) has done well in the past few months. This is a worthwhile activity when the group's energy seems to be waning, when the group has reached a specific milestone, or when you simply want to spotlight the growth that has occurred.

If no one volunteers, begin with yourself. Ask each group member to be specific. When recognizing a team effort, be sure to acknowledge hidden as well as obvious contributions, so no one feels slighted. When everyone has had a turn to speak, thank the group and move on. This activity may feel awkward at first, but after a few times most groups get a charge out of it.

3. Ask which items the group feels a need to improve and why

Ask your group which items on your assessment do you need to pay the most attention to and why? You might find that this discussion will surface important differences in perception, and help clarify your priorities.

4. Solicit ideas for improving areas where the group is experiencing weaknesses

By asking how you can work to improve these shortcomings, you will return the group to an action mode. Don't rush to judgment here. It is beneficial to generate alternatives and build consensus around the best initiatives.

5. Develop an action plan to resolve those issues of highest priority

Together with the group, divide the ideas that have been developed into categories:

1. Tasks that the group should take on now
2. Tasks the group should take on eventually
3. Tasks that should probably be addressed by the group leader

QUESTIONNAIRES

In assessing your group's performance, you also need to test how well members feel it is functioning. We suggest that you consider circulating (and publicly reporting) two questionnaires. One is designed to take the temperature of the group. The second is to ask the group to evaluate your performance as group head. Here are the two questionnaires:

GROUP MEMBER QUESTIONNAIRE

Ask your group members whether they agree or disagree with the following statements:

1. Members of our group are committed to accomplishing our objectives.
2. Members of our group get a lot of encouragement for new ideas.

3. Members of our group freely express their real views.

4. Every member of our group has a clear idea of the group's goals.

5. Everyone is involved in the decisions we have to make.

6. We tell each other how we are feeling.

7. All group members display respect for each other.

8. The feelings among group members tend to pull us together.

9. Everyone's opinion gets listened to.

10. There is very little bickering among group members.

11. We have the right skills, personalities and sufficiently motivated group members.

12. This group is challenging and fun to work with.

13. What needs to be done next is clear and correct.

14. I am satisfied with the progress of the group to date in moving toward its objectives.

List the three major accomplishments that you are proud of the group having achieved over the past three months (quarter):

List three things that should have been accomplished by now, but haven't been:

EVALUATING YOU

There is an old military saying that goes, "Leadership is not saying 'Charge'; it is saying 'Follow Me!'" Accordingly, **if you want to send a message that your group should be willing to review and be held accountable for its performance, it follows that you should be willing to go first.**

We recommend that, once a year, you invite all your people to evaluate your performance as a practice leader, using a form that asks questions similar to those given below. The results should be tabulated by a third party, and the averages published to all the members of your group. You can then have a candid discussion about where they think you are strong in your role, and where you have room for improvement.

This is scary, but powerful. And at the end of the process, you are better positioned to say, "OK, I've been willing to discuss my performance, now it's your turn!" Here are some of the questions we would suggest you include:

The Group Leader:

1. Causes me to stretch for performance goals

2. Is concerned about long-term issues, not just short-term profits

3. Provides constructive feedback that helps me improve my performance

4. Is a source of creative ideas about our business

5. Helps me to grow and develop

6. Conducts team meetings in a manner that breeds involvement

7. Makes me feel that I am a member of a well-functioning team

8. Emphasizes cooperation as opposed to competitiveness between work groups

9. Is prompt in dealing with underperformance and underperformers

10. Helps me understand how my tasks fit into the overall objectives for the firm

11. Keeps me informed about the things I need to know to perform my role properly

12. Actively encourages me to volunteer new ideas and make suggestions for improvement of the practice

13. Encourages me to initiate tasks or projects I think are important

14. Is good at keeping down the level of "politics and politicking"

15. Is more often encouraging than critical

16. Is accessible when I want to talk

17. Is fair in dealings with people

18. Is consultative in his/her decision making

19. Acts more like a coach than a boss

20. Is publicly generous with credit

21. Is effective in communicating with people

We are confident that if you do well on these questions, you and your group will work in harmony and accomplish a superb performance.

CLIENT SATISFACTION

We have both long been advocates of putting in place some form of client feedback, highly visible to all in the group, so that success with clients comes to be considered as at least equally important as all other means of measuring group success. Tim Morton, president of the U.S. and Latin American E-solutions group at EDS, describes their approach to this:

> We have in place a web-based "service excellence dashboard," which, among other things, allows clients to provide, in real time, comments, positive or negative, about our service. Our company's chairman, Dick Brown, looks at the dashboard every day, calling it up on his laptop when he's on the road, and can check the status of every client project we have. Many of our clients use the dashboard on a weekly basis!
>
> All this has made us much more responsive to clients, and feel much more accountable. There is more to the dashboard than just the client feedback. It also tracks project status which is accessible to a wide range of relevant professionals, and has led us to anticipate issues better, and have people pitch in when they see other teams with a problem.

At a time when some groups are still debating whether to do annual surveys of clients, and who should see the results, the stakes have now been raised. Welcome to the world of enforced excellence and strict accountability to clients!

NONFINANCIAL MEASURES: ASSESSING THE CALIBER OF THE PRACTICE

Bringing in more business is always nice, but the real key to success is bringing in better business: more profitable, more challenging and skill-building. We suggest that, once a quarter, you get your group together, review every piece of new work that you obtained, and discuss for each piece of new business the following questions:

Did this engagement:

1. Allow us to learn new skills?

2. Deepen (not just sustain) an important existing client relationship?

3. Introduce us to an important new client?

4. Allow us to work with more important people in an existing client relationship?

5. Get us into an exciting new industry or client sector?

6. Allow us to command higher fees than in the past?

7. Allow us to leverage more than in the past?

Another way of examining your marketing success is to examine the following ratios:

1. Client loyalty ratio: What percentage of your revenues will recur next year without any effort?

2. Win-loss ratio: What percentage of assignments that you pursue do you win?

3. Assignment size: What is the size (total fees) of your average assignment?

4. Penetration ratio: What percentage of all fees spent by a client on services in your area do they pay to you?

5. Sole source ratio: What percentage of your business is won on a noncompetitive, sole-source basis?

6. New client ratio: What percentage of this year's revenues are from clients you had never worked for prior to this year?

7. Client retention ratio: What percentage of your top ten clients were top ten clients three, or five, years ago?

8. New service ratio: What percentage of your revenues come from services you didn't offer three or five years ago?

9. Rainmaker ratio: What percentage of your senior people have a demonstrated capability of bringing in a volume of business at least triple our average revenue per person?

PEOPLE MEASURES

Karl Kristoff shared this observation:

> I think you measure success on a number of different levels. Certainly, we can't lose sight of the fact that we're a business, so profitability is important, and maybe in some views the most important criteria.
>
> However, I also measure success based on the satisfaction of the people who are practicing in the group. I think experience teaches that people who are satisfied and happy with what they're doing will perform better and, at the end of the day, be more profitable for the firm.

You must also assess the people health of your group. You will want to look at:

a. Your turnover rates (percentage of people leaving you; In many businesses it is helpful to break this down into the percent joining competitors, the percent joining clients and the percent leaving the profession)

b. Your success in getting your people promoted

c. How good you are at exporting talent to other groups

d. How good you are at importing talent from other groups

While quantitative measures of "people performance" are hard to create, it is a good idea to use regular questionnaires to take the temperature of your (senior and junior) people's enthusiasm, and their own perception of self-development. On the website for this book (www.firstamongequals.com) there is an extensive (and downloadable) set of questionnaires you can use to get people to rate their work experience. A few sample questions from that source are shown in the sidebar.

ASSESSING FINANCIAL PERFORMANCE

Different businesses have different ways of measuring financial success. For example, it makes sense to calculate a "profit per partner" in a partnership but not, obviously, in a corporation. In-house professionals might not use the concept of "profit," and may not charge fees.

Sample items for a group member satisfaction survey. (Ask your group members whether they agree or disagree with the following statements.)

The Work Itself

My work makes good use of my knowledge and ability.

I feel I am still learning and growing.

I am very satisfied with the sense of personal accomplishment my work provides.

I am very satisfied with the chance to do interesting work.

I am very satisfied with the overall challenge my work offers.

Collaboration

When I am on a difficult assignment I can usually count on getting assistance from my colleagues.

I am satisfied with the teamwork in the group.

I am satisfied with the level of communication in the group.

I feel that I am a member of a well-functioning team.

Performance Evaluation

I am satisfied with the opportunities to discuss my performance.

I understand the measures used to evaluate my performance.

I think my performance is evaluated fairly.

Performance reviews have been useful in helping me improve my job performance.

I receive useful performance feedback throughout the year.

Development

Overall, our training and development program meets my needs well.

The group has done a good job of providing the training I've needed to do my job well.

I am encouraged by the group to learn new skills.

Sample items for a group member satisfaction survey. *(Cont.)*

I am given the chance at the group to learn new skills.

Coaching

I receive good coaching to help me improve my performance.

I receive prompt feedback on my work, good or bad.

When I do a good job, I am usually recognized and complimented for it.

When there is a need to correct me for something I did or failed to do, it is usually done in a constructive way.

I can usually get help with conflicting deadlines and priorities when they arise.

When I need help or have questions, colleagues are readily available and accessible to talk to.

People in my group are publicly generous with credit.

The group treats people with trust and respect.

Group Culture

The group is responsive to individual professional needs.

Most people in our group do "whatever it takes" to do a good job for their clients.

In this group we set very high standards for performance.

The quality of the professionals in our group is as high as can reasonably be expected.

I feel free to voice my opinion openly in the group.

Poor performance is not tolerated at the group.

I am very satisfied with the friendliness of my colleagues and professionals.

The level of politics and politicking around here is low.

My colleagues and professionals have high enthusiasm and morale right now.

The following measures should, however, be generally applicable:

1. Profit margin.

   The most widely used overall profitability measure.

2. Average (implied) rate per hour.

   Even if you do not price your services on an hourly basis, it is immensely valuable to divide total revenues by total work hours to calculate an implied rate per hour. This is a good indicator of your relative positioning in the market.

3. Average billable (or client-service) hours per person (chargeability).

   Again, even if you do not bill by the hour, it is useful to know the average production workload per person.

4. Leverage.

   The proportion of your work that is done by junior people, relative to that done by senior people. In general, increasing leverage (assuming the same quality) is an indicator of increased efficiency.

5. Unbilled work-in-progress.

6. Receivables.

   These two measures test your fiscal hygiene. Are you billing the work you do promptly, and are clients paying those bills promptly?

7. Fees generated for other groups of the firm.

8. Fees generated for the group by others in the firm.

   These two measures ("import" and "export" of work to and from your group measure how interconnected your group is with the rest of your firm.)

9. Growth in fees.

   Getting bigger is a nice indicator of market acceptance of your group. But always remember, the goal is performance, not size. You should worry about doing better work, being more profitable, and challenging your people. These are the things that result in growth. Growth without these things is of dubious value.

Given the variety of possible financial measures, how do you decide which to focus on? Here's one way of looking at it:

Start with a simple formula:

Profit = (Profit per Officer) times (Number of Officers)

In this formula, the word "Officer" is meant to refer to a senior person. Thus, in a partnership, officer might mean partner, while in a corporation, officer might mean a senior vice president.

The point of this simple formula is to note that there are two broad categories of profit improvement approaches. First, you could keep the profit per officer the same, and grow your bottom line by adding officers (in essence, a simple growth strategy).

This approach is valuable to the owners of the firm, because total profits go up. However, the problem with this method is that it leaves the profit per officer the same, and hence there are no extra funds to distribute to any one given officer (or members of their team). Profits have increased, but not profitability.

Because of this, increasing profits per officer is a much more attractive strategy. It provides both extra profits for firm owners and a surplus to pay more to those in the operating groups.

Figure 22-1 shows a way to look at profit per officer.

What this reveals is that profit per officer is the simple multiplication of four key submeasures: *margin, rate, utilization* (also referred to as chargeability or billability), and *leverage.*

Two of these four factors (margin and utilization) are what we term "hygiene" issues, while two others (rate and leverage) reflect changes in fundamental profit health. To understand the difference between these

Figure 22-1

$$\frac{PROFITS}{OFFICERS} = \frac{PROFITS}{FEES} \times \frac{FEES}{HOURS} \times \frac{HOURS}{PEOPLE} \times \frac{PEOPLE}{OFFICERS}$$

$$= \text{MARGIN} \times \text{RATE} \times \text{UTILIZATION} \times \text{LEVERAGE}$$

categories, consider (as an illustration) two of the four ways of improving profit per officer: increasing utilization or increasing rate. One group may have improved its profitability by working more hours per person. Another may have achieved exactly the same profit improvement by working the same number of hours per person as the previous year, but raising its rate per hour through some combination of client service, specialization, innovation, or bringing in higher-rate transactions.

These two groups may have achieved the same profit per officer improvements, but their accomplishments are not commensurate. **Increasing utilization (or hours worked) means you made more money because you worked harder. It is a nontrivial accomplishment, but it is primarily a short-term achievement. (We call it the cart-horse strategy: achieving more by pulling a heavier load.)**

However, a group that made more money, not by working harder but by getting the market to place a higher value on each hour worked, has accomplished something much more profound and long-lasting. By definition, they have made themselves more valuable on the marketplace.

The same argument can be made for the difference between margin and leverage. Improving margin is (mostly) about controlling overhead expenses. Important, but nevertheless hygiene. But a group that finds a way to deliver its services with less senior officer time and more junior time must, by definition, have built an asset: It has found a way to get work done by using lower-cost people. To have leveraged successfully, it must have found new ways to deliver its services, to train and manage people to handle what they could not before, and to establish new methodologies.

To see how these categories can be used, examine Figure 22-2, which shows the financial results for a firm of six (fictional) groups.

It can be seen that all groups improved their profitability, but in very differing ways. It is even easier to see what has happened if all results for each group are expressed as a percentage of the respective firmwide averages, as is done in Figure 22-3.

It is clear that group 1, with the highest firmwide profit per officer, achieves this result almost entirely by being in a high-fee-level market, with none of its other performance measures being particularly high. Is the group to be

Figure 22-2: *BASIC DATA FOR SIX GROUPS*

	Last Year					This Year				
	Margin	Rate	Utilization	Leverage	PPO*	Margin	Rate	Utilization	Leverage	PPO*
Group 1	0.318	$190.8	1425	4.3	$371.8K	0.299	$186.6	1503	4.6	$385.7K
Group 2	0.390	$115.2	1710	4.6	$353.4K	0.387	$117.1	1720	4.9	$381.9K
Group 3	0.413	$127.2	1500	4.5	$354.6K	0.414	$128.1	1612	4.2	$359.1K
Group 4	0.398	$ 91.2	1725	4.7	$294.3K	0.425	$103.7	1472	4.8	$311.4K
Group 5	0.356	$121.2	1335	4.8	$276.5K	0.368	$117.1	1612	4.4	$305.6K
Group 6	0.375	$112.8	1740	3.2	$235.5K	0.341	$115.3	1658	3.9	$254.2K
FIRM AVGE	0.377	$122.7	1560	4.5	$314.3K	0.379	$124.3	1599	4.5	$334.5K

*PPO = profit per officer

Figure 22-3: *RESULTS EXPRESSED AS AN INDEX OF FIRM AVERAGES*

	Last Year					This Year				
	Margin	Rate	Utilization	Leverage	PPO*	Margin	Rate	Utilization	Leverage	PPO*
Group 1	84	155	91	96	118	79	150	94	102	115
Group 2	104	94	110	103	112	102	94	108	108	114
Group 3	110	104	96	101	113	109	103	101	93	107
Group 4	106	74	111	105	94	112	83	92	106	93
Group 5	95	99	86	107	88	97	94	101	97	91
Group 6	100	92	112	71	75	90	93	104	86	76
FIRM AVGE	100	100	100	100	100	100	100	100	100	100

rewarded for good performance or does this reflect good fortune and good location?

Group 2 shows good overall results, but these are achieved mostly through hygiene factors of chargeability (utilization) and margin control. Neither of its "health factors" (rate or leverage) is strong, although leverage improved a little in the latest year.

A final productive way of summarizing and presenting this information is to calculate a hygiene index (by multiplying the margin index by the utilization index) and a health index (multiplying the rate index by the leverage index). This is done in Figure 22-4.

It is now easier to see what has happened in each group. Group 1 has increased its profitability by pushing even further on its fundamental health, but its hygiene continues to deteriorate relative to the rest of the firm. It may be the most profitable group, but clear guidance for even further improvement could be given. Group 2 has done a good job of improving its profit health, and should be commended. Group 3, while it improved its cash profit per officer, has slipped relative to the rest of the firm, and in particular has let its profit health decline badly.

Group 4 has done a good job of profit health, but lost its superior position in hygiene: it still has work to do. Group 5 has the opposite (and much worse) problem. It has fixed a hygiene problem, but at the expense of dealing with profit health. While it, too, improved its cash profits per officer (up from $276.5K to $305.6K), it still has problems. Group 6 has made little progress.

Figure 22-4: *HEALTH AND HYGIENE*

Last Year				This Year		
Hygiene Index	Health Index	PPO Index		Hygiene Index	Health Index	PPO Index
77	149	118	Group 1	74	153	115
113	96	112	Group 2	110	102	114
105	104	113	Group 3	110	96	107
117	78	94	Group 4	103	92	91
81	106	88	Group 5	98	92	91
111	66	75	Group 6	93	80	76

CONCLUSION

We must stress again that none of this analysis presumes what type of group you have. We don't assume that you are a profit center, or bill by the hour, or are in private practice rather than in-house. We believe that the concepts of measuring clients, people, and financial outcomes is generally applicable, and that important distinctions must be made in all groups between health and hygiene. The suggestions made here will, we hope, stimulate your thinking about the right set of outcome measures for your group.

chapter 23

Why Bother?

Why would you want to do all this?

WE HAVE DESCRIBED IN THIS BOOK a role full of chal-
lenges. Group leaders, as player-coaches, must give up some portion of the
client or production work they were trained to do, are certainly skilled at,
and probably find deeply satisfying. For what? The chance to deal with the
emotions of their colleagues. The responsibility to be the one to let people
know they could do better. The obligation to resolve conflicts and crises.
All of which requires skills that no one ever trained you for.

The most common reaction we hear when we discuss group leadership
with professionals is: "But no one ever taught us this stuff! Nowhere in our
education or growth within the firm were we ever given practice at these
skills! How are we going to find good managers in such an environment?"

We don't underestimate the challenge. One of the tragedies of professional
life is that throughout our schooling we are taught to focus on the logical,
the rational, and the analytical. This orientation continues through the
many years of our apprenticeship, when we are usually junior members of
project teams, responsible for analytical work. The message we receive is:
"Keep your head down, get it right, do it fast, and don't mess up."

Nowhere along the way does anyone emphasize the importance of social, interpersonal, and emotional skills in determining our success in professional life. Then the day arrives when we make a terrifying discovery: The world is filled with people: clients, colleagues, subordinates and superiors. And that dealing with them draws upon attitudes and skills that no one ever taught us. The fact that many of us come to the realization late in our careers that these skills are important is a reason to try harder to acquire them, not an excuse to abandon all efforts.

Another common reaction we get is: "Why should I want to take on this role? If it means giving up some of my client work, or production work, won't I be putting my career at risk by spending time managing and not practicing my profession?"

The first point to make is that you are probably a player-coach, not a full-time coach. You haven't given up your profession by becoming the group leader. Whether or not you keep up your professional skills is more a matter of the caliber of work you do, not its quantity.

The news is even better. Consider the range of skills we have discussed: listening, empathizing, understanding and influencing another human being, being able to get things done through others. All of these skills are immensely valuable to a client counselor. We started the book by asking you to consider whether the talents of a trusted advisor to clients were similar to those of being a trusted advisor to one's colleagues. We now ask you to consider the question in reverse: would learning how to win and earn trust from your colleagues, learning how to be a person that others accept guidance from, would all that help you become more valuable to your clients, and be more valuable on the marketplace? We think the answer is a resounding "Yes!"

There are financial benefits as well. In *Practice What You Preach* David was able to provide solid evidence that there is a strict sequence for making superior profits. First, he showed, you must energize and excite your people. If you do that, your people will serve your marketplace with outstanding quality and service. And if you do that, you'll earn superior profits. So how do you launch this sequence? The evidence was clear: by having group managers in place who are dedicated to bringing out the best in those around them.

But the reasons for wanting to perform this challenging role are not all self-ish, even if direct benefits to you do exist. There is also the comfort and sat-isfaction that comes from knowing that you have made a difference in people's lives. That you have helped them accomplish more than they ever dreamed that they could. That you helped people understand themselves more deeply and more accurately, and helped them find a path in profes-sional life that would play to their special strengths. **It gives you a chance to put your head on your pillow and say: I made a difference in some-one's life today. It doesn't happen every day, but when it does, it is deeply fulfilling.**

Rob Duboff said it this way:

> I recognize how lucky I was at the beginning of my ca-reer. The first boss I worked for argued with me all the time (and I with him). He cared enough about a young kid to ar-gue, to try to teach and to make sure I got the lessons. He didn't just dictate and he made sure to meet my family and talk to them as well. That's the attitude that I've always tried to convey: that I care about the person that produces the work. And that's the type of person I've put in leadership po-sitions when I've had the chance.

Think back on your own career. Did you ever have a great mentor, leader, or manager who made a difference to your career (and your life)? Most people who succeed did. There was that one person who gave us a chance, gave us significant responsibility that stretched us, but was there, watching from the sidelines, to make sure we didn't go down in flames. Maybe you had a chance to say "Thank you," to that person, and maybe you didn't, but the group leadership role gives you a chance to pass the favor on.

We have given a great deal of advice in this book. Naturally, you cannot act on it all at once. To help you plan your implementation, we present here a brief summary of the lists in this book, grouped into the following cate-gories:

A) Diagnostic tests

B) Defining the group and its rules

C) About you

D) Influencing individuals

E) Group management processes

F) What to do each week

 SOME DIAGNOSTIC TESTS

If you already have a group, then the wisest first step is to do a "temperature-taking" of the current state of affairs. We included in the text some lists that will help you evaluate how well your group is currently functioning and also use to reflect on which issues you care most about. The relevant lists are:

   i. A diagnostic test to see if you have a well-functioning group (Introduction)

  ii. Diagnostic signs of lack of group trust (chapter 13)

 iii. Diagnostic signs of interpersonal conflict (chapter 17)

 iv. Warning signs of bad meetings (chapter 15)

   v. A group member questionnaire (chapter 22)

 vi. Assessing the caliber of the group's engagements (chapter 22).

 vii. Another way of examining your marketing success (chapter 22)

viii. Example questions for a group member satisfaction survey (chapter 22).

 ix. Examine financial measures (chapter 22)

 DEFINING THE GROUP AND ITS RULES

As we indicated at the beginning of the book, there are certain things you must do to get started, to establish or clarify the rules by which you and your group will operate, and what kind of group or team you want to be. Here are all the lists that are relevant to that task:

   i. Get agreement on what you should spend time on (chapter 1)

  ii. Establish your terms of engagement with firm management. (chapter 2)

 iii. Establish group rules of conduct (chapter 11)

 iv. Establish common non-negotiable minimum standards (chapter 11)

   v. Decide what your group should be intolerant of (chapter 11)

  vi. Decide what your group will require of each other (chapter 11)

 vii. Decide your group's purpose (chapter 11)

viii. Establish the desired benefits from acting as a group (chapter 12)

  ix. Test your group's readiness to be a group (chapter 12)

   x. Questions to ask each group member (chapter 12)

  xi. Establish agreement on trust behaviors (chapter 13)

 xii. Identify a compelling challenge (chapter 14)

xiii. Establish your reasons to hold meetings (chapter 15)

xiv. Decide your meeting rules (chapter 15)

ABOUT YOU

As we pointed out in the text, the most important predictor of group success is your own performance as leader. Here are the lists in the text that are about you:

   i. Decide how you will make a difference (chapter 1)

  ii. Assess your current behavior (chapter 3)

 iii. Compare yourself to the characteristics of a trusted advisor (chapter 3)

 iv. Follow the rules of romance and relationship building (chapter 3)

  v. Compare yourself to the list of what good listeners do (chapter 6)

 vi. Examine the behaviors of leaders in a success culture (chapter 3)

vii. Use a questionnaire to get your people to evaluate you (chapter 22)

INFLUENCING INDIVIDUALS

Now we turn to the lists that deal with how you interact with individuals.

   i. Ask each colleague about his or her aspirations and interests (chapter 3)

  ii. Use guidelines to determine when coaching is required (chapter 5)

 iii. Win permission to coach (chapter 5)

iv. Give corrective feedback (chapter 5)

v. Establish the goals of your counseling process (chapter 5)

vi. Formalize the stages of your counseling process (chapter 5)

vii. Establish formal criteria for performance (chapter 5)

viii. Assess the contribution to the group of each member (chapter 5)

ix. Establish the list of skills to be assessed and nurtured (chapter 5)

x. Use techniques to communicate with bad listeners (chapter 6)

xi. Consider the different forms of commitment (chapter 7)

xii. Apply the styles grid (chapter 7)

xiii. Use the distinguishing characteristics of each style to determine how to deal with each individual (chapter 7)

xiv. Consider the various common causes of underperformance (chapter 8)

xv. Follow the steps to be taken to help a person (chapter 8)

xvi. Make use of non-financial currencies as a form of recognition (chapter 16)

xvii. Tackle the prima donnas (chapter 9)

xviii. Gain individual support for change (chapter 10):

E GROUP MANAGEMENT PROCESSES

Now we turn to the processes you use to manage your group, as a group.

i. Follow the process to build commitment (chapter 14)

ii. Manage investment time collectively (chapter 12)

iii. Bond your group together (chapter 13)

iv. Bring fun (and belonging and trust) into the workplace (chapter 13)

v. Follow the guidelines for an action-planning meeting (chapter 15)

vi. Prepare possible meeting topics (chapter 15)

vii. Follow guidelines for brainstorming sessions (chapter 15)

viii. Look for opportunities that warrant recognition (chapter 16)

ix. Follow guidelines for giving recognition (chapter 16)

x. Consider ways to provide recognition (chapter 16)

xi. Have an annual awards program (chapter 16)

xii. Understand four basic categories of conflict (chapter 17)

xiii. Follow the steps to resolve conflict (chapter 17)

xiv. Use the principles of crisis management (chapter 18)

xv. Tips for dealing with the loss of a client (chapter 18)

xvi. Tips for when you have to let some people go (chapter 18)

xvii. How to act when a valued colleague dies (chapter 18)

xviii. Establish your standards for work supervision (chapter 19)

xix. Steps to integrate new additions (chapter 20)

F   WHAT TO DO EACH WEEK

A friend suggested we compile a list of the questions a group leader should ask himself or herself each and every week. Here it is.

1) Is anyone in noncompliance with our group standards?

2) Is anyone struggling?

3) Who needs help, even if they're not struggling?

4) Who needs energizing?

5) Who needs recognition or appreciation?

6) Is there anyone I haven't had coffee or lunch with (or otherwise paid personal attention to) in a while?

7) Is anyone doing things that are disrupting the group?

8) Who do I have the least solid relationship with?

9) Are the juniors being looked after?

10) Are there any conflicts going on between group members?

You can us this list in two ways. Use it to look back on the past week, and ask yourself how many of these things you dealt with. Then use it to plan the coming week. Maybe you should put this list on a card, laminate it and keep it in plain view on your desk!

By accepting the responsibility to affect the performance of those around you, **you have a chance to make a difference and to leave a legacy.** Good luck!

NOTES ON SOURCES

INTRODUCTION

Philip Greenspun: *ArsDigita Systems Journal*, October 22, 2000 (on-line).

James Emerson, Jon Katzenbach, Laura Holmes: Communication with the authors.

David H. Maister, *Practice What You Preach*, Free Press, 2001.

Chapter 1: CLARIFY YOUR ROLE

Benjamin Haas, Deborah Koeffler, Jack Newman: Interviews with The Edge Group.

"A business group is like a sports team": David H. Maister, *Managing the Professional Service Firm*, Free Press, 1993, chapter 19.

John Schoenewald: Communication with the authors.

Chapter 2: CONFIRM YOUR MANDATE

Portions of this chapter are based on David H. Maister, "Are You Ready for Practice Group Coaches?", Maister Associates, 1999.

John Graham: quoted in *The Holmes Report*, The Holmes Group, New York, 2001.

Karl Kristoff, Robert Gilbert: Interviews with The Edge Group.

Katzenbach: Communication with the authors.

Chapter 3: BUILD RELATIONSHIPS—ONE AT A TIME

Characteristics of a trusted advisor: David H. Maister, C.H. Green, and R. M. Galford, *The Trusted Advisor*, Free Press, 2000, p. 4.

Ron Daniel: quoted in Marvin Bower, *The Will to Lead*, HBS Press, 1997, p. 24.

"Managers were notable less for their beliefs and actions than for their underlying character": Maister, *Practice What You Preach*.

"Get people to dream": Dale Carnegie, *How to Win Friends and Influence People*, Simon & Schuster, 1936.

267

Cliff Farrah: Communication with the authors.

Attributes of a successful coach: David H. Maister, *True Professionalism*, Free Press, 1997.

Robert E. Gilbert: Interview with The Edge Group.

Nonnegotiable standards: Maister, *Practice What You Preach*.

Chapter 4: DARE TO BE INSPIRING

Jack Welch: speech at Harvard Business Commencement Day, 2001, as quoted in *Harvard Business School Bulletin*, August 2001.

Rosamund Stone Zander and Benjamin Zander, *The Art of Possibility*, Harvard Business School Press, 2000.

Leo Burnett: *100 Leo's: Wit & Wisdom from Leo Burnett*, NTC Business Books, 1995 (a speech Leo Burnett delivered to employees at the company's annual breakfast meeting in 1967).

Peter Friedes: Communication with the authors.

Chapter 5: WIN PERMISSION TO COACH

Helen Hunt/Larry Moss story: *Los Angeles Magazine*, March 2001.

Daniel Fensin: Interview with Patrick McKenna.

Rob Duboff: Communication with the authors.

Albert Bandura, *Social Learning Theory*, Prentice-Hall, 1976.

Formal counseling: This section is adapted from Maister, *Managing the Professional Service Firm*, chapter 22.

Nick Jarrett-Kerr: Interview with The Edge Group.

Chapter 6: LISTEN TO BUILD RAPPORT

"What good listeners do": Maister et al., *The Trusted Advisor*, page 104.

Chapter 7: DEAL DIFFERENTLY WITH DIFFERENT PEOPLE

Dr. David Merrill, *Personal Style and Effective Performance*, St. Lucie Press, 1983. (Dr. Merrill's initial research has since been incorporated into training programs offered by Tracom Corporation and Wilson Learning.)

Phil Gott, Rob Duboff, Joachim Frank: Communication with the authors. Our thanks to Phil Gott for suggesting some of the terminology in figure 7–2.

Chapter 8: HELP UNDERPERFORMERS

Daniel Fensin: Interview with Patrick McKenna.

Chapter 10: BUILD SUPPORT FOR CHANGE

Jim Shaffer: Communication with the authors.

Patrick J. McKenna, G. Riskin, M. Anderson, *Beyond Knowing,* The Edge Group, 2000, pp. 17 and 18.

Chapter 11: CLARIFY GROUP GOALS

Karl Kristoff: Interview with The Edge Group.

Chapter 12: DEVELOP YOUR GROUP'S RULES FOR MEMBERSHIP

Deborah Koeffler, Jack Newman: Interviews with Patrick McKenna.

Collective management of investment time: This section is adapted from Maister, *Managing the Professional Service Firm,* chapter 21.

John Graham: Quoted in *The Holmes Report,* 2001.

Deborah Koeffler: Interview with The Edge Group.

Maister, *Practice What You Preach,* chapters 20, 21 and 22.

Chapter 13: BUILD TEAM TRUST

Daniel Fensin: Interview with Patrick McKenna.

Maister, *Practice What You Preach,* Chapters 21 and 22.

John Feinstein: Communication with the authors.

Chapter 14: THROW DOWN A CHALLENGE

Alfie Kohn, *Punished by Rewards,* Houghton Mifflin, 1999.

Jon Katzenbach: Communication with the authors.

Chicago Study: Mihaly Csikszentmihalyi, *Beyond Boredom and Anxiety,* Jossey-Bass, 1975.

McKenna et al., *Beyond Knowing,* p. 41.

Chapter 15: ENERGIZE YOUR MEETINGS

Daniel Fensin, Jack Newman, Benjamin Haas: Interviews with Patrick McKenna.

Chapter 16: GIVE RECOGNITION

Peter Friedes, Phil Gott, Jeremy Silverman: Communication with the authors.

Chapter 17: RESOLVE INTERPERSONAL CONFLICTS

Jean Lebedum, *Managing Workplace Conflict*, Amer Media Inc., 1998.

Roger Fisher and William Ury, *Getting to Yes*, Houghton Mifflin, 1981.

Chapter 18: DEAL WITH YOUR CRISES

Daniel Fensin: Interview with Patrick McKenna.

Chapter 19: NURTURE YOUR JUNIORS

Maister, *Practice What You Preach*, chapter 7.

Karl Kristoff, Nick Jarrett-Kerr: Interviews with Patrick McKenna.

Ogunlesi: Communication from Eileen Urban to the authors.

Francine Popoli Edelman: Communication with the authors.

Chapter 20: INTEGRATE NEW PEOPLE

Robert Dell: Interview with Patrick McKenna.

Major, Hagen & Africa: "Lateral Partner Satisfaction: Who has it, How they got it, and How to enhance it," a 1998 survey authored by Jonathan Lindsey and June Eichbaum, principals and co-founders of the New York office of Major, Hagen & Africa.

A special thanks to Merrilyn Astin Tarlton for her assistance in writing this chapter. Merrilyn is an Adjunct Professor at the University of Denver College of Law and editor of *Law Practice Management* magazine.

Chapter 21: CONTROL YOUR SIZE

Peter McKelvey: Communication with the authors.

Nick Jarrett-Kerr: Interview with Patrick McKenna.

Chapter 22: MEASURE GROUP RESULTS

John Harris: Interview with The Edge Group.

Assessing marketing results: Adapted from Maister, *True Professionalism*, chapter 20.

Rate the Group Leader: Maister, *Managing the Professional Service Firm,* p. 218.

Tim Morton: Communication with the authors.

Profit-per-Officer formula: Maister, *Managing the Professional Service Firm,* chapter 3.

Numerical example: David H. Maister, "Results and Rewards in the Multi-Site Firm," Maister Associates, 1994.

Chapter 23: WHY BOTHER?

Maister, *Practice What You Preach,* chapter 9.

Rob Duboff: Communication with the authors.

FURTHER READING

Among the many hundreds of books about groups, leadership, and professionals, here are a few that we would recommend to any group leader.

R. Meredith Belbin, *Beyond the Team,* Butterworth-Heinemann, 2000.

Kenneth Blanchard and Spencer Johnson, *The One-Minute Manager,* William Morrow, 1982.

Jim Calhoun, *Dare to Dream,* Broadway Books, 1999.

Dale Carnegie, *How to Win Friends and Influence People,* Simon & Schuster, 1936.

James Flaherty, *Coaching: Evoking Excellence in Others,* Butterworth-Heinemann, 1999.

John W. Gardner, *On Leadership,* The Free Press, 1990.

Jon R. Katzenbach and Douglas K. Smith, *The Wisdom of Teams,* Harvard Business School Press, 1993.

George David Kieffer, *The Strategy of Meetings,* Simon & Schuster, 1988.

James M. Kouzes and Barry Z. Posner, *The Leadership Challenge,* Jossey-Bass, 1995.

Max Landsberg, *The Tao of Coaching,* Harper Collins, 1997.

Jean Lipman-Blumen and Harold J. Leavitt, *Hot Groups,* Oxford University Press, 1999.

BIBLIOGRAPHY

Marvin Bower, *The Will to Lead,* Harvard Business School Press, 1997.

Dale Carnegie, *How to Win Friends and Influence People,* Simon & Schuster, 1936.

Alfie Kohn, *Punished by Rewards,* Houghton Mifflin, 1999.

Jean Lebedum, *Managing Workplace Conflict,* Amer Media Inc., 1998.

Patrick J. McKenna and Gerald A. Riskin, *Herding Cats: A Handbook for Managing Partners and Practice Leaders,* Institute for Best Management Practices, 1995.

Patrick J. McKenna, Gerald A. Riskin, and Michael J. Anderson, *Beyond Knowing: 16 Cage-Rattling Questions to Jump Start Your Practice Team,* Institute for Best Management Practices, 2000.

David H. Maister, *Managing The Professional Service Firm,* Free Press, 1993.

David H. Maister, *True Professionalism,* Free Press, 1997.

David H. Maister, C. H. Green, and R. M. Galford, *The Trusted Advisor,* Free Press, 2000.

David H. Maister, *Practice What You Preach,* Free Press, 2001.

David Merrill, *Personal Style and Effective Performance,* St. Lucie Press, 1983.

Mihaly Csikszentmihalyi, *Beyond Boredom and Anxiety,* Jossey-Bass, 1975.

Rosamund Stone Zander and Benjamin Zander, *The Art of Possibility: Transforming Professional and Personal Life,* Harvard Business School Press, 2000.

ACKNOWLEDGMENTS

FOR A NUMBER OF YEARS we have worked together (along with Patrick's colleagues in Edge International) in the development of a video- and workbook-based practice management program called PracticeCoach®. This package is used by groups to self-manage themselves and their groups. This work has given us numerous opportunities (particularly at the annual PracticeCoach® users conference) to exchange views with each other and our clients on the practical problems of being a group leader.

The first draft of this book (significantly different from what you hold in your hands) was written by Patrick, who, in part, drew upon David's writings and the ideas we exchanged in person. He therefore invited David to be his co-author. Together, they rewrote the material extensively, adding and discarding chapters, concepts, and language. The result is truly a joint effort.

Patrick's research into effective practice leadership began in 1993 when he and his fellow partners at The Edge Group (now Edge International) interviewed managing partners and practice leaders from a selection of the top one hundred U.S. law firms. Thereafter, they initiated a separate project entitled "best management practices," receiving submissions from sixty-three legal, accounting, consulting, and other professional services firms from over half a dozen different countries. In 1996, The Edge Group conducted a survey of managing partners and practice leaders in law firms and member firms of two international accounting associations. Over the past five years, Patrick and his partners have met with managing partners, executive committee members, and practice leaders from over three hundred law, accounting, management consulting, and public relations firms throughout Canada, the United States, Australia, South Africa, and the United Kingdom to interview them on practice leadership issues.

In all of this, Patrick has benefited enormously from the long-term collaborative input of his partners at Edge International, most notably his good friends Gerald A. Riskin, Michael J. Anderson, and Ed Wesemann. He is also grateful to his courageous administrator, Christine Birdseye, for continually coming to his rescue in helping to meet challenging deadlines.

Patrick is indebted to Stuart Rochester; Bruce W. Marcus, author of *Competing for Client;* and Merrilyn Astin Tarlton, editor of *Law Practice Management* magazine, for their continuing encouragement and support over the years.

For David, the work reflected here is the culmination of ideas and experiences from twenty years of reflecting on and working with clients on the basic questions: "But how do I make things *happen?* What do I *do?*" As his work unfolded, both in writing and consulting, he became increasingly convinced that the central key to success was (and is) the individual skills of the individual group manager. Whether his work has been on strategy, marketing, profit improvement, or people development, he has always found himself eventually working with "front-line" group leaders who must implement the grand schemes developed at the firm level. As a result, he has worked with (and developed sympathy for) literally thousands of group leaders.

To properly credit those who have helped him, he would need to thank every client he has ever worked with and every audience member in a seminar who ever posed a question. In fact, he does thank all of them! Especially those who posed the tough questions for which he had no ready answer. He hopes that some of them, at least, will find some of the answers in this work.

David, as always, must acknowledge the help that he receives from his wife, Kathy, in discussing his ideas and helping him (in uncountable ways) to juggle the numerous demands of the "writing, traveling, speaking, and consulting" lifestyle. He is grateful that she allows him to not retire.

David's business manager, Julie MacDonald O'Leary, for the fifth book in a row, provided irreplaceable assistance in reviewing numerous drafts and helping not only with the book's readability but also making (as usual) very useful and substantive suggestions on content.

We must acknowledge, with immense gratitude, those individuals mentioned in the text who gave us insights and the permission to quote them: Robert Dell, Rob Duboff, Francine Popoli Edelman, James Emerson, Cliff Farrah, John Feinstein, Daniel J. Fensin, Peter Friedes, Robert Gilbert, Phil Gott, Benjamin Haas, John Harris, Michael Hodges, Laura Holmes, Nick Jarrett-Kerr, Jon Katzenbach, Deborah Koeffler, Karl Kristoff, Peter McKelvey, Tim Morton, Jack Newman, Helen Ostrowski, John Schoenewald, Jim Shaffer, Jeremy Silverman, and Eric Vautour.

A special thanks goes to those (not otherwise mentioned above) who were so generous in providing the time to review our initial drafts and provide meaningful feedback: Dianne Bennett, Simon Chester, Robin Ferracone, John Heywood-Farmer, Michael von Herff, Allan Koltin, Paul McMahon, Bruce Marcus, Larry Roslund, and Alicia Whitaker.

Our gratitude also goes to Byron Dowler at Coastlines Creative for the book cover design.

INDEX

Accomplishments reports, 194, 200
Actionable ideas, 185–86
Action-planning meetings, 181–91
Action plans
    counseling for, 74
    in group self-evaluation, 244
    in group strategy, 145–47
    identifying possible courses in, 64
    for prima donnas, 117–18
    for relationship building, 40–43
    for underperformers, 110–11
Active listening, 63–64, 76–77
Administrative Support Awards,
    200
Advice
    in best interests of others, 38–40
    providing feedback on results,
    158–59
AFSM International, 4
Amiables, 90f, 91, 96, 98f
    characteristics of, 93–94
    working with, 101–2
Analyticals, 90f, 91, 96, 98f
    characteristics of, 92–93
    working with, 99–101
Appraisal function, 69
ArsDigita Corporation, xviii
As Good As It Gets (film), 59
Asking, 87, 90f
Assante Asset Management, xx
Assertiveness, 86–88, 89, 90f, 91, 92, 93,
    94, 97
Assignment size, 248

A.T. Kearney, 37
Attitude, 4, 227–29
Average (implied) rate per hour,
    252
Awards Programs, 194, 199–200

Bailey, Liza, 167–68
Bain & Co., 196
Bandura, Albert, 68
Behaviorally defined rules, 141
Best Suggestion to Clients Awards,
    200
Bevan Ashford, 69, 225, 239
Beyond Knowing (McKenna et al.), 127,
    168
Billable hours, xxiii, 143–44
BKD, LLP, 241
Blackman, Kallick, Bartelstein, 61,
    160
Blame, avoiding, 243
Boston Philharmonic, 46
Bower, Marvin, 45
Brainstorming, 183–85
Bridgestone/Firestone, 51
Brown, Dick, 247
Budgets, 147
Burnett, Leo, 47–50, 52, 55

Card list exercise, 154–55
Career goals, 41–43
Career planning, 73–74
Carnegie, Dale, 33
Cart-horse strategy, 254

Challenges, 165–73
  building for early success in, 172
  declaration of commitment to, 170–71
  encouraging experimentation in, 171
  with existing resources, 171
  focusing on excitement of, 172–73
  individual advantages of, 170
  opportunities to create or outdo, 172
  setting unreasonable expectations in, 172
Change, 121–28
  addressing people's needs in, 125–26
  gaining support for, 122–24
  successful introduction of lasting, 127–28
Change of heart (commitment failure excuse), 156, 157
Character, 32–33, 227–29
Chargeability, 252. See also Utilization
Cheerleading, 23–24
Client loyalty ratio, 248
Client retention ratio, 248
Clients
  commitment to, 84
  loss of, 214
  measuring satisfaction of, 247
  right to visit colleagues', 18
Closed-ended questions, 78
Coaching
  active listening in, 63–64
  agreement on next step in, 64
  of amiables, 101–2
  of analyticals, 99–100
  asking about progress in, 62
  caring about others in, 32–33
  confirming individual readiness for, 62–63
  creating a safe environment for, 65–69
  of drivers, 97–99
  of expressives, 103–4
  identification of possible actions in, 64
  liking for people and, 31–32
  offering information on, 63
  offers of support in, 63, 64–66
  right to, 18–19
  seeking clarification in, 63
  of underperformers, 111
  winning permission for, 59–74
Commitments
  declaring, 170–71
  differences in, 83–84
  following through on, 155–57
  honoring, 140
  small, 187–88
  voluntary, 186–87
Communication
  during a crisis, 210–11
  direct approach to, 81
  with firm leadership, 22–23
  indirect approach to, 82
  with new people, 235–36
  preventive approach to, 81
  therapeutic approach to, 81–82
Compensation. See also Money
  input on, 20–21
  performance and, 19–20
Competition, 131, 134–35
Confidentiality, 140
Confirming specifics, 157–58
Conflict resolution, 201–6
  areas of agreement and disagreement in, 205–6
  comments on causes of conflict in, 204
  description of conflict in, 203
  suggestions solicited in, 206
  summarizing in, 205
Constructive disagreement, 159–60
Consulting capsules, 179–80
Contracts for action, 146, 188
Controlled behavior, 88, 90f
Core group, 239
Corrective feedback, 65, 66

Counseling, 69–74
Credit Suisse First Boston, 167, 225
Crises, 207–18
    caused by layoffs, 215, 217–18
    caused by mistakes, 213–14
    death of a colleague, 215–17
    defection of key player, 212–13
    key principles for managing, 207–10
    loss of a client, 214
    support during, 53
Culture of success, 39, 148

Daniel, Ron, 31
Death of a colleague, 215–17
Delegating, 17, 148, 150
Dell, Robert M., 231
Diagnostic tests, 262
Differences, 83–104
    blending similarities and, 85–86
    guidelines for understanding, 86–89
    key to understanding colleagues',
        89–95
    responding to, 96–97
Direct approach to communication, 81
Dreams, 33–34, 46
Drivers, 90f, 96
    characteristics of, 91–92
    working with, 97–99
Duboff, Rob, 61–62, 89–90, 261

Edelman, Francine Popoli, 226–27
EDS, 37, 247
Einstein, Albert, 184
Emerson, James, xix
Emotions, 37
Emotive behavior, 88, 90f
Enthusiasm, 38
Ernst & Young, 61
Evaluations
    of leaders, 245–47
    self-. See Self-evaluation
Excitement, 172–73
Expectations, unreasonable, 172
Experimentation, encouraging, 171

Export of work/talent, 249, 252
Expressives, 90f, 91, 96, 98f
    characteristics of, 94–95
    working with, 102–4

Failure, celebrating, 155
Farrah, Cliff, 37, 60–61, 68, 178, 211
Fees, growth in, 252
Feinstein, John, 162
Fensin, Daniel J., 61, 112, 160, 179–80,
    189, 190, 210
Financial performance assessment,
    249–56
First impressions, managing, 233
Fisher, Roger, 202
Fish Tank Factor, 172–73
Flaws, admitting, 36–38
Fleishman-Hillard, 12, 148
Flip charts, 184, 233
Follow-up, 147, 188–90
Formal counseling, 69–74
Frank, Joachim, 90–91
Free pass rule, 37
Friedes, Peter, 50, 196, 197
Frontenac Company, 196, 240
Fun at work, 162–63

General Electric, 45
Getting to Yes (Fisher and Ury), 202
Gilbert, Robert E., 43
Giving of oneself, 36
Goals
    career, 41–43
    clarifying, 131–36
    meeting, 176–77
    setting, 74
Golden Rule Awards, 200
Goldman Sachs, 45
Gott, Phil, 198–99
Graham, John, 12, 148
Greenspun, Philip, xviii–xix
Groninger, Don, 51–52
Ground rules, 139–42
Group effectiveness quiz, xxii

Group leaders. See Leaders
Group leaders councils, 24
Group meetings, 175–91
  action-planning, 181–91
  ground rules for, 140
  knowledge-sharing/skill-building, 179–81
  meeting goals in, 176–77
  reluctance to attend, 137–38
  rules for, 176, 177–79
  volunteering to attend, 23
  warning signs of problems, 175–76
Group member questionnaires, 244–45
Group member satisfaction survey, 250–51
Group results measurement, 241–57
  financial performance, 249–56
  group self-evaluation in, 242–44
  nonfinancial, 247–48
  questionnaires in, 244–47
Groups
  advantages for competition, 131, 134–35
  bonding, 161–63
  challenges for. See Challenges
  characteristics of financially success-ful, 150
  common symptoms of problems in, 151
  conflict resolution in. See Conflict resolution
  controlling size of, 237–40
  core, 239
  crises in. See Crises
  downsizing, 239
  goal clarification for, 131–36
  individual advantages in, 131, 135–36, 170
  management processes in, 264–65
  membership rules for, 137–50, 262–63
  price of membership in, 143
  reason for existence, 131, 132–34

  recognition for, 193–200
  splinter, 240
  trust in. See Trust
  unacceptable behavior in, 149–50
Group self-evaluation, 242–44
Group strategy, 145–47

Haas, Benjamin, 3–4, 118–19, 188
Half-pint party, 198–99
Hall of Fame wall, 198
Harris, John, 241–42
Health index, 256
Help, offers of, 54, 63
Hewitt Associates, 50, 196
Hewlett Packard (HP), 90
Hiring, 227–29
Hodges, Michael, 126
Hodgson Russ, 20, 136, 224
Holmes, Laura, xxv
Humor, 211
Hunt, Bunker, 165
Hunt, Helen, 59
Hygiene index, 256
Hygiene issues, 253–56

Import of work/talent, 249, 252
Inconvenience (commitment failure excuse), 156, 157
Indirect approach to communication, 82
Informal meetings, 40–41
Inspiration, 45–55, 167
  for amiables, 102
  for analyticals, 101
  for drivers, 99
  for expressives, 104
  informal check-in and, 53–54
  interest in group achievements and, 51–52
  interest in personal lives and, 52–53
  offers of help and, 54
  in times of crisis, 53
Interest, showing, 35–36, 51–53

Interruption (commitment failure excuse), 156, 157
Interviews, 228–29
Investment hours
    amount committed to group, 143–44
    use of, 144–47

Jarrett-Kerr, Nick, 69–70, 225, 239
Juniors, 221–29, 254
    hiring, 227–29
    mentors and, 225–27
    work assignment system and, 221, 222
    work supervision system and, 221, 222–25

Kaiser Associates, 37
Katzenbach, Jon, xviii, 16–17, 147–48, 161
Keller, Helen, 166
Key client program, 242
Knowledge-sharing/skill-building meetings, 179–81
Koeffler, Deborah P., 140–41
Kohn, Alfie, 165
Kristoff, Karl, 20, 136, 224, 249

Lasalle, Jones Lang, 126
Latham & Watkins, 231
Layoffs, 215, 217–18
Leaders
    evaulation of, 245–47
    firm, 22–24
    role of, 10
    time allotment and, 6–8
Leadership Solution, The (Shaffer), 113
Lebedum, Jean, 204
L.E.K., 238
Leo Burnett Company, 47–49
Leverage, 252, 253–56
Listening, 75–82
    active, 63–64, 76–77
    characteristics of effective, 75–76
    dealing with bad listeners, 80–82
Loyalty, 235

Maister, David H., 10, 29, 38, 75, 260
Major, Hagen & Africa, 232
Managing the Professional Service Firm (Maister), 10
Managing Workplace Conflict (Lebedum), 204
Mandate, 11–25. See also Rules
Margin, 253–56
McKelvey, Peter, 238
McKenna, Patrick J., 127, 168
McKinsey, 16, 31, 45
Meaning in work, 107
Meetings
    group. See Group meetings
    informal, 40–41
Memory lapse (commitment failure excuse), 156
Mentors, 225–27
Mentors of the Year Award, 200
Mercer Management Consulting, 61, 89
Merrill, David, 86, 88
Metaphors, 68
Miller Canfield Paddock and Stone, 43
Minimum-maximum requirement, 17
Mistakes, 213–14
Mitchell Silberberg & Knupp, 140
Money, 165. See also Compensation
Morgan, Lewis & Bockius, 5, 147, 180
Morton, Tim, 247
Moses Strategy, 9
Moss, Larry, 59–60
Mutual accountability, 138–42

Nagging rights, 34, 40, 43, 150
Negotiation, 202
New client ratio, 248
Newman, Jack, 5, 147, 180

New people, 231–36
  affirming value of, 234–35
  communicating with, 235–36
  first impressions and, 233
  immersion experience for, 235
  support for, 233–34
New service ratio, 248
Newsletters, 197
Nixon, Richard, 213
Nonfinancial measures, 247–48
Non-reimbursed time, xxiv, 21–22
Note taking, 79, 184

Ogunlesi, Bayo, 225–26
O'Leary, Julie MacDonald, 178, 184–85
Open-ended questions, 78
Oracle, 37
Orientation programs, 233, 235
Ostrowski, Helen, 217

Paraphrasing, 79–80
Penetration ratio, 248
People measures, 249
Performance criteria
  compensation and, 19–20
  specifying, 70–72
Porter Novelli, 217
Position pay, 19–20
Practice Development Awards, 200
Practice What You Preach (Maister),
    xviii, 39, 149–50, 161, 223,
    260
Preventive approach to communica-
    tion, 81
Prima donnas, 23, 113–20
  confronting problem behavior,
    114–18
  double standard for, 118–19
  two options for handling, 120
Professional pride, 84, 147–48
Professional Services Review, xix
Profitability, 15–17
Profit health, 253–56

Profit margin, 252
Profit per officer/partner, 249,
    253–56
Progress reviews, 24, 111
Punished by Rewards (Kohn), 165
Punitive approach to communication,
    82

Questionnaires, 244–47
Questions, 77–79

Rainmaker ratio, 248
Rate, 253–56
Ratios, 248
Receivables, 252
Recognition
  for amiables, 102
  for analyticals, 101
  for drivers, 99
  for expressives, 104
  for groups, 193–200
Rehearsal, 67–68
Relationship building, 27–43
  action plan for, 40–43
  advice giving in, 38–40
  caring about others and, 32–33
  dealing with flaws in, 36–38
  dream realization and, 33–34
  investing time in, 34–36
  liking for people and, 31–32
  as trusted advisor. See Trusted advi-
    sors
Resource member approach, 239
Responsiveness, 86, 88, 89, 90f, 91, 92,
    93, 94, 97
Role clarification, 3–10
Role models, 69
Role-playing, 67, 68, 181
Rules, 14–24
  behaviorally defined, 141
  consequences for breaking, 142
  ground, 139–42
  for group meetings, 176, 177–79

of group membership, 137–50, 262–63
input on compensation, 20–21
participation of firm leadership, 22–24
performance criteria and compensation, 19–20
right to coach, 18–19
time to do the job, 14–18
value of non-reimbursed time, 21–22
Russell Reynolds Associates, 232

Safe environment, creating, 65–69
Schoenewald, John, 4
Self-evaluation
group, 242–44
individual, 72
Servant leadership, 9
Service Quality Awards, 199
Shaffer, Jim, 113–14
Shared contribution, 138, 143–47
Shared values, 138, 147–50
Sharing, 154–55
Silverman, Jeremy, 196–97, 240
Singular focus, 182
Skills, 4, 221, 227
Smythe Dorward Lambert, xxv
Sole source ratio, 248
Splinter groups, 240
Stengel, Casey, 4–5
Streamliner Awards, 200
Styles grid, 89, 90f, 91
Success
building for early, 172
celebrating, 190–91
contributing to others, 71–72
creating mental pictures of, 68–69
culture of, 39, 148
Summarizing, 79–80, 205
Support, 64–66, 117
during crises, 53

for new people, 233–34
for underperformers, 108–9
Swanson, David, xx

Telling, 87, 90f
10-80-10 rule, 32
Terms of engagement. *See* Mandate
Therapeutic approach to communication, 81–82
Time. *See also* Investment hours
to do the job, 14–18
investment in relationship building, 34–36
leaders' use of, 6–8
to meet informally, 40–41
off the issue, 36
Towers Perrin, 3, 113, 118, 188
True Professionalism (Maister), 38
Trust, 50, 64–66, 151–63, 238
elements of, 154–60
initiatives for building, 152–54
Trusted Advisor, The (Maister), 29, 75
Trusted advisors, 28, 29–31, 32–33, 260
Turnover rates, 249
12i Communications, 226

Unbilled work-in-progress, 252
Underperformers, 105–12
common reasons for problems, 105–7
protracted problems in, 112
suggestions for assisting, 108–11
Understanding of colleagues, 36
University of Chicago, 165–66
Urban, Eileen, 225–26
Ury, William, 202
Utilization, 253–56. *See also* Chargeability

Values
conflict over, 204
shared, 138, 147–50

Vanasse Hangen Brustlin, Inc., 162
Vautour, Eric, 232–33
Videotaping meetings, 181
Virtuous circle, 135
Vision thing, 8–9, 84

Weekly "to do" list, 265–66
Welch, Jack, 45, 107

Win-loss ratio, 248
Wisdom of Teams, The (Katzenbach), 147
Work assignment system, 221, 222
Work supervision system, 221, 222–25

Zander, Benjamin, 46–47, 49, 50, 52, 54, 55

ABOUT THE AUTHORS

PATRICK J. MCKENNA is a partner in Edge International, where since 1983 he has worked exclusively serving professional service firms worldwide. Mr. McKenna did his MBA graduate work at the Canadian School of Management, is an alumnus of Harvard University's Leadership in Professional Service Firms, and has professional certifications in both accounting and management.

He is the author of *Building Business Abroad* and co-author of *Practice Development: Creating a Marketing Mindset,* recognized by an international journal as "one of the top ten books that any professional services marketer should have on their bookcase." His most recent publications include *Herding Cats: A Handbook for Managing Partners and Practice Leaders* (1995); and *Beyond Knowing: 16 Cage-Rattling Questions To Jump-Start Your Practice Team* (2000), both of which achieved recognition on the Canadian Management Top 10 bestsellers list.

Mr. McKenna has worked with at least one of the Top Ten major law or accounting firms in each of over a dozen different countries.

He may be reached at:

Email: patrick.mckenna@attglobal.net
Website: www.patrickmckenna.com
Tel: 1-780-428-1052

DAVID H. MAISTER is widely acknowledged as one of the world's leading authorities on the management of professional service firms. For two decades he has advised firms around the world in a broad spectrum of professions, covering all strategic and managerial issues.

He is the author of the bestselling books *Managing the Professional Service Firm* (1993), *True Professionalism* (1997), *The Trusted Advisor,* (co-author, 2000) and *Practice What You Preach,* (2001). In his previous academic career he also wrote (or co-authored) seven books on such diverse subjects as truck drivers, managing an airline, and factory operations. This is his twelfth book.

A native of Great Britain, David holds degrees from the University of Birmingham, the London School of Economics, and the Harvard Business School, where he was a professor for seven years. He lives in Boston, Massachusetts.

He may be reached at:

Email: David_Maister@msn.com
Website: *www.DavidMaister.com*
Tel: 1-617-262-5968

WEB SITE DEDICATED TO THIS BOOK

For more information about the subjects discussed in this book, go to *www.firstamongequals.com*

PRACTICE COACH

For information on the PracticeCoach® program, go to *www.practicecoach.ai*